M000237389

RESEARCH *to* REVENUE

**The Luther H. Hodges Jr. and
Luther H. Hodges Sr. Series on
Business, Entrepreneurship,
and Public Policy**

Maryann Feldman, *editor*

This series provides a forum for social scientists, public policy scholars,
historians, and others investigating the economic, political, societal,
and geographic contexts and conditions that foster entrepreneurship,
innovation, and economic development in the United States and around the
world. As place-based inquiry has gained currency, scholarship in the areas
of business, entrepreneurship, and public policy increasingly consider spatial
and cultural issues. A basic aim of the series is to challenge analyses that
privilege globalization with the view that place—and human attachment
to—place influence the expression of creativity and innovation.

DON ROSE and **CAM PATTERSON**

RESEARCH *to* REVENUE

A Practical Guide to University Start-Ups

The University of North Carolina Press   CHAPEL HILL

*Published with the assistance of the Luther H. Hodges Jr. and
Luther H. Hodges Sr. Fund of the University of North Carolina Press.*

© 2016 The University of North Carolina Press
All rights reserved

Manufactured in the United States of America. Designed and set in Merlo
and The Sans by Rebecca Evans. The paper in this book meets the guidelines
for permanence and durability of the Committee on Production Guidelines for
Book Longevity of the Council on Library Resources. The University of North
Carolina Press has been a member of the Green Press Initiative since 2003.

Jacket illustration: depositphotos.com/© SergeyNivens

Library of Congress Cataloging-in-Publication Data
Rose, Don, 1960– author.
Research to revenue : a practical guide to university start-ups / Don Rose and
Cam Patterson.
pages cm — (The Luther H. Hodges Jr. and Luther H. Hodges Sr. series on
business, entrepreneurship, and public policy)
Includes index.
ISBN 978-1-4696-2526-3 (cloth : alk. paper)
ISBN 978-1-4696-2527-0 (ebook)
1. University-based new business enterprises. 2. Academic spin-outs.
3. Technology transfer. I. Patterson, Cam, author. II. Title. III. Series: Luther H.
Hodges Jr. and Luther H. Hodges Sr. series on business, entrepreneurship,
and public policy.
HD62.5.R67 2016   658.1′1—dc23
2015028434

MIX
Paper from
responsible sources
FSC   FSC® C013483
www.fsc.org

Contents

For additional resources on university start-ups, please visit the book's companion website, researchtorevenue.com.

Figures and Tables

Foreword

The Greek philosopher Democritus mused, "Everything in the universe is the fruit of chance and necessity." Jacques Monod, a 1965 Nobel Laureate in Medicine and Physiology, adopted Democritus's aphorism as the title for his book *Chance and Neccessity*, in which he presented a contemporary view of evolution. Monod described random mutational events as "chance" chemical events and couched "necessity" as the natural selection of the ever-changing environment for new life forms arising from the mutational events.

Years after Robert Swanson and I founded Genentech, in 1976, we were asked on occasion to discuss some of the factors that contributed to the success of the company. Sometimes I would use a slightly modified title of Monod's book as the epigraph and talking points for my discussion, namely, "Chance and necessity . . . and . . . naïveté." Although Bob and I were comfortable in our respective fields of business and science, we were entering into a new type of commercial endeavor that soon presented unanticipated (at least to us) challenges. Hence, my title aimed to bring attention to the necessity at the time for new types of medical drugs (biologics) and the chance convergence of several technologies that presented the opportunity to take a risk with a bold new venture. In a short period of time we faced the realization that we were quite naive about the wide-ranging problems waiting for us. And perhaps if we had known of all the pitfalls beforehand, we might not have taken the risk in the first place. However, we did not admit this because our financial backers might have become uneasy, to say the least, and after all, we were young and naive. We certainly did not anticipate the first and probably the most significant and unexpected hurdle we encountered, namely, registering as lobbyists and spending two weeks in Washington convincing Congress not to prohibit genetic engineering.

I will not enumerate the numerous pitfalls Genentech encountered as we moved forward. For the most part they are clearly and systematically presented in *Research to Revenue: A Practical Guide to University Start-Ups*.

Academics interested in translating their research interests to a commercial enterprise are advised to use the systematic and well-documented experiences presented by Don Rose and Cam Patterson in *Research to Revenue*. From intellectual property, to raising funds, to business models, to naming the company, no topic imaginable for success is omitted. Of particular interest is what the authors describe as the university ecosystem. In contrast to the academic atmosphere of thirty-five years ago, universities today are proactive in the role of translational research as valuable to themselves, their faculty, and society. The discussion of the university ecosystem here is of considerable value.

I can assure anyone (not only academics) interested in commercializing technological innovation emanating from a university backdrop that *Research to Revenue* is an invaluable guide for success. *Research to Revenue* would have solved most of our naïveté had we been fortunate to have had this guide in 1976.

Herbert W. Boyer
Cofounder Genentech
Professor Emeritus, UCSF

Acknowledgments

Writing a book of this breadth is beyond the scope of just two authors. A number of people contributed to various aspects of the book. The following helped review certain technical and legal sections and provided some of the research reflected in the book: Jackie Quay, Andrea Portbury, Andy Kant, Jeff Kennedy, Ken Eheman, Clay Thorp, Anil Goyal, John Austin, and Lister Delgado. The lessons learned sections of the book came from faculty entrepreneurs Richard Boucher, David Clemmons, Tony Hickey, Holden Thorp, Richard Superfine, Tom Eagan, Nancy Demore, Keith Kocis, Bob Johnston, and Ned Sharpless and business leaders and entrepreneurs David Spencer, Al Bender, Greg Mossinghoff, Myla Lai-Goldman, Bruce Oberhardt, Chris Price, Chris Morriso, Rich Shea, Anil Goyal, and Karen LeVert.

Abbreviations

AUTM	Association of University Technology Managers
BOD	board of directors
CBO	chief business officer
CDA	confidentiality disclosure agreement
CEO	chief executive officer
CFO	chief financial officer
CLIA	Clinical Laboratory Improvement Amendment
CMO	chief medical officer
COGS	cost of goods sold
COI	conflict of interest
COO	chief operating officer
CRO	contract research organization
CSO	chief scientific officer
CTSA	Clinical and Translational Science Award
DOD	Department of Defense
EIR	entrepreneur-in-residence program
ESOP	employee stock option plan
FDA	Food and Drug Administration
FTO	freedom to operate
GM	gross margin
IND	investigational new drug
IP	intellectual property
IPO	initial public offering
ISO	incentive stock option
ISP	Internet service provider
LCD	liquid crystal display
LDT	laboratory-developed test

LLC	limited liability corporation
M&A	mergers and acquisitions
MVP	minimal viable product
NCI	National Cancer Institute
NDA	nondisclosure agreement or new drug application
NHLBI	National Heart, Lung, and Blood Institute
NIH	National Institutes of Health
NSF	National Science Foundation
PCR	polymerase chain reaction
PCT	Patent Cooperation Treaty
PD	principal director
PI	principal investigator
PMA	premarket approval
R&D	research and development
RFA	requests for applications
ROI	return on investment
SAB	scientific advisory board
SBIR	Small Business Innovation Research
STTR	Small Business Technology Transfer Research
TICAM	real estate taxes, insurance, care and maintenance charges
TTO	technology transfer officer
VC	venture capitalist
VP	vice president

RESEARCH *to* REVENUE

Introduction

Once Upon a Time . . .

Doctors John Kinser and Linda Gregson of Woodfin University Cancer Research Center made a groundbreaking discovery. As collaborators, they discovered a very promising anticancer compound. In a mouse tumor model, the compound completely eliminated angiogenesis (the growth of blood vessels in tumors), stopping tumor growth in its tracks. When a graduate student presented the lab results during a poster session at a national meeting, the response was overwhelming. Michael Troxler, an entrepreneur at the meeting contacted Kinser and Gregson about starting a company to commercialize the compound. Kinser and Gregson liked the idea of a start-up, but their business knowledge was virtually nil. They knew one colleague who had started a company, but it had failed and he was not very encouraging. The three met with the technology transfer office (TTO), but their enthusiasm was tempered by the fact that the poster was a public disclosure (disclosure of information in a public forum, which can be used against the inventor who is claiming a novel discovery) and significant patent rights had been forfeited.

Not to be deterred, the professors went back to the lab, reexamined their data, and rescreened additional compounds to find even more potent compounds. They disclosed the compound to the TTO, who determined it might be patentable and filed a provisional patent. With renewed excitement, the professors contacted Troxler, and the three decided to start Angiostatix, LLC. Excitement over starting the company quickly dissipated as heated discussions ensued about ownership of the company. Troxler wanted to be the chief executive officer (CEO) and, as such, thought he should own a third of the company with the academic founders (Gregson and Kinser) each getting a third as well. The professors thought this was preposterous since they had made the discovery, which, they believed, was the real value of the company. The discussion about ownership became contentious even between Kinser and Gregson. Equal ownership between the faculty founders did not seem fair to Kinser, since he had worked on the biological target his entire twenty-year career and Gregson had only screened the compounds. In the end, the parties begrudgingly split the company ownership evenly three ways.

Troxler's first job was to license the technology from the TTO. The negotiations were contentious and drawn out, especially over the fraction owned by the university (and over the antidilution clause that prevented subsequent investors from decreasing their ownership percentage). The negotiations also consumed critical capital through attorney fees. Kinser and Gregson were glad Troxler was handling the negotiations, but they eventually had to intervene with the TTO on some terms. Troxler then turned to fund-raising. He pitched the company to a number of venture capital firms (VCs), but the general response was that the idea of a company was too early. Kinser and Gregson became frustrated with the progress Troxler was making, confirming their suspicion that his value to the company was limited. At one point, they called into question his ability to understand the science, let alone pitch the company effectively. Troxler countered by pointing out the lack of research the professors had done in testing the compound and their lack of availability for presenting to VCs. The situation came to a head when the professors decided to fire Troxler. However, because he had been given stock at founding (without a vesting period), Troxler walked away with a third of the company.

Over the next year, the professors applied for Small Business Innovation Research (SBIR) grants to conduct preclinical testing of the compounds, but none were funded because they did not have a strong principal investigator (the graduating graduate student did not have the scientific credentials). Through a chance encounter, they met a clinical oncologist who had worked at a large pharmaceutical company for years and was looking for a new opportunity (he was let go after a megamerger). He reworked the SBIR proposals and was able to get Phase I and Phase II grants for a total of $1 million. As Phase II was winding down, however, it was discovered that funds were misspent during Phase II, which triggered an audit by the National Institutes of Health (NIH).

Meanwhile, the university had filed provisional patents on the compounds. Because of recent budget cuts, the TTO was unable (or unwilling, from the founders' perspective) to pay for the international filings. When Kinser and Gregson were planning to hire a part-time CEO, the negotiations were prickly because the former CEO had a large ownership stake. Adding to the stress was the clinical oncologist, who thought he should be CEO. Eventually, they convinced Mary Parker, who had been part of senior management in several biotech start-ups, to join them. She used the data from the SBIR studies to pitch the company to an early-stage VC, which was very excited about the opportunity. The VC began to look deeper into the deal and identified multiple problems, some minor, some not so minor, including the following:

- The U.S.-only patent coverage was a limitation.
- The NIH audit created concern.
- The license with the university covered only lung cancer and no others, and it contained a troublesome antidilution clause that prevented the university from being diluted by investments. Both issues could be addressed but would require significant renegotiation.
- The former CEO was vocal about his dismissal and was threatening a lawsuit.
- The founders were considering a lawsuit against the former CEO to retrieve his equity.
- The legal entity would have to be changed from a limited liability corporation (LLC) to a corporation, a minor issue.

Even with these problems, the VC was ready to make an investment. The investment was for $2 million in return for 35 percent of the company, a position on the board of directors, and one of the firm's partners serving as interim CEO. The company's internal discussions were fierce: the founders argued for the deal, given the difficulty in attracting capital. The CEO, fearing for her future with the company, thought they should stall in order to find another deal, especially one where the company did not have to give up so much control. In the end, the company walked away from the deal and spent two years trying to find another investor. Eventually, the founders lost interest in the start-up, the interim CEO found a full-time position elsewhere, and the idea of Angiostatix faded.

The fictional story of Angiostatix represents the potentially transformative power of a start-up to move a groundbreaking discovery into the market place and to have significant impact on society. The story also shows the roller-coaster ride many founders face in launching and building a start-up. It highlights the many critical decisions to be made along the way. Many faculty members are not prepared to make these decisions effectively or able to judge the wisdom of decisions being made by others. This knowledge gap is understandable, given their lack of training in entrepreneurial activities, their lack of business experience, and their deep focus on funding and publishing scientific research. Gaining the required knowledge or finding the right people to help was, at best, difficult. In addition, this story points to how many would-be or even experienced entrepreneurs lack the experience of commercializing very early-stage science and technology, working with faculty founders, or interacting with a university who owns the intellectual property.

In this book we hope to bridge the knowledge gap for faculty founders, research administrators, first-time CEOs, and technology transfer officers as they engage in the process of supporting, launching, and building a university start-up. It is also a tool for business leaders, especially those considering getting involved with a university start-up. We explain the university start-up within the context of the entrepreneurial ecosystem and provide a practical guide to launching the start-up. These two aspects of the book have been gleaned from Cam's years of experience on the faculty side in attempting to launch a university start-up and Don's on both the private side (spinning out a university start-up and being a venture capitalist funding early-stage companies) and the administrative side, developing programs to mentor faculty who are starting companies and support those companies with funding and incubation space.

What's in the Book

Chapter 1 provides an overview of how universities commercialize technologies and how start-ups play a role in that process. We consider the many factors that contribute to a successful start-up.

In Chapter 2, we go on to describe the many moving parts involved in a university start-up. We start with a minitutorial on the business aspects of a university start-up (business model, technology, and product development). From there, we consider three major components of the entrepreneurial ecosystem: the university (intellectual property [IP] and license), the people (advisers and management), and the funding (investors and money). We described each component in detail, providing the perspective and incentives of each component relative to the start-up. This part is the "What" of the book.

Chapter 3 guides you through the significant steps in preparing, launching, and building a university start-up. It starts with recognizing the opportunity and moves through the steps of protecting the IP, building the business case, recruiting advisers and management, writing the business plan, and raising capital. Each step provides practical information based on our experience. Although the steps are arranged in a linear fashion, it should be noted that 1) many start-ups don't follow this precise order; 2) some steps are more important than others for different companies; and 3) some steps might not apply in all situations. Broadly speaking, however, certain steps will follow a particular order; for example, capital must be raised to build the product in order to sell the product.

In Chapter 4 we present three case studies that cover the range of technologies one might find among university start-ups: a therapeutic drug for treating cancer, a sensor for measuring gases in the environment, and cloud-based computing technology for optimizing server performance. For each case study, we consider the key steps described in Chapter 3. These case studies provide a realistic view of the possible twists and turns one might encounter along the way to launching a start-up.

In Chapter 5 we consider the specific perspectives of three key stakeholders in the start-up process: faculty founders, business leaders, and university research administrators. We explore the personal motivations faculty founders might have for starting a company; we also discuss issues around conflict of interest and commitment; how to effectively separate, mentally and physically, the start-up from the university research lab; and how to think about company control. We polled a number of faculty founders about key lessons they learned from their experiences, and those lessons are excerpted and presented here. For business leaders, those who help a faculty founder start and grow a company, we examine the many aspects of working with the university. For example, it is important to understand the perspective of the TTO when negotiating a license from the university. We also present some of the lessons experienced entrepreneurs learned from launching university start-ups. For research administrators, we examine the rationale for supporting university start-ups and the programmatic approaches to fostering entrepreneurship on campus while upholding the mission of the university. Three broad themes are addressed: entrepreneurship education of faculty and students; engaging the external community to participate at various levels with start-ups; and programs, policies, and guidelines that can foster the launching and building of successful university start-ups.

1

Commercializing University Technology and the Role of Start-Up Companies

Universities are a rich source of knowledge, ideas, discoveries, and innovation. A major role of the university is to disseminate these resources to society in a way that can have beneficial impact. The traditional methods of dissemination have been either through the education of students, who leave the university to make their mark on the world, or through faculty publications of scientific research. In the last several decades, a new channel has developed: commercialization of university research, inventions, and innovations. Although the commercialization of university research has been happening for centuries, the university's role in it began in earnest in the 1950s with the establishment of the modern research university. That role increased significantly starting in the 1980s with the passage of the federal Patent and Trademark Law Amendments Act, better known as the Bayh-Dole Act, which gave universities title to inventions derived from federal funding and an imperative to commercialize these inventions. More recently, commercialization has changed again as entrepreneurship has begun to play a more defined role in it.

The following are several groundbreaking, impactful products and services that can be traced to university innovations.

Insulin. Insulin was discovered in 1922 by Frederick Banting, a Canadian surgeon working at the University of Toronto, along with his assistant, Charles Best. Crude extracts from the islets of Langerhans in the pancreas of laboratory dogs were injected into other dogs that had been rendered diabetic through the removal of their pancreas. Injection of this substance (which Banting and Best named "insulin," from the Latin for "islet") lowered the diabetic dogs' blood sugar. In 1923, the Nobel Prize was awarded to Banting and John James Rickard Macleod for the discovery. Banting sold the patent for insulin to the University of Toronto for $1. The university went on to use the income generated from the production and sale of insulin to fund new research. The pharmaceutical company Eli Lilly began large-scale production of the extract in 1923.

Gatorade. In 1965, at the bequest of the Florida Gator's assistant football coach Dwayne Douglas, Robert Cade, who was then the director of the University of Florida College of Medicine's renal and electrolyte division, began researching the athlete's body's response to excessive sweating. Cade, along with research fellows Dana Shires, Jim Free, and A. M. deQuesada, concocted a drink containing salts, sugars, and lemon juice and had student athletes drink it during their practice sessions. They called this drink Gatorade. In 1967, Cade and his fellow inventors sold the rights (but retained a percentage of royalties) for Gatorade to Stokely–Van Camp, who began mass production. In 1983, Stokely–Van Camp was taken over by the Quaker Oats Company, which subsequently launched an aggressive, international marketing campaign to increase the sales and marketing of Gatorade. In 2001, Pepsico bought Quaker Oats, further increasing the revenue from Gatorade sales. The University of Florida has invested the royalties from Gatorade sales in further research in exercise physiology and other biomedical areas.

Recombinant DNA pharmaceuticals. In 1972, Stanford medical professor Stanley Cohen and the University of California, San Francisco, biochemist Herbert Boyer used their respective molecular biology skills to create recombinant DNA, a hybrid DNA strand made up of two different DNA molecules from separate plasmids. This innovation is often cited as the birth of biotechnology. In 1976, Boyer teamed with venture capitalist Robert Swanson to set up the world's first biotechnology company, Genentech. By patenting recombinant DNA technology, Stanford and the University of California system earned $255 million from licensing revenues, which the schools subsequently used to continue to develop research endeavors. While under patent, recombinant DNA was licensed to 468 companies worldwide, resulting in over an estimated 2,400 new technologies.

Improved hypertext searching. Google began in 1996 as a research project of Sergey Brin and Larry Page, two Ph.D. students at Stanford University. At the time, both were working on the Stanford Digital Library Project. As part of his dissertation project, Page developed a web crawler called BackRub that could explore the relationship between a single web page and all the back links associated with it. In order to analyze the data they were accruing, Page and Brin developed a search engine designed to identify linked pages based on their importance to the originating web page. The search engine, with the domain name google.stanford.edu, was run off the Stanford website. In 1997, Page and Brin registered the domain google.com, and in 1998, Google Inc. was incorporated as a company. Google went public in 2004. Page and

Brin's development of this highly efficient program for hypertext searching revolutionized the way people used the Internet. The Google algorithm has brought over $331 million to Stanford University, much of which has been channeled into the school's department and program funding.

Liquid crystal display (LCD). The physicist James Fergason, the inventor of LCD, first started experimenting with liquid crystals while he was working at Westinghouse Research Laboratories in Pittsburgh. Westinghouse was interested in liquid crystals as thermal sensors, but Fergason was more interested in the idea of applying liquid crystal technology to displays. This interest prompted Fergason to move to the newly established Liquid Crystal Institute at Kent State University in Ohio. As part of his research at Kent State, Fergason discovered the principle of twisted nematic structure (TN), which would prove to be an essential component in LCDs. In 1970, Fergason left Kent State University to form his own company, ILIXCO. When he applied for a patent for TN LCD technology in February 1971, however, he learned that in December 1970, two Swiss researchers, Martin Schadt and Wolfgang Helfrich, from the company Hoffmann–La Roche in Basel, Switzerland, had published a paper on and filed a patent for TN LCD. A long legal battle ensued between Hoffman La Roche, ILIXCO, and Kent State University (who claimed intellectual property on some of Fergason's TN LCD research). Eventually, Hoffmann–La Roche bought Fergason's patent.

Pacemakers. In 1952, Dr. Paul Zoll at Beth Israel Hospital in Boston used an external device to electrically stimulate the heart of a patient suffering from heart block. Zoll's device, which was large and bulky (and had the potential to electrocute the patient), was improved upon in 1958, when electrical engineering graduate student Earl Bakken designed and built a hand-held external device that delivered electrical impulses to the heart via myocardial leads. This form of the pacemaker also had the advantage of being battery-powered, decreasing the risk of electrocution and giving patients the ability to move about while undergoing treatment. In 1958, this model of the pacemaker was improved even further due to the work of Wilson Greatbach, an electrical engineer in New York, who set about designing an implantable device. In 1960, the first successful human trial of an implantable, battery-operated pacemaker designed by Greatbach was achieved. In 1961, Greatbach signed a license agreement with Medtronic, Earl Bakken's company, and together Greatbach and Bakken continued to work on improving the reliability and wearability of the pacemaker.

Technology Commercialization

None of the aforementioned innovations would have had their impact on society without technology commercialization, an activity that is unique within universities since it typically involves both public (government funding) and private (industry, investors) entities. The majority of a university's technology commercialization activities in the United States are made possible by the Bayh-Dole Act. Passed by Congress in 1980, the act gives universities title to any innovations or discoveries arising from research supported by federal funds (e.g., from the National Institutes of Health, the National Science Foundation [NSF], or the Department of Defense [DOD]). In return, the university has obligations to report inventions to the government, protect the IP through patents and copyrights, promote the IP for commercialization, and share any licensing income with the inventors. As a result of the Bayh-Dole Act, most research universities have established technology transfer offices (TTOs) to comply with the legislation. The number of TTOs has grown from fewer than 10 when the act was established in 1980 to hundreds today.

The goal of university technology commercialization, other than complying with Bayh-Dole, is multifaceted, with each university emphasizing different goals to different extents. The following are some common goals:

FACULTY RECRUITMENT AND RETENTION. Although it's often overlooked, a robust technology commercialization program at a university can be used to keep talented faculty or recruit new faculty. Many younger faculty who are considering academic positions are interested in how their research will have impact or how they can create wealth through commercializing research.

UNLOCKING INNOVATION. Translating innovative research into impactful products and services, such as curing a disease, creating safer drinking water, or reducing waste, is seen as benefiting society, and is aligned well with the mission of a university.

RETURN ON INVESTMENT. From a financial perspective, technology commercialization can return revenue to the university based on its investment—that is, its funding of the research infrastructure (e.g., buildings, labs, core facilities, IT services, etc.) as well as the cost of running the TTO operation (e.g., personnel, patent costs, etc.).

EDUCATIONAL IMPACT. One of the ancillary benefits of a strong commercialization effort is teaching students about how research is translated into commercial products. Courses in technology commercialization provide students with an understanding of the business side of science, better preparing them for research and development (R&D) jobs. Entrepreneurial education equips students with the tools necessary to embark on their entrepreneurial efforts after they leave the university.

ECONOMIC DEVELOPMENT. Many start-ups start locally and grow locally (i.e., near the university whose innovation is being commercialized). As such, they tend to hire locally and spend locally, making them engines for economic development.

A survey of over 100 TTOs shows the multifaceted nature of technology commercialization.[1] Respondents ranked the following as the number one driving factor for their technology commercialization activities: faculty service (39 percent), translating research results (35 percent), revenue maximization (12 percent), other (12 percent), and research support (3 percent). The authors noted that economic development was not a choice in the survey and could have accounted for the large response to the "other" category.

Start-Ups versus Licensing to Established Companies

For a university-derived technology, there are two major paths for bringing the technology to market (fig. 1.1). The first involves the university licensing the technology to an established company where the company incorporates the technology into its product development, manufacturing, and sales processes. The other path involves founding a start-up company to commercialize the technology. In the latter, the new venture is more closely associated with the university because of involvement of the faculty member with the start-up and the "care and feeding" required to launch the start-up, an activity being taken on by more and more universities.

So what determines the path of technology, the start-up or the established company? In his book *Academic Entrepreneurship*, Scott Shane describes the characteristics of technologies that are most suitable for licensing to established companies (table 1.1).

1. I. Abrams, G. Leung, and A. Stevens, "How Are U.S. Technology Transfer Offices Tasked and Motivated—Is It All About the Money?," *Research Management Review* 17 (1) (Fall/Winter 2009), http://www.bu.edu/otd/files/2011/02/How-are-US-Tech.-Transfer-Offices-Tasked-and-Motivated.pdf (accessed 14 July 2015).

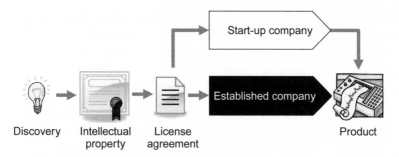

FIGURE 1.1 Two paths to a commerical product

TABLE 1.1 Comparison of characteristics of technology suitable for start-ups vs. established companies

CHARACTERISTIC	START-UP COMPANY	ESTABLISHED COMPANY
Type of technology	Radical	Incremental
Type of knowledge	Tacit	Codified
Stage	Early	Late
Purpose	General	Specific
Customer value	Significant	Moderate
IP protection	Strong	Weak

Source: Adapted from Shane, *Academic Entrepreneurship*, 103.

According to Shane, technologies most suitable for start-ups have the following important characteristics:

RADICAL. Technologies that are radical create a paradigm shift or are game changing, having the ability to create entirely new product categories or new ways of doing things. Established companies prefer incremental technologies over radical technologies because the latter can 1) cannibalize an established company's sales of existing products, 2) undermine the competencies and skills of an existing firm, requiring additional investment in acquiring new skills and competencies, and 3) be viewed with skepticism and disbelief since they are coming from outside the organization.

TACIT. Tacit knowledge of a technology is largely held in the minds of the inventors, as compared to codified technology, which can be written down and transferred to another person. Tacit knowledge tends to favor a start-up since the faculty founder is typically more engaged, by way of founding and ownership. This engagement helps establish the applications of the technology as well as technology- and product-development activities. An established company, by way of a license, usually does not have access to this tacit knowledge unless it hires the faculty as consultants or sponsors research at the university.

EARLY STAGE. Early-stage technology has not been developed enough to attract a license from established companies. Established companies seek more mature technologies not only because of the high risk associated with early-stage technologies but also because the timeline to revenue is shorter and the value is difficult to assess (e.g., as it relates to the license).

GENERAL PURPOSE. A general-purpose technology (often referred to as platform technology) has many market applications, some of which may not be apparent at first. Diverse utilities give the start-up an option to choose the most promising market, as compared to an established company that will focus on the primary market addressed by their business. This option value also provides alternatives in the event that one application proves unsatisfactory due to problems with product development or lack of market traction.

HIGH CUSTOMER VALUE. Because a start-up must develop a product from scratch, it requires a significant investment of people, capital, and time. In order for a start-up to receive a return on that investment, the product's value to the customer must be significant. In contrast, established companies can leverage their current infrastructure in product development, sales, and marketing, and thus do not have to invest as much to develop the product. This lowers the return on investment for the company.

STRONG INTELLECTUAL PROPERTY POSITION. IP is just one aspect of bringing a product to market. Established companies have a number of assets they can draw on to develop and launch a product: knowledge capital, R&D facilities, and established distribution channels. For a start-up, IP is typically its *only* asset, therefore IP needs to be strong for a start-up to attract management, key employees, and capital.[2]

Since most universities do research on fundamental aspects of biology, chemistry, materials, and software and research faculty possess much of

2. Scott Shane, *Academic Entrepreneurship: University Spinoffs and Wealth Creation* (Cheltenham, UK: Edward Elgar, 2004).

the know-how beyond patents and publications, one could assume most technologies coming from a university are suitable for start-ups. Why, then, do only approximately a third of university innovations reach the market through start-ups?

Beyond the inherent nature of the technology, a number of factors both within and outside the university affect start-up formation. Dante Di Gregorio and Scott Shane studied a number of universities from 1994 to 1998 and examined the rate of start-up formation (not the success of the start-ups) as it related to four factors: 1) the availability of venture capital in the region, 2) the commercial orientation of the university research, 3) intellectual eminence of the university, and 4) university policies. The authors concluded the following:

- The lack of local venture capital does not constrain start-up activity. The reason may be related to the fact that VC investments are not typically made at the company-formation stage or the fact that VC investments occur across a region, not just locally.
- Industry funding does not influence the rate of start-ups. Although a commercial orientation for research would presumably lead to more commercializable technology, it is assumed that industry, which funds the research, is more likely to take a license than to release the technology for a start-up.
- University eminence significantly influences start-up activity. It is presumed that technology from a more eminent university reduces the barriers to attracting management and capital.
- University policies influence start-up activity. Policies related to royalty sharing can disincentivize faculty to start companies: The greater the royalty retained by the university, the lower the start-up activity. Furthermore, as one would expect, universities that were willing and able to make equity investments increased start-up activity. Two factors were found to have little influence on start-up activity: the presence of a university incubator and a university venture fund. A university incubator may increase the likelihood of success but does not appear to influence the decision to start a company. The reasons a university venture fund has little influence may be the same reasons that the lack of local VC availability does not constrain start-up activity.[3]

3. Dante Di Gregorio and Scott Shane, "Why Do Some Universities Generate More Start-Ups Than Others," *Research Policy* 32 (2003): 209–27.

A number of other factors can play a role in university start-up activity:

AN ENTREPRENEURIAL CULTURE. The desire of the faculty to be involved in a start-up can be driven, to a large extent, by the culture of the university. A university with a large number of faculty with positive entrepreneurial experiences will greatly influence faculty who are considering a start-up for the first time. According to authors Janet Bercovitz and Maryann Feldman, diffusive learning occurs in academic settings where faculty who are experienced in commercialization activities interact with less experienced faculty. Specifically, they state, "Considering the localized social environment, we find that when the chair of the department is active in technology transfer, other members of the department are also likely to participate, if only for symbolic reasons. We also find that technology transfer behavior is calibrated by the experience of those in the relevant cohort. If an individual can observe others with whom they identify engaging in the new initiative, then they are more likely to follow with substantive compliance.[4]

EXTERNAL ENTREPRENEURIAL ENGAGEMENT. Most faculty founders do not have the skills and experience to launch a company, develop a business strategy, and raise the capital required to execute the strategy. Engaging external entrepreneurs to partner with the faculty founder is important in developing the start-up. The more entrepreneurs interact with faculty, the more likely faculty will form start-ups. The interaction can be passive, in that entrepreneurs read literature or contact the TTO looking for interesting technology, or the interactions can be facilitated by the university through showcases, "speed-dating," or symposia.

UNIVERSITY SUPPORT. Many universities lack the resources to support early-stage start-ups spinning out of the university. Most TTOs are staffed by employees with a mix of technical and legal experience who have the skills to protect IP and negotiate licenses. Rarely are these offices staffed by entrepreneurs who understand the process and can manage the chaos associated with the nonlinear nature of the steps one needs to take to build a start-up.

In 2005, Gideon Markman et al. examined the structure of university TTOs and their licensing strategies and how those strategies influence university en-

4. Janet Bercovitz and Maryann Feldman, "Academic Entrepreneurs: Organizational Change at the Individual Level," *Organizational Science* 19 (2008): 69–89.

trepreneurship.[5] The authors conducted seven in-depth interviews with TTO directors and used those results to conduct more focused interviews with 121 additional TTO directors. The 128 U.S. institutions in the study represented 92 percent of the Association of University Technology Managers (AUTM) membership and 60 percent of the total federal and industry research funding as of 1999. After the interviews, the authors were able classify TTOs as one of three types of organizations: 52 percent were traditional university administrative units, 41 percent were nonprofit 501(c)1 research foundations, and 7 percent were for-profit private venture extensions of the university. In the area of licensing, the authors grouped TTO licensing strategy into three distinct transactions: licensing in return for sponsored research, in return for cash, or in return for equity.

Since most university licenses incorporate more than one of these elements (e.g., a start-up might pay an up-front licensing fee as well as issue equity to the university), Markman et al. asked how these strategies were distributed across all licenses (What is the average distribution of licensing strategies [out of 100 percent] across these three possibilities at your institution?). The institutions' responses indicated that 11 percent of TTOs primarily sought sponsored research, 17 percent primarily sought equity, and 72 percent primarily sought cash as their licensing objectives. Looking at the relationship between TTO *structure* and new venture creation, the most positive correlation existed for the for-profit TTO structure. The reason for this is since the for-profit model provides the most flexibility in entrepreneurial activities (raising money, incubating companies, etc.), most for-profit TTOs are built for the express purpose of spinning out companies. No other TTO structures were positively correlated with creating start-ups. In terms of the relationship between *licensing strategy* and new ventures, a negative correlation existed between sponsored research and new venture creation since most sponsored research involves large corporations. As expected, a positive correlation existed between licensing for equity and the creation of university start-ups. Finally, the most popular strategy, licensing for cash, was negatively correlated to new venture creation. This is because most start-ups don't have cash for licensing, whereas more established companies do.[6]

The authors conclude: "Taken together, these findings suggest that universities most interested in generating short-term cash flows from their IP

5. Gideon D. Markman, Phillip H. Phan, David B. Balkin, and Peter T. Gianiodis, "Entrepreneurship and University-Based Technology Transfer," *Journal of Business Venturing* 20 (2005): 241–63.
6. Ibid.

licensing strategies are least positioned to create long-term wealth through venture creation. Although two-thirds of the universities in this study have invested significant resources in incubators and have expressed an interest in new business start-ups and economic development, most of them have not linked this to their technology transfer strategy choices or to the mission of their [TTOs]. This disconnect may be one reason why university incubators tend to remain at the fringe of regional economic development efforts, in spite of the espoused goals of community development in many university mission statements."[7]

Limited research has been done on what factors lead to the successful commercialization of technology by a university start-up. Christopher Hayter interviewed 117 academic entrepreneurs involved in commercializing technologies licensed from a wide range of U.S. universities and concluded the following factors led to successful commercialization:

- Faculty founders' participation in a joint venture
- Multiple or externally sourced technologies
- Start-up receiving venture capital (had only a slight affect)
- Faculty founders' participation in industry-sponsored research
- The technology not being a life science technology
- The company having a nonfaculty CEO

Surprisingly, a number of factors did *not* have a significant impact on successful commercialization:

- Founders having previously founded a start-up
- TTO policies (obstructionist or otherwise)
- Equity position held by the university
- Peer culture (positive but insignificant)
- University entrepreneur services
- Development funding from SBIR or state government

Hayter acknowledges several limitations of his research that may account for some of the findings. The first and most significant was the sample size. The database of companies considered in the study contained 193 university start-ups founded since 1980, of which 117 were surveyed. Some estimates put the total number of start-ups founded over this time period at over 3,000, indicating that sampling error may have impacted Hayter's conclusions. Second, many companies don't ever commercialize the technology originally licensed from the university but rather commercialize one they themselves

7. Ibid., 258.

have developed; that is, a company may pivot (change its strategic direction or make improvements that don't rely on the original university technology). Accounting for these pivots is difficult. Third, Hayter's definition of commercialization is not well-defined and, admittedly, difficult to define: Successful commercialization is a self-reported binary indicator of commercial success where 1 equals some level of commercialization, while 0 indicates that the spinoff has not, to date, commercialized the technology. Commercial success comes in many forms and is open to interpretation. Does a certain level of revenue, an acquisition, or an initial public offering (IPO) signify success? Finally, the area of academic entrepreneurship has changed significantly over the last decade with more universities developing programs, policies, and funding to support university start-ups. Many of the start-ups studied may not have had the benefit of this support, and, more likely, the entrepreneurial culture would not have been established at the university.[8]

Types of University Start-Ups

A start-up company spinning out of a university can come in many forms. Two key ingredients determine the type of the start-up: 1) the nature of the idea, innovation, or invention around which the company is founded and 2) the people involved in starting the company. Figure 1.2 shows schematically these different components as they relate to different types of start-ups.[9]

Type I start-ups include start-ups where a faculty member is involved in the founding of a company to commercialize some body of research, invention, or IP. Here, the faculty member will play some role in the company (e.g., as a consultant or scientific adviser), and less frequently, he/she will leave an academic position and join the company's management team.

Type II start-ups involve university IP but do not involve the research faculty. In our experience, these are less common because the specialized nature and immature development of most university IP requires some input from the faculty inventor.

Type III start-ups are founded by an entrepreneurially minded faculty member with an idea that is not viewed by the university as protectable IP (i.e.,

8. Christopher S. Hayter, "Harnessing University Entrepreneurship for Economic Growth: Factors of Success Among University Spin-offs," *Economic Development Quarterly* 27 (1) (2013): 18–28.

9. One may see the terms university "spin-out" and "start-up" as well as distinctions between the two (e.g., one may involve a faculty founder, another may not). There is no standard distinction; we use "start-up" exclusively throughout the book to mean any start-up associated with a university discovery, innovation, or invention.

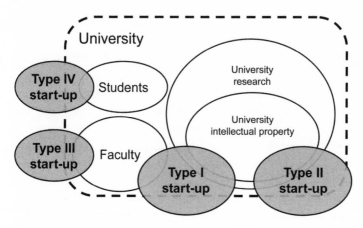

FIGURE 1.2 Types of university start-ups

by patents or copyrights) and may or may not be related to his/her faculty position. For example, an English professor with a passion for beer might start a microbrewery or an education faculty member may form a company for consulting to school systems.

Type IV start-ups are student-led and are built around an idea conceived while a student is at the university (e.g., Facebook). Because students are not students for very long, these companies usually move out of the university, leaving no long-term ties to it. This type of start-up raises questions about the university's rights for companies developed by students while living on campus using university resources (e.g., the library or computer systems). In general, schools retain rights to any intellectual property developed by students and faculty as part of their education and employment but will grant exceptions to student if the work is done as part of an university entrepreneurship activity or a class project (e.g., see University of Illinois guidelines, http://otm.illinois.edu/studentownership).

Technology-Based University Start-Ups

Type I start-ups, and to a lesser extent Type II start-ups, are the main focus of this book. These technology-based start-ups are unique in several ways.

Licensed intellectual property. University research results in novel discoveries or inventions that are then either copyrighted or, more commonly, patented.

The copyrights and patents form the basis of the IP licensed to the start-up company. The licensed IP represents the most significant asset and competitive advantage for the company. From a university's perspective, licensing to a start-up rather than to an established company presents several challenges. First, the start-up may not have a well-formed management team or a business leader, leading to delays in negotiations and resulting in the faculty founder's involvement in negotiations. Second, the start-up rarely has capital to pay the up-front costs or to reimburse the university for patent fees. Instead, the start-up has equity to offer the university as something of future, and generally unknown, value.

Faculty founder. Most technology-based university start-ups have a faculty founder whose research is the core capability of the company. As mentioned, the founder has significant tacit knowledge of the technology—its flaws, its potential, and its applications. As such, his/her involvement is critical for success. However, the faculty founder has to wear several hats, one as company owner/founder/technical lead/interim management and the other as university employee/teacher/researcher. Distinguishing between those two roles can be challenging. Furthermore, because the faculty member has a financial interest in the company, namely ownership, conflicts of interest (COI) arise. Conflict of commitment can also be an issue as it relates to how much time the faculty member spends with the start-up compared to the time spent on university duties.

High risk. Compared to technologies licensed to established companies, most technologies for university start-ups are revolutionary and relatively immature. As such, these start-ups are high-risk endeavors, with risk ranging from technical risk (Will it work?), to scale-up risk (Can we manufacture it?), to market risk (Will anyone buy it?), to management risk (Is it the right team?).

Significant capital requirements. Most technologies coming out of university start-ups, with the exception of information technologies, require significant capital to bring the product to market. This is especially true for life science technologies where regulatory approval is required. Given the high risk associated with university start-ups and their requirement for capital, they face a challenge when raising funds.

University engagement. Since the university has an interest in having the start-up succeed (success will help pay license fees, satisfy the faculty member's interest in commercialization), support by the university can increase the likelihood for success. This could include start-up funds, incubation space, or connections to investors and management.

Since the 1990s, the number of university start-ups has steadily increased. According to the AUTM, the rate of annual start-up creation has more than doubled since 1998, from less than 150 per year to over 300 per year in 2010. A number of factors contribute to this trend:

UNIVERSITY POLICIES AND PROGRAMS. From seeking a return on society's research dollar, to recruiting and retaining talented faculty, to driving local economic growth, universities have begun to embrace entrepreneurship as part of the university mission. To support academic entrepreneurship, universities have expanded the mission of their TTOs, established venture funds, and created programs like entrepreneurs-in-residence to help support faculty with start-ups. Many have also updated or clarified conflict of interest and commitment policies to account for faculty start-up activities.

STATE POLICIES AND PROGRAMS. Mirroring university activity in this area, many state governments view university start-ups as economic development engines for their region. Many states have established grant programs (e.g., SBIR match or bridge), venture funds, and incubators to help these fledgling companies.

CHANGING VIEWS AMONG PROFESSORS. Many academic faculty, especially younger faculty, see commercialization and start-up activities as part of their academic role. For some, these activities are seen as a way to build personal wealth; for others, commercialization provides an opportunity to translate their research into real-world impact. This changing attitude yields less distinction and more compatibility between academics and industry.

INNOVATION AND ENTREPRENEURSHIP. Many universities are embracing I&E as a theme across campus. As part of this, undergraduate majors and minors in entrepreneurship are being established. "Maker spaces" are being created for students to produce prototypes. "Hackathons" are bringing ideas together with coders to develop novel apps and websites. "Start-up dorms" are used to foster new ideas and incubate student-led start-ups. These campus activities have begun to influence faculty and tech transfer offices as they relate to research-based university start-ups.

The increase in the commercialization of university research is not without its critics. Daniel Greenberg sees the trend as troubling and worthy of discourse and possible public policy changes. He argues that the influences of capitalism have negatively influenced the objectivity and purity of academic research. He raises a number of questions worth considering as one embarks on the entrepreneurial path to commercialization: "Have today's commercial values contaminated academic research, diverting it from socially beneficial goals to mercenary service on behalf of profit-seeking corporate interests? What are the gains and losses in the visibly tightening linkage of science and mammon, and to whose benefit and whose detriment? Can academic institutions, with their insatiable appetite for money, reap financial profits from their production of valuable knowledge without damage to the soul of science?"[10]

There is no doubt that the interaction of academics with capitalism as it relates to commercialization has resulted in less than desirable outcomes. Today, however, most universities have recognized the potential for negative effects and have policies and guidelines in place to manage this interface between academics and private enterprise.

In this book, we emphasize the positive effects of commercializing university technology. The interaction of private enterprise with academics has resulted in institutions, administrators, and faculty taking a more "translational" approach to research. Instead of acquiring knowledge for knowledge sake, many are asking how that knowledge can be translated into benefit for society. In their book *Engines of Innovation: The Entrepreneurial University of the Twenty-First Century*, Holden Thorp and Buck Goldstein go further. "Now more than ever," they write, "funding sources and other supporters [of universities] are looking for a measureable return on their investment. It is no longer merely desirable for universities to be the source of innovations. It is now a national priority. Institutions that have received so much over the years—and then are generally perceived as one of the crown jewels of American culture—must now step up at a time of crisis and play a central role in addressing pressing issues facing the world."[11]

It is with this charge that we embrace the role of university start-ups as essential in translating university innovations into impactful products, research to revenue.

10. Daniel S. Greenberg, *Science for Sale: The Perils, Rewards, and Delusions of Campus Capitalism* (Chicago: University of Chicago Press, 2007), 2.

11. Holden Thorp and Buck Goldstein, *Engines of Innovation: The Entrepreneurial University of the Twenty-First Century* (Chapel Hill: University of North Carolina Press, 2010), 3.

2

The University Start-Up

Characteristics and Context

Start-ups, in general, include everything from restaurants to online retailers, from consultancies to manufacturers of widgets. University start-ups are a subset of businesses within the world of entrepreneurship. They share many of the same attributes of other start-ups: they need capital to grow the company and smart people to make key decisions. However, they are unique in other ways. They are borne out of discoveries made within the university setting by faculty focused on academic research, and as such, they require a different type of "care and feeding" from that of other start-ups. This chapter discusses the unique qualities of a university start-up and places it within the broader entrepreneurial ecosystem.

Anatomy of a Start-Up Company

A university start-up can be thought of as a translation engine, translating university discoveries into impactful products that solve a customer problem, meet an unmet need in the market, or address a societal problem. Extending the analogy, the engine, fueled by capital, drives the process of developing the product, manufacturing the product, marketing the product, and selling the product to customers. A number of key aspects of a start-up are considered here and elaborated on further in Chapter 3. Figure 2.1 provides an overview of the start-up company and its processes. Briefly, and in more detail below, *technology development* is focused on the earliest studies and experiments to demonstrate the utility and feasibility of the technology. *Product development* embodies the key attributes of the technology into a product, defining the features and benefits. *Manufacturing* develops the infrastructure and process to create a reliable product, balancing quality and cost. *Sales and marketing* create demand for the product by considering the customers need for the features and benefits of the product relative to competitive products. Finally, the customer engages with the company through a *business model*, which de-

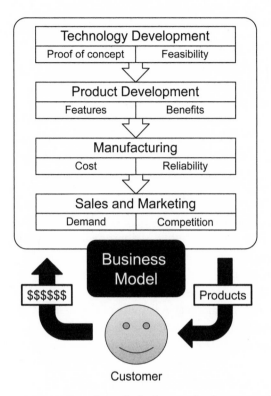

FIGURE 2.1 Overview of bringing a technology to market

fines the transaction of delivering the product or service to the customer in exchange for cash.

Business Model

To be successful, every business must have a business model, and a start-up is no exception. Although deciding on a business model may seem premature at the early stages of a university start-up, it can have deep implications on how the company is formed, raises money, and develops products. The company does not need to lock down a model at this point, but it does need to be considered alongside product development since they go hand-in-hand.

A business model is broadly defined as the roadmap for how a company is going to create value and capture returns on investments (i.e., make money). A narrower definition, sometimes referred to as the revenue model, focuses on defining the nature of the transaction between the customer and the start-up: What will the customer buy and how will they buy it?

There are number of business models applicable to university start-ups:

DIRECT SALES. The simplest business model is direct sales, where the company sells the product directly to the customer by deploying a sales force. Although the simplest transactional model, direct sales requires the development of many aspects of a mature business: product development, manufacturing, sales, marketing, customer support. For start-ups to do a direct sales model, they need the time and capital to implement these aspects of the business (e.g., hiring and training salespeople).

DISTRIBUTOR MODEL. A company may decide that the cost and time to sell directly to customers is prohibitive. In that case, it may choose a distributor to market and sell the product. Although the company will have to share the profits from sales, the right distributor will have rapid access to customers and regions to sell the product. Distributors are popular for low-cost (commodity) products that need to reach a large customer base (e.g., via catalogs or websites) or for products destined for global markets (e.g., the Asian market). A liability of the distributor model may surface when an early-stage, technology-based product is trying to gain market adoption. In this case, the start-up often needs to have a direct line of communication with the customer to understand the application, to make changes to the product to better solve a problem, etc. A distributor who does not fully understand the product or has less incentive to communicate can interfere with this consumer relationship.

(SUB)LICENSING/PARTNERING MODEL. For some technologies, the route to bringing a product to market is long, expensive, and complicated. For these technologies, finding a corporate partner with the requisite resources is the preferred route. One approach is for the start-up to license (or sublicense, from the university's perspective) the technology to a partner. In this case, the partner does most of the work to bring the product to market (and retains most of the value). At the other extreme, the start-up may have enough internal capabilities to collaborate with a partner in developing the product. For example, given the costs of developing a drug, pharmaceuticals typically fall into this model. A large pharmaceutical company may license the drug compounds from the start-up or may sign a codevelopment agreement where both parties contribute time, money, and expertise.

SERVICE MODEL. For this model, the company provides a service (i.e., a unique capability) to the customer. For technology-based companies, the typical service is providing a unique analysis or measurement for a fee ("fee-for-service"). For example, a novel analysis of a polymer material can be provided as a service to a chemical company developing new products. In this case the customer sends a sample to the start-up where it is analyzed and the results returned to the customer. In other service models, the start-up may have a unique capability to produce a novel material (nanoparticle) or component (optical element). In this case, the customer will contract with the start-up to produce the material that goes into the customer's product.

SUBSCRIPTION MODEL. The subscription model usually applies to software and web-based companies. In this case, the customer pays an annual subscription fee to use the software or website. The advantage to the customer is a "pay-as-you-go" approach. If the software is not needed after several years, the subscription will not be renewed. For the start-up, subscriptions provide a recurring revenue stream and access to customers who can help refine the product.

SOFTWARE AS A SERVICE (SAAS) MODEL. This is a blend of the two previous models, which was made popular by Salesforce.com. In this case, the customer subscribes to an enterprise software system. Rather than implementing the software at the customer's business, the provider hosts the software on its servers. This model reduces integration costs and lowers the bar for customers who want access to the software but don't want to make a large investment in computer infrastructure.

RAZOR AND RAZOR BLADE MODEL. This model, a hybrid of some of the above-mentioned models, takes advantage of a customer's use of a product that requires a continuous supply of components. This model was made popular by inkjet printers: The printers (razors) are relatively inexpensive but require the periodic purchase of inkjet cartridges (razor blades). For technology-based companies, this type of model often translates into an instrument (razor) that requires a disposable unit or reagents (razor blade).

The business models described are not mutually exclusive, and businesses can have a model that combines several aspects of two models. For example, a platform technology company may commercialize using several models. It may license the technology to a third party for independent development of a product for one application, partner with a company to jointly develop a product for a second application, and internally develop and sell a third product. For example, in therapeutics development, a series of drugs can have applications across several therapeutic areas. A large pharmaceutical company may partner with the start-up to develop a drug for a specific disease for a large market, leaving the start-up to develop a drug targeting a smaller patient population.

Furthermore, it's not uncommon for a company to change its business model over time. The change can be part of a planned business strategy or emerge if one model is not gaining traction (sometimes referred to as a "pivot"). An example of the former involves the start-up formed around a novel process for synthesizing biodegradable polymers. The initial business model may be providing custom synthesis of polymers for customers (service model). As the company gains more expertise, infrastructure, market understanding, and revenue, it creates a product line of off-the-shelf biodegradable polymers for customers to purchase and incorporate into their products. Finally, as the company grows, it may consider making its own products (e.g., garbage bags) to sell directly to customers. This example shows the relationship between a business model and how it captures value. Initially, the company is providing custom synthesis services and is capturing little value compared to its clients, who are creating products from the polymers. In the second case, the company is capturing more value by providing products that are desired by more customers, plus it can make the polymers in larger batches, creating better efficiency. Finally, by creating its own final products, the start-up captures the value that was previously captured by its clients and customers.[1]

Technology Development (Proof of Concept)

One of the first activities a university start-up will engage in is technology development. Most technologies at the core of a start-up company arise from university research, but at some point the research must transition to development (initially technology development and then product development). Although the lines between these activities are not distinct and the activities will differ for each technology, it is important to distinguish between research and technology development in the context of a start-up. Research within the domain of universities is typically hypothesis-driven: a question is posed and the research attempts to discover whether to validate or dispute the hypothesis. The result of research is knowledge around the research question, as well

---

1. This example further illustrates the complexity of shifting business models. By moving from the service to the product model, the start-up can begin to compete with (and alienate) its current (and former) customers and clients.

as additional questions or subquestions yet to be answered. This knowledge, made public through published works (e.g., journal articles), is the subject of future grant-funding proposals and makes up the economic system of major research universities. Technology development is distinct from research in that 1) it answers more questions than it raises and 2) many of the questions it answers are important in creating a product and less important to academic endeavors (i.e., not very intellectually interesting or worthy of publication). Technology development is sometimes referred to as "proof of concept" or "proof of principle." Examples of technology-development activities include the following:

DEMONSTRATION OF APPLICATION AND CAPABILITIES. Often a technology derived from university research is described in terms of an application that demonstrates the principle of the technology but the application may have little commercial relevance. This often arises because the faculty member does not have access to "real-world" problems, or the commercial application may be too difficult or too expensive to demonstrate. For example, a novel antifouling polymer coating may have been shown effective in inhibiting algae growth in a lab experiment, but deciding how to use the polymer in a real-world application (ship's hulls, sewage pipes, piers, medical devices) is the work of technology development.

VALIDATION. Often a technology has been demonstrated with a small sample size, again, for the purpose of generating data for a publication. Validation involves reproducing the effect many times on one set of samples and/or demonstrating the effect for a large set of samples. For example, biomarkers are typically discovered using a small set of patient samples. Technology development would involve not only analyzing the samples multiple times to validate the biomarker assay but also analyzing a large cohort of patients to examine the sensitivity and selectivity of the test in real-world populations.

BENCHTOP/BREADBOARD PROTOTYPE. An important principle or scientific effect may have been demonstrated in a university lab. The embodiment of that principle in a benchtop or breadboard prototype involves technology development. For example, a spectroscopic detection phenomenon might have been discovered using an elaborate optical laser bench, but for demonstrating its commercial feasibility, it will need to be reduced to a breadboarded prototype, which is more suitable for customer use and manufacturing.

SCALE-UP. An academic research investigator often discovers a novel molecule, compound, or polymer that has groundbreaking properties. One of the challenges encountered during technology development is the scaling of that process to produce larger quantities or reproducibly producing batches. Effective scaling requires development and optimization, and difficulties in this area can be an indication of challenges down the road for manufacturing.

EFFICACY AND SAFETY. A disease mechanism may be elucidated through academic research, but demonstrating a molecule that can modulate the disease in an animal disease model is an important, commercially relevant first step. Further development is demonstrating the safety of the molecule in humans.

Technology development can be challenging. For some technologies, the first challenge is choosing the commercially relevant application. For platform technologies (technologies that have multiple applications), it can be difficult to select the application with the greatest commercial potential because a) the technology's capabilities have yet to be demonstrated in that application, b) the fit between an application and the core capabilities of the technology may be different across different applications, and c) the insights of an experienced management team may not be available at this point of development. Once the application is chosen, the funding of technology-development activities can be challenging. These activities are often too risky for conventional equity investment (e.g., high-net-worth individuals, or angels, or VCs), and, given that it's often outside the scope of academic research (lack of innovation, lack of a hypothesis, nonpublishable results), it rarely gets federal research funding (NIH, NSF). For example, a novel therapeutic discovered at a university will generate publications and grants around target validation, mechanism of action, or efficacy in various animal models. However, experiments to determine the therapeutic's oral availability or renal toxicity are difficult to fund at the university.

Product Development

Technology-development activities lead naturally to the next major activity: product development. More formal than technology development, it has identifiable steps that management and investors can look to as value-creation milestones. The nature of the product-development activities depends on the type of product and the associated risks. One can divide product-development activities into two broad categories, based on the type of associated risk. For example, some products have significant *technical risk* (Will it work? Will it be safe and effective?) and a defined process for addressing the this risk. Developing a drug, diagnostic, or medical device involves a series of well-defined (FDA mandated) steps, starting with testing in animals followed by testing in humans. Other product-development activities relate to *market risk* (Is there a significant market need? Will the customer buy the product?). This involves taking a seed concept, developing a working prototype with specific features and functionality, getting market feedback early, refining the product to increase the market acceptance, retesting with customers, and so on. These different product-development activities are outlined below. (Note: Although they are presented separately here, many products have a mix of technical and market risk, requiring a blending of these two sets of activities.)

Product Development Addressing Technical and Regulatory Risks

Technical success is defined as meeting a series of technical specifications such as reproducibility, effectiveness, accuracy, safety, robustness, strength, effectiveness, weight, or cost. Three aspects of technical specifications for a product should be clear:

1 MARKET-BASED. Product specifications are rooted in the application being addressed by and derived from market insight or customer input. This points to the need for clearly defining the application to be addressed, the problem to be solved, and the perceived value the customer attributes to solving the problem.

2 MEASUREABLE. It sounds obvious, but the specification must be measurable, otherwise it will be difficult to know if it has been achieved. For example, a sensor needs to detect 100 parts per million of carbon monoxide to be useful to a customer.

3 VALUE-CREATING. It is important that the specifications be framed in a way that when they are achieved, significant value will have been created. This may be more perception than reality, but investors need a way to measure the progress of a company. Value-creating milestones, based on achieving one or more specifications, are usually agreed upon by the management team and the investors.

Once market-based, measurable, value-creating technical milestones have been identified, a development plan is created to address each milestone. The plan will include a timeline, activities to be pursued (studies, experiments), skills needed (personnel, consultants, vendors), and costs associated with each milestone.

TABLE 2.1 FDA approval regulatory routes

PRODUCT	APPROVAL ROUTE	TIME AND COST	PROCESS AND REQUIREMENTS
DRUG	IND/NDA*	5–10 years $50M–300M million	1 Preclinical (animal) animal studies 2 Approval of an IND by FDA 3 Clinical (human) studies (Phase I/II/III) 4 Approval of new drug application (NDA)
MEDICAL DEVICE DIAGNOSTIC TEST	Premarket notification	N/A	Class I device (gloves, bandages, hand-held surgical instruments) No PDA review required
		< 2 years $100K–$1M	Class II/III device (Predicate device on the market) 1 Pre-IDE meeting with PDA to discuss study 2 Study to demonstrate substantial equivalence to device currently on the market 3 Submit 510K for approval
	Premarket approval (PMA)**	3–5 years $2M–10M	Class II/III device (No predicate device on the market) 1 Pre-IDE meeting 2 Pilot phase: <100 patients over 3–6 months for safety/efficacy 3 Pivotal phase: 1,000 or more patients at multiple sites over 1–2 years for safety/efficacy 4 Submit PMA (180 days for approval)

*The typical FDA requirements will differ if the drug has a high impact on a life-threatening condition (fast track) or treats a relatively small population (orphan).

**Only ~2% of diagnostic tests follow the PMA route.

Product development for technologies spinning out of the university often involves approval by the FDA. The FDA is responsible for keeping our food supply safe and ensuring drugs, devices, and diagnostics provide a benefit to patients and that the benefits outweigh the risks. For most start-ups in the life science space, regulatory approval by the FDA is required. Table 2.1 is a quick snapshot of the regulatory aspects of drugs, devices, and diagnostics.

Overview of Drug Development

The development of novel therapeutics follows a path largely dictated by the FDA. The company first tests the drug in animals to demonstrate efficacy and safety—that is, efficacy in animal models that are surrogates for the disease in humans (e.g., obese mice) and safety in healthy animals given a wide range of drug dosages. In addition, the company conducts studies to examine the distribution and how long the drug stays in the animal (pharmacodynamics and pharmacokinetics). These preclinical studies are part of the investigational new drug (IND) application the company must submit to the FDA.[2] The application contains the data to demonstrate that the drug will not expose humans to an unreasonable risk when the clinical studies are initiated. The IND application contains pharmacology and toxicity studies, manufacturing information to demonstrate a stable and pure source of the drug for clinical studies, and the planned clinical protocols that outline the risks involved and the approvals required in conducting clinical trials with humans.

Once the IND has been approved, the company can initiate clinical trials ("first-in-human" trials). Phase I trials generally enroll a small number of healthy subjects (fewer than 100) to study the safety of the drug at different doses. If no adverse reactions occur, Phase II trials are initiated with a larger cohort of diseased patients (up to 1,000) which not only expand the study of drug safety but begin the process of demonstrating, for the first time, the efficacy of the drug in treating the disease. Phase II trials are often pivotal since they show treatment of the disease. Phase III trials include an even larger cohort (thousands) and demonstrate safety and effectiveness for broader segments of the patient population.

Overview of Medical Device and Diagnostic Development

Medical devices and diagnostics are also regulated by the FDA.[3] The process is similar in that preclinical work helps to support and justify the risk to evaluating the test or device with humans. First, the FDA evaluates the test or device in terms of risk to the patient, classifying it as low (Class I), moderate (Class II), high (Class III) risk. The risk can be associated either with the use of

2. INDs can also be submitted by physician investigators ("investigator-initiated INDs"), where the physician initiates, conducts, and controls the investigation. This activity is not part of a start-up but may lead to commercial development where the study involves an unapproved drug, an approved drug for a new indication, or a drug for a new patient population.

3. For an overview of the FDA regulations of diagnostic tests, see Elizabeth Mansfield, Timothy J. O'Leary, and Steven I. Gutman, "Food and Drug Administration Regulation of *in Vitro* Diagnostic Devices," *Journal of Medical Diagnostics* 7 (2005): 2–7. For an overview of medical devices, see John B. Reiss, ed., *Bringing Your Medical Device to Market* (Washington, D.C.: Food and Drug Law Institute, 2013).

the product (e.g., implants) or how the information will be used to diagnose the disease and how life-threatening the disease is (a test for obesity carries less risk than a test for pancreatic cancer in terms of a missed diagnosis). The second factor considered by the FDA, also related to risk, is the existence of similar approved products on the market. A similar product on the market ("predicate device") demonstrates a level of safety that a unique product cannot. For products with the highest potential risk (Class III), the FDA will require a Premarket Approval (PMA) application. This will include studies that support a reasonable assurance of safety and effectiveness. For lower risk tests and devices (Class I/II), the FDA requires a Premarket Notification (510[k]) submission. In these cases, the FDA compares them to a substantially equivalent, or predicate, product already on the market. In cases where there is no predicate, the company can seek de novo review. In this case, the product is tested as a PMA (e.g., clinical trials) but reviewed as a lower risk product (510[k]-type review).

A special case exists for certain diagnostic tests that are developed within a clinical testing laboratory and offered by that laboratory. These "home-brew," or laboratory-developed, tests (LDTs) are regulated at the state level through Clinical Laboratory Improvement Amendments (CLIAs) and fall outside FDA regulation, offering a faster, lower cost path to market.[4]

Product Development Addressing Market Risk

Some products must be developed with more emphasis on market risk (Is there a market need? Will anyone buy the product?). A practical guide to product development from this perspective comes from Steve Blank's book *Four Steps to Epiphany*. He argues that too many products are developed without customer input from the beginning, which leads the traditional product-development process down a path toward failure in the marketplace. The alternative is to engage in "customer development," where the initial product concept is validated by customers in terms of their needs. "A start-up begins with a vision," Blank writes. "A vision of a new product or service, a vision of how the product will reach its customers and a vision of why lots of people will buy that product. But most of what a start-up's founders initially believe about their market and potential customers are just educated guesses. To turn the vision into reality (and a profitable company), a start-up must test those

---

4. Peter M. Kazon, "Laboratory Developed Tests," in *In Vitro Diagnostics: The Complete Regulatory Guide*, edited by Kenneth R. Piña and Wayne L. Pines (Washington, D.C.: Food and Drug Law Institute, 2012).

guesses or hypotheses, and find out which are correct. So the general goal of customer discovery amounts to this: turning the founders' initial hypothesis about their market and customers into facts. And since the facts live outside the building, the primary activity is to get in front of customers."[5]

The following are Blank's four steps of customer development:

1 CUSTOMER DISCOVERY. As the name implies, this step seeks to find out who the customers are and how important the problem you are solving for them is. It involves creating a number of hypotheses about the product and testing those hypotheses with customer input.
2 CUSTOMER VALIDATION. This step tests the perceived value of the product and corroborates the business model by selling the product to customers, moving a potential customer to actual customer. Often called the "check test" (Will the customer write a check for the product?), this and customer discovery are the two most critical steps in building a successful company.
3 CUSTOMER CREATION. Once initial sales have begun, the next step is to drive demand for the product through effective marketing.
4 COMPANY BUILDING. With significant customer demand for the product, the company can begin scaling the business; i.e., establishing formal departments to carry out the mission of the company.[6]

The customer discovery process is discussed in more detail in Chapter 3.

Manufacturing

As the product is developed, attention begins to turn to manufacturing. Late in product development, a limited production of "beta prototypes" or "production prototypes" is made. The prototypes can be used for customers to test as alpha or beta units. By having a select group of customers test-drive the product, important information can be gained in terms of usability, functionality, and reliability. Second, the prototypes begin to establish the manufacturing process and help to lock down the product to the point where no more significant changes can be made, allowing the manufacturing group to begin ordering larger lots of materials, parts, and components and begin to establish the manufacturing processes.

The business model takes into account the options for manufacturing.

5. Stephen G. Blank, *The Four Steps to Epiphany: Successful Strategies for Products That Win* (cafe press.com, 2006), 33.
6. Ibid.

Decisions need to be made as to whether the manufacturing is going to be done in-house (completely built at the company site) or outsourced (manufacturer builds and ships units from its factory) or via a combination of the two (components outsourced and assembled by the company). As with any major decision for a start-up, it comes down to time and money. Initially, outsourced manufacturing may be the best option since it gets the product on the market quickly without the significant capital costs of building a manufacturing operation.

Sales and Marketing

Sales and marketing is where the business model gets fully implemented. This is the true test of whether large numbers of customers will purchase the product or whether sales never develop to the point of sustaining the company. It is often said that, "marketing creates the appeal, sales close the deal." Marketing focuses on communicating effectively the key features and benefits of the product through advertising, trade shows, a website, e-mail blasts, webinars, and other channels. Marketing's job is to create leads or potential customers that sales can follow up on. In some companies, marketing also covers customer support (presales questions and postsales support and repair). Sales focuses on the transaction (i.e., selling the product for money). Given the wide variety of business models, the sales effort can vary from company to company. As mentioned, sales may be done directly by the company or outsourced to a distributor (see page 24).

The University Start-Up Ecosystem

A university-born start-up company is part of a complex ecosystem comprised of many moving parts. To be successful, the start-up relies on three key components of the ecosystem. The first component is the university, which can impact the start-up in several significant ways, from licensing of the technology to helping support the start-up. The second component involves the people outside the university engaged with the start-up. These people play important roles by either working for the company (scientists, engineers, management) or with the company (advisers, consultants, service providers). The final component is funding (capital or cash), which provides the fuel to enable the company to develop its product or service. Funding comes from a variety of sources: federal agencies, individual investors (angels), institutional investors (venture capital), and/or corporations (corporate partners). In ad-

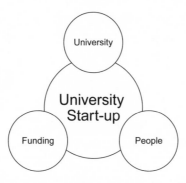

dition, the funding is often accompanied by expertise (e.g., an investor can make key connections or provide experienced governance).

The University

The university plays a number of roles in the start-up ecosystem. At minimum, it owns and protects the intellectual property and licenses the IP to the start-up; it also employs the faculty member who is founding the company. Beyond these roles, the university can provide support for the start-up by educating faculty members, helping to recruit entrepreneurs and service providers who can engage with the start-up; offer grants and investments in the early-stage company; and furnish space for incubating the company.

Let's unpack each one of these roles individually.

The University Protects Intellectual Property

Intellectual property encompasses the inventions discovered at and owned, protected, and licensed by the university for commercial development. With the passage of the Bayh-Dole Act in 1980, universities are able to retain the ownership to any inventions arising from federally funded research.[7] In exchange, the university has certain obligations, as outlined previously in the Introduction. Intellectual property falls into a number of different categories: copyrights, trademarks, patents, industrial design rights, and trade secrets. For most universities, the two relevant categories are copyrights and pat-

7. "Chapter 18—Patent Rights in Inventions Made with Federal Assistance," Title 35 of the United States Code—Patents, http://www.gpo.gov/fdsys/pkg/USCODE-2011-title35/pdf/USCODE-2011-title35-partII-chap18.pdf (accessed 10 December 2014).

8. Given the open nature of the university system, few formal trade secrets (e.g., formulations, processes, etc.) exist. However, given the complex nature of science and the fact that experiments

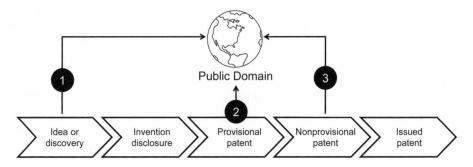

FIGURE 2.2 Flow of intellectual property through the university

ents.[8] Copyrights play a key role in protecting software, although enforcing copyrighted software has been difficult. Patents are the most significant (and most expensive) form of IP that universities use for protection. In a university setting, the patent holder is the university and the inventor is the faculty, staff, or student who made the discovery. The granting of the patent provides 20 years of exclusivity, giving the owner the right to go to court to attempt to prevent others from making, using, selling, or distributing the invention without permission. In return for this period of exclusivity, the inventor must publicly disclose the details of the invention (the patent) in order to facilitate innovation by others (e.g., improvements). Patents fall into three categories: design patents, plant patents, and utility patents, with the latter being the most common. An example of a utility patent with an explanation of its components can be found at researchtorevenue.com.

Figure 2.2 shows the typical flow of intellectual property (patents) through the university along with the points of public disclosure. University research results in new knowledge, most of which is published in journals or disclosed at meetings (fig. 2.2, path 1). Some of this knowledge has the potential to solve problems of commercial interest; that is, it meets a customer's needs. These discoveries and ideas (inventions) have the most value for commercialization if they are protected by patents. In order to protect these inventions, a disclosure must be made to the university (typically the TTO), which captures the nature and scope of the invention. The TTO makes decisions about what to file and when to file for patent protection (discussed in more detail in Chapter 3). Once a provisional patent application has been filed, the faculty member

---

fail and successful experiments are not always reported, a certain amount of "trade secret" resides with the faculty member. For this reason, the commercialization of some technologies requires the intellectual input of the faculty member.

TABLE 2.2 Examples of patent coverage and costs

PATENT TYPE AND COVERAGE	COST
Broad international coverage (14 countries)	$272K to issue plus ~$20K annual annuities
Broad international coverage (23 countries)	$526K to issue plus ~$60K annual annuities
Limited international coverage (U.S., 3 European)	$133K to issue plus ~$5K annual annuities
U.S. only (no PCT [patent cooperation treaty]), complicated prosecution	$27K to issue plus maintenance fees at 3, 7, 11 years
U.S. only (no PCT), simple prosecution	$13K to issue plus maintenance fees at 3, 7, 11 years

Source: UNC Office of Technology Development

can disclose the discovery while retaining protection (fig. 2.2, path 2).[9] The provisional application is converted to a nonprovisional application no later than 12 months after its filing. Eighteen months after the nonprovisional is filed, the patent application is published (fig. 2.2, path 3). Meanwhile, the patent office is reviewing the patent and issuing "office actions" or opinions and requests (e.g., doesn't allow certain claims, divides the patent in two). Eventually, the patent office makes a ruling of allowance or disallowance, the former resulting in the issuance of a patent.

The cost of protecting IP can be significant. With the larger number of inventions disclosed each year, universities struggle to decide which patents to file. The challenge is magnified by the fact that many of these disclosures are made with limited information on the viability of the technology (Will it work?) or the commercial application (What is the product?). Table 2.2 shows examples of different patent coverage and the associated costs.

The University Licenses Intellectual Property

The commercialization of university technology is enabled by the university granting a license or releasing the technology without a license. While the university retains ownership of the intellectual property, usually in the form of a patent, it can provide a license to a company that allows the company

9. If the invention is disclosed prior to filing the provisional patent, patent protection can still be obtained but only for the United States (assuming the invention is made in the United States).

to develop, manufacture, sell, and distribute products and services based on the IP. A typical license contains the following elements:

SCOPE OF USE. This defines both the geographic region for sale (e.g., United States only, worldwide) and the fields into which the product can be sold (e.g., consumer electronics, defense, medical devices). If the scope is divided, a patent can generate multiple licenses to multiple companies.

DEVELOPMENT MILESTONES. These define a timetable by which certain product-development milestones will be met. For example, if the IP is a pharmaceutical compound, the milestones will typically be the regulatory hurdles (IND, Phase I, II, III, and NDA). The timetable protects the university from companies that do not make the appropriate progress in commercializing the technology. Additional milestones may be put in place around company formation and growth (e.g., business plan, seed funding, establishing facilities, first product launch).

PAYMENTS. In return for the license, the company pays the university a variety of payments:

- Up-front fees. These are due upon signing the licensing agreement, with the rationale that the university needs to cover the sunk cost of patenting the IP.
- Milestone payments. Cash payments made to the university upon the company reaching certain milestones, as outlined above.
- Royalties. The company will pay the university a percentage (typically less than 10 percent) of sales of the product based on the technology.

For a start-up with limited financial resources, these payments tend to be back-loaded. For example, an up-front payment might not be required, or it might be small compared to what an established company might be required to pay, but the royalties on products sold could be higher.

EQUITY. Given the financial constraints of start-ups, many universities will acquire equity (stock representing ownership in the company) as part of the license agreement. The ownership can be as high as 50 percent in cases where the university has or will provide significant support, but typically the equity percentage is in the high single digits or low double digits. In addition to the equity, the university will sometimes include an "antidilution" provision for its equity, which prevents the university's ownership from being diluted by additional investors but typically only applies up to a certain level of investment (e.g., university ownership dilution occurs after the company has raised $1 million in equity-based financing). (See page 62 for more on dilution.)

Maryann Feldman et al. explored the rise in equity in licensing of university technology. They found three advantages for a university taking equity as part of the licensing transaction:

> First, equity provides a university with options or financial claims on a company's future income streams. The attractiveness of the option is consistent with the uncertainty associated with the technical and economic characteristics of academic patents and with the experience-based assessment that the opportunity cost of foregone license and royalty revenue is generally low. Second, equity deals, in which the university becomes part owner of the company, . . . align the interests of the university and the firm towards the common goal of commercializing the technology. . . . Third, . . . equity may serve a certification function that provides a signal to relevant third parties.
>
> From the perspective of the university, taking equity may signal to the outside world that the university is entrepreneurial. For the firm, an equity deal may signal to other investors that the firm has received a valuable technology from the university and that the university is confident in the value of technology that the firm holds. This may enhance the firm's ability to receive additional funding.[10]

Building on the first advantage cited, equity provides the university a certain level of risk reduction. As the start-up evolves, it often changes its business strategy, which might mean abandoning the original university technology in favor of another technology licensed from another entity or the development of internal IP. Even so, as a shareholder, the university will share in the success of the company—it is very rare for a university to lose its equity, even when the license is terminated.

UNIVERSITY OBLIGATIONS. The university must continue to pay patent costs as well as prosecute and defend the patent. Most universities reserve the right to defend the patent from infringement but may not have the incentive and financial resources to mount an appropriate defense.

---

10. Maryann Feldman, Irwin Feller, Janet Bercovitz, and Richard Burton, "Equity and the Technology Transfer Strategies of American Research Universities," *Management Science* 48 (1) (2002): 106–7.

If not licensed to a third party, the IP may be released to the faculty member, who can personally file for patent protection and develop it outside the university. Releasing the IP to the inventor is rare but can happen if 1) university deems the IP to have been developed by the faculty outside of the university without federal grants and/or 2) the university does not think the IP is patentable or commercializable. The terms of release vary by university, and releasing the IP to the faculty inventor can be problematic since it may create a conflict of interest: a faculty member continuing to do university research that may be related to a personal asset.

An example license between a start-up and a university can be found at researchtorevenue.com.

The University Employs Faculty Founders

In the case where faculty members are involved in founding a company, a conflict of interest or a conflict of commitment may arise. A conflict of interest occurs when the faculty member has an interest in both the university (his/her employer) and the start-up (as a shareholder), and some activities may present a conflict between those interests. Since start-ups are not new to the university setting, research administrators have developed policies to address conflicts of interest. These policies are usually implemented through a conflict of interest committee, since many of them require some level of interpretation and discussion based on the specific situations and department differences. Most of the conflicts involve either student mentoring or clinical trials. For example, a graduate student working in the lab of the founder may have the option to pursue experiments that would benefit the student's research and be publishable, while other experiments may benefit the start-up but not be publishable. The faculty member has a conflict when it comes to how to direct the student. Clinical trial conflicts, the most serious type of conflict, arise when the faculty member overseeing a clinical trial involving a product (e.g., drug, device, diagnostic) being commercialized by a start-up is also the founder. The results of the trial can have significant financial consequences for the faculty member, creating the potential for a lack of objectivity.

Conflicts of commitment, which involve the level of commitment by the faculty member to the university and the start-up, are less clear-cut. They usually arise when a faculty member's time commitment to university duties (teaching, research) and start-up activities (consulting, fund-raising) conflict. Some universities have specific policies (e.g., they allow the faculty member one day a week for consulting or working on the start-up), whereas others offer guidelines and leave it up to the department chairs to monitor.

Another area of contention between the university and faculty founders is the use of university facilities for start-up activities. Many universities restrict university space for research and education purposes only, whereas many faculty would like to have their start-ups incubated close to their lab (or even in their lab). For some universities, there is a strict "separation of church and state," where all start-up-related activities must be performed in nonuniversity space. In this case, office space, e-mail accounts, meeting rooms, libraries, and so forth, cannot be used for start-up activities. Given the difficulty in monitoring and enforcing this prohibition, some universities have opted for more flexibility through guidelines. Other universities do permit start-up activity on campus, typically in designated incubation space under close management by conflict of interest committees.

The University Supports Start-Ups

Beyond protecting and licensing IP to start-ups, the role of the university varies greatly when it comes to supporting the start-up. On one extreme, TTOs might provide contacts and limited advice during the company formation and growth. On the other extreme, some universities have developed sophisticated programs to support start-ups, from entrepreneurs-in-residence to university investment funds.

The impetus for this support varies. For some universities, supporting faculty entrepreneurship is good for faculty recruitment and retention. Many faculty consider commercialization of their research an integral part of their career, and entrepreneurial commercialization is becoming increasingly common. Economic development is another driver for many universities, who cite the fact that start-ups that start local tend to stay local and hire local. Another rationale for supporting university start-ups relates to translation, or the unlocking of basic science for the public good. This bench-to-bedside movement has been especially driven by the NIH, which has provided hundreds of millions of dollars into translational institutes through its Clinical and Translational Science Award (CTSA).

University support of entrepreneurial activities can include the following:

EDUCATIONAL PROGRAMS. These programs range from webinars, to day-long bootcamps and workshops, to semester-long courses taught by business schools. The goals of these programs range from teaching general entrepreneurial literacy (teaching terminology and providing context) to the formal development of a business plan, including the product-development plan, market research, financial plan, competitive landscape, value proposition, and go-to-market strategy.

EXTERNAL CONNECTIONS. One of the keys to success for a university start-up is making connections to the people and companies outside the university. These connections provide essential expertise for start-ups: management, product development, legal assistance, and funding. Making these connections is most common via informal introductions from experienced faculty founders or TTOs, but in many cases a more formal means is required. For example, forums set up to strategically foster networking relationships between faculty inventors and the broader entrepreneurial community may be particularly useful.

FUNDING. Traditionally, university start-ups have been funded by a combination of angel investments and venture capital. However, given the recent changes in the capital markets, angel investors are looking for a short (less than three years) time to revenue, which can be challenging for technology-based university start-ups. Venture capitalists have become more conservative in their investments, making them out of reach for all but the most promising start-ups. In response to this funding gap, universities are beginning to develop alternative funding to support these companies. University-based funding can range from competitive grants to equity investments. The grants can be awarded to faculty members to help with technology development or given to the start-up for product development that would not be supported by traditional extramural research funding mechanisms. Equity investments provide a return for the university in the event the start-up is successful.

INCUBATION. In addition to funding, university start-ups require incubation (i.e., space and facilities) to launch and grow the company. Although private incubators exist in many communities, universities also provide incubation, which varies in terms of space and other kinds of support offered. Some universities have the ability to designate space within the faculty founder's lab for the start-up, with the requisite oversight as mentioned before. Others have dedicated buildings to house start-ups. Support can vary from space only to fully integrated programs involving workshops, accounting services, pitch sessions, and funding. One of the most valuable aspects of an incubator for technology-based start-ups is access to common or shared equipment. Having access to capital equipment (e.g., freezers, centrifuges) can be critical to advancing the company since most start-ups lack the funds to purchase expensive capital equipment.

For more detailed information about how a university can build a supportive entrepreneurial ecosystem, see Chapter 5.

People

The second major element of the start-up ecosystem is the people directly involved in the start-up and those in the supporting cast. They include both people from the university (faculty, students) and people outside of the university who make up the management team or serve as consultants and advisers.

Faculty Member

The roles the faculty member plays in the start-up are diverse and can change over time. As mentioned before, university start-ups are usually built around science and technology that is tacit; that is, resident in the mind of the faculty member. Thus it is essential that he or she play an active role in the start-up, at least during the early stages. For some technologies, faculty research can serve as the early validation, demonstrate feasibility, or provide proof of concept for the company. In terms of company engagement, faculty founders are usually involved in the early days when the company is formed, since their research is the core asset of the start-up. Beyond being a founder, the faculty member will initially play roles as consultant and technical adviser. A more active role will be assembling and organizing a team of scientific colleagues to serve as the scientific advisory board (SAB, see page 46). The most engaged role a faculty founder can play, though rare, is leaving the university to take a full-time position with the company as chief scientific officer (CSO) or chief technical officer (CTO). Some universities allow the faculty member to take a leave of absence or a sabbatical for a year or two to work at the start-up. The role of the faculty member is discussed in more detail in Chapter 5.

Former Students to Fill the Talent Gap

Although faculty founders can provide the scientific and technical talent to help guide the start-up, they rarely leave their academic position to join the start-up. Hiring technically trained scientists can help fill this talent gap, but with the specialization of science today, the domain expertise may not be readily available. One solution is to tap into graduating doctoral students or postdoctoral fellows who have been working in the lab where the technology originated. These students are ideal for a number of reasons:

SKILLS. They have necessary laboratory skills to execute experiments, skills directly relevant to the technology.

DIRECTION. Having lived and breathed the science and technology for many years, they know what works, but more important, they know what does not work.

COMPETITION. In writing publications and thesis, they know other groups working in this same space.

RISK. Being young in their careers, many are willing to take a risk with a start-up.

ACCESS. Given their relationship with the faculty founder, they often have access to data, insight, and unpublished results from the founder's lab. Sometimes a student has built a greater level of trust with the founder than the CEO has, and this can provide better access.

AFFORDABILITY. Their wages as a grad student or postdoc have been low. A few more years working at these wages may seem worth it if they can see some upside (experience, ownership).

In short, former students can act as a technical surrogate for the faculty founder. With proper guidance from the faculty founder and/or management team, they can be a valuable resource for the start-up. Their role can range from assisting in writing the technical sections of the business plan, to providing figures for the pitch deck, to writing and executing SBIR grants for the company to working with early adopters.

To help facilitate the transition of these students from university to company, some universities are providing fellowships to students. These "commercialization fellowships" provide a stipend for the graduating student to devote themselves full time to the start-up, usually under the guidance of company adviser or CEO.

An insightful example is Bassil Dahiyat, who made the transition from graduate student to CEO of a biotech start-up, Xencor. He chronicles his journey and offers lessons learned for any academic making the transition to a start-up in his article "Stranger in a Strange Land?," which is reprinted on our website, researchtorevenue.com.

Advisers and Mentors

For many faculty-founded start-ups, a management team may not be in place during the early days of the company, so getting the leadership necessary to make key decisions early on can be difficult. In these cases, advisers and mentors can help guide the early decisions of the company. Advice can come from many different people. An immediate source of advice and mentoring are academic colleagues who have been down the entrepreneurial path.[11] Not only can they provide advice on what and what not to do; they can also provide introductions to key people. As Dahiyat recalls with Xencor: "The take-home message here is that if you are in academia and aspire to start a company, it really helps if you are at an institution where you are surrounded by peers and professors already experienced with the biotech industry—they can often help you with the right introductions. Once you have gotten that foot in the door, you still have to sell your idea, but being at a place that has a network in the commercial world will accelerate the process of opening doors."[12]

Another source is local entrepreneurs. One of the big challenges for a faculty founder is connecting with these advisers, since faculty members don't usually associate with them. Often, the TTO can provide names of people who can offer guidance.

Another source of advice can come from a corporate attorney either as informal advice before incorporation or as more formal advice once the company has been formed. Some founders think they can save money by incorporating online and get legal advice from websites. This is often short-sighted thinking since, relative to the cost of bringing the product to market, the cost of using an attorney is minuscule. Plus, corporate attorneys, especially ones who work with start-ups, have a wealth of experience to draw from. They can help address issues about incorporation, company governance, equity distribution, employment agreements, fund-raising, and acquisition.

Boards and the Management Team

With any company, a number of key roles and personnel are involved in governing, managing, and building the business. The following are typically found in any university start-up:

11. A word of caution: Take each colleague's advice in the context; the colleague who took a company public will have a different perspective from that of the colleague whose company came down in flames.

12. Bassil Dahiyat, "Stranger in a Strange Land?," *Nature Biotechnology*, 23 August 2012, http://www.nature.com/bioent/2012/120801/full/bioe.2012.8.html (accessed 13 June 2014).

BOARD OF DIRECTORS (BOD). "The board" is a legally established, preferably diverse group of people whose composition will change over time as the company grows. Starting out, the board is composed of the founder(s) and perhaps a neutral, experienced person outside the university (corporate lawyer, seasoned entrepreneur). The outside board member provides balance on the board when it is making key decisions and may rotate off as the company grows. As the company grows, the board will expand to include the CEO (if not a founder), investors, and experienced individuals who can provide industry-relevant advice, insight, and connections. The board has ultimate authority in making high-level company decisions (e.g., hiring/firing of the CEO, accepting investment, distributing equity, employee compensation, and mergers and acquisitions).

SCIENTIFIC ADVISORY BOARD (SAB). The SAB is composed of scientists who can provide technical insight into the company's technology and its applications. These SAB members would have scientific and technical expertise in relevant application or industrial areas. The SAB can serve several purposes. At one level, it can be a great sounding board for the management team to explore new strategic directions, especially when the direction is outside the technical domain expertise of the academic founders. The other purpose of the SAB is to provide some window dressing for the company. These members are preeminent scientists who are well regarded in the field, perhaps at the National Academy of Science or Nobel level, and provide a certain amount of scientific street cred and validation to help attract investors, early customers, and management. Although some members can serve both roles, the preeminent scientist might not have the time or interest to engage in evaluating strategic decisions, and the people who can take the time to engage may not be at the preeminent level.

CEO AND MANAGEMENT TEAM. The CEO reports to the board and serves as the quarterback for the company. His/her primary role in the early days of the start-up is establishing the business plan for the company and fund-raising. Needless to say, the CEO position is of utmost importance, and the person who will serve in that role should be chosen wisely (more on this in Chapter 3). Working with the CEO are the other "chiefs": chief scientific officer, the chief financial officer (CFO), and maybe a chief business officer (CBO) or a chief operating officer (COO). Reporting to the chiefs are a number of vice presidents (VPs):

VP of sales and marketing, VP of business development, VP of Human Resources, etc.

The people that become involved in the start-up are one of the most important factors for determining success or failure of a start-up. A groundbreaking technology with a clear path for commercialization may never see the marketplace if the wrong people are involved. We discuss the management team in more detail in Chapter 3, but two factors are worth considering here. First, chemistry is paramount. If people can't interact in productive, supportive ways, then the road will be bumpy. This doesn't mean there can't be disagreements, but to move things forward, they work as a team, being respectful and constructive in their interactions. Recalcitrance and bitter fights are counterproductive. Second, leadership matters. At the end of the day, leaders must lead in order to accomplish goals. And leaders must be allowed to lead. This notion can be foreign to founders coming from an academic setting where committees and task forces use consensus to make decisions. In a company, individuals need to be given authority to make important decisions and be held accountable for those decisions.

Funding

The third major element of the start-up ecosystem involves the funding, or the fuel for launching and growing the university start-up. Funding of start-ups comes in many forms and is acquired at various stages of the company's development—referred to as "stage-appropriate capital." Funding enables a company to meet major product-development milestones (prototype development, product testing and optimization, validation), to establish the operations of the company (manufacturing, business development, customer acquisition), and to pay the salaries of those who devote their time and energy to growing the company.

Funding comes in two basic forms: dilutive and nondilutive. Dilutive capital involves the company selling a portion of its equity (a portion of ownership) to an investor. During this transaction the company usually issues additional equity (e.g., stock) beyond the current equity holders. This results in a dilution of the current shareholders so that even though they have more cash in the bank, they own less of the company. Examples and the effects of dilution are discussed in detail below. Nondilutive funding, as the name implies, does not result in dilution of ownership. Here, the money comes not from an investor but from an entity interested in the company commercializing the technology that is not seeking a return for providing that funding. A common source of nondilutive capital is government grants.

Funding usually proceeds as the company develops. Some type of pre-start-up funding may come from the university in the form of proof-of-concept grants. Once the company has formed, it can seek government or foundation grants (nondilutive) or investments from angel investors or venture capital firms (dilutive). Finally, alternatives to these involve bootstrapping, taking out loans, partnerships, or crowdfunding, each of which are discussed below.

Pre-Start-Up Funding

Since most univeristy start-ups are built around a university-born innovation, it is important to understand how these innovations are funded in the early stages and how some of that funding can be leveraged to lower the risk of a technology prior to spinning out the company. As discussed earlier, research gives rise to the innovation, technology development addresses the technology's feasibility, and product-development activities bring the product to the point of launch, sales, and marketing.

For a university start-up, it is important to understand what technology development is and how it is funded. Technology development involves studies that are *non–hypothesis driven*; that is, the results of the studies demonstrate a principle of the technology, a proof of concept, or a validation. These studies are extremely important since they provide the first glimpse into the commercial viability of a technology, but the funding for them is exceedingly difficult to obtain for several reasons. First, sometimes the faculty member who is trained in hypothesis-driven research does not have the expertise to formulate the studies necessary for technology development (e.g., the skills required to discover a biomarker are not the same as those required to develop an assay to validate it). Second, with the exception of SBIR and STTR (Small Business Technology Transfer Research) grants discussed below, the federal agencies that fund hypothesis-driven research typically do not fund technology-development studies, especially if this work is to be done in the university lab. Furthermore, universities don't often support this type of research because it does not result in data that can be used for securing additional grants and does not meet the level of scientific inquiry required for graduate student dissertations or publications (e.g., data on the thermal stability of a polymer may not be innovative enough for the next NIH Research Project Grant [R01] application). Finally, obtaining funding from external investors is difficult because 1) a company into which an investment can be made is rarely formed at this stage and 2) if there is a company, the risk is usually too high for most investors.

An example of this funding gap is often seen in the development of diagnostics and therapeutics. Federal agencies (e.g., NIH) will fund the research of a biological mechanism of a disease, the identification of a target, and the development of an animal model for the disease. The research may uncover a natural ligand or analog that is involved in the modulation of the disease in the animal model. In some cases, funding can be obtained to screen a library of compounds using an assay containing the ligand to discover a chemical entity that modulates the disease, or at least modulates the target. The funding gap usually occurs when one is trying to acquire the funds to test that entity in the animal model to demonstrate efficacy. Even more difficult, and many times impossible, is securing funding for additional safety testing studies for the potential therapy. These efficacy and safety studies have little innovation and are not publishable but are essential for attracting a corporate partner or venture investor.

There are, however, several other sources of pre-start-up, technology-development funding. Many universities are developing funds to enhance the viability or licensabilty of a technology. Tech transfer offices may have funds they can deploy via $10,000–$50,000 technology enhancement grants to faculty to help reduce the risk of their technology, making them more attractive to external parties. Sources of pre-start-up technology-development funding include the following:

PROOF-OF-CONCEPT CENTERS. Some universities wrap support, in the form of courses and infrastructure, around a grant to create a proof-of-concept center. Two notable centers are the Massachusetts Institute of Technology's Deshpande Center for Technological Innovation and the von Liebig Entrepreneurism Center at the University of California, San Diego, where the university provides infrastructure, advisers, networking events, classes, and funding to help a start-up demonstrate a proof of concept.[13] The von Liebig Center provides grants ($15,000 to $75,000), advisers (six advisers work at the center), networking events (open houses, lunch-n-learns), and courses (e.g., Venture Mechanics, Entrepreneurship Dynamics). Over $2.8 million in grants for 66 projects over five years has resulted in 16 start-ups (and four licenses).

13. C. A. Gulbranson and D. B. Audretsch, "Proof of Concept Centers: Accelerating the Commercialization of University Innovation," 2008, Kauffman Foundation, http://sites.kauffman.org/pdf/poc_centers_01242008.pdf (accessed 14 July 2015).

The start-ups have leveraged the funding to acquire over $71 million in private capital, a 25:1 leverage.[14]

COULTER FOUNDATION. The Coulter Foundation has established the Coulter Translational Partnership Award in Biomedical Engineering and, to date, has awarded 16 universities to provide technology-development and proof-of-concept funding. Funding ranges from $50,000 to $500,000 but is typically $100,000 for a one-year project, with additional funding if milestones are met.

NIH CENTERS FOR ACCELERATED INNOVATION (NCAI). A forward-thinking federal program has been being piloted by the National Heart, Lung, and Blood Institute (NHLBI). The funding goes to a group of univer-sities to establish a Center for Accelerated Innovations. Each center assembles a team of external advisers (entrepreneurs, business leaders) to select promising technologies (drugs, devices, diagnostics) aligned with NHLBI's mission. Each project receives $200,000 to $500,000 to help de-risk the technology and prepare it for either licensing or a start-up. The first grant for $31 million was awarded in 2013 to three centers composed of a consortium of universities. The concepts of the NCAI have recently been extended to the entire NIH by the REACH program, in which smaller centers have been established for promoting precom-mercial development of biomedical innovations.

NSF INNOVATION CORPS (I-CORPS). The I-Corp program enhances the impact of NSF-funded research by supporting technology-development studies to de-risk commercially viable technologies. The program is built around teams composed of the faculty member (PI), an entrepre-neurial lead, and a mentor. The team follows a structured curriculum, based on Steve Blank's product- and customer-development principles, and can receive up to $50,000 in funding for six months to conduct proof-of-concept studies. The funding typically goes directly to the team, and many of the projects evolve into start-ups.

CLINICAL AND TRANSLATIONAL SCIENCE AWARD. The NIH has funded over 60 medical centers in the United States to build the infrastructure to accelerate discoveries toward better health. The funds are used to estab-lish academic homes for clinical and translational research. The homes provide tools, core facilities, and training to support translational

---

14. The Deshpande Center had comparable numbers: $7 million over 64 projects resulting in 10 start-ups acquiring almost $90 million in private capital.

research. Part of this support comes in the form of "pilot grants," which can be used for translational research and technology development.

Once a start-up has spun out of a university, additional funding for both technology and product development is needed, as well as for operations and intellectual property. Funding typically comes in two forms, grants and equity investments.

Grant Funding

Companies can apply for grants from a variety of public and private sources. A number of groups provide grants to early-stage university start-ups:

STATE AND REGIONAL AGENCIES. Some states recognize the economic development potential of start-ups: most start-ups stay in the region in which they were founded and spend money and create jobs. As such, states and, more infrequently, local communities often provide grants or loans to early-stage companies to meet early milestones. The sources of these funds can range from tax revenue to bond referenda. For example, through a bond referendum, the Connecticut legislature created Connecticut Innovations, which provides both preseed (up to $150,000) and seed (up to $1 million) investments for Connecticut-based start-ups.[15]

FOUNDATIONS. Most foundations provide grants to universities for research in the area aligned with their interests, be it diseases (cancer, cystic fibrosis, Parkinson's) or global issues (clean water, poverty, global warming). In addition, some foundations will provide grants to start-ups that are developing products aligned with the foundation's mission. (A list of foundations that are funding start-ups can be found at researchtorevenue.com.)

FEDERAL AGENCIES (SBIR/STTR). The largest source of nondilutive funding for technology and product development is from federal agencies. Federal agencies that provide more than $100 million in extramural funding (i.e., funding for university research) are required to set aside not less than 2.6 percent of that funding for the SBIR program. In addition, federal agencies that provide in excess of $1 billion for extramural research and development must set aside 0.3 percent of that funding for

15. See its website at ctinnovations.com.

TABLE 2.3 SBIR/STTR funding statistics for fiscal year 2009

		SBIR	STTR
Phase I grant applications	Submitted	22,444	2,804
	Awarded (%)	4,008 (18)	592 (21)
Typical Phase I award amount		$250K	$250K
Phase II grant applications	Submitted	3,352	467
	Awarded (%)	1,801 (54)	251 (54)
Typical Phase II award amount		$450K–1M max total cost for 2 years	

the STTR program. This results in a total of over $2 billion in funds for SBIR programs and $250 million in STTR grants annually. Statistics for funding through this mechanism, including funding rates, are shown in table 2.3. The SBIR and STTR programs can provide enough funding for developing a product to the point of being marketable or de-risking the technology to the point of attracting an investor or corporate partner. Both programs provide funding in two phases: Phase I, proof of concept and feasibility, and Phase II, development and commercialization. The major differences in eligibility requirements and grant spending restrictions between SBIR and STTR grants are shown in table 2.4. Note that different agencies use the STTR mechanism differently. For example, the NIH allows applicants to choose which mechanism suits them best. Others, such as the NSF, will reserve certain topics for STTR grants only. Some agencies do not offer STTR grants as an option because their extramural budgets are insufficient. A discussion of how to prepare an SBIR/STTR proposal can be found in Chapter 3.

SBIR contracts (solicitations) are another form of funding administered by the SBIR program. SBIR contracts, unlike SBIR grants, are initiated by the funding agency and pertain to a specific research topic or question. Federal funding agencies must issue at least one program solicitation for SBIR contracts annually, and the topics of these solicitations, as well as the date they will begin taking applications, are posted on each agency's website. The research topics tend to be much more focused than those for which SBIR grants are given. From a lightweight battery for military applications to nanoparticles for drug delivery, these contracts are designed to deliver a technology, product, or capability needed by the agency. If a company has a technology an agency needs, the contract can help to further develop the technology and, in some

TABLE 2.4 Comparison of eligibility requirements for SBIR and STTR grants

	SBIR	STTR
Principal investigator	Must be employed at least 51% of the time at a small business at the time of the award for the duration of the award. Must have at least 10% effort on the specific award project.	Can come from university or small business. Must have at least 10% effort on the specific award project.
Collaboration between university and small company	Allowed	Required
Subcontracting of work	Phase I: up to 33% Phase II: up to 50%	At least 30% to university (total subcontracts not to exceed 60%)

cases, yields the company's first customer, the U.S. government. Similar to the grant proposals, SBIR contract solicitations are divided into Phase I and Phase II awards, with Phase II awards available only to applicants who have successfully completed milestones during their Phase I award time frame.

OTHER FEDERAL FUNDING PROGRAMS. Outside the SBIR/STTR grants and contracts, several government agencies offer funding for innovative technologies and product development. For example, four U.S. Department of Defense agencies provide funding to companies developing novel technologies: the Defense Advanced Research Projects Agency (DARPA), the Defense Threat Reduction Agency (DITRA), the Office of Navy Research, and the Army Research Office. In addition, some government agencies provide support to start-up companies not through direct grants but through access to services. For example, the NIH's National Center for Advancing Translational Sciences offers the Bridging Interventional Development Gaps (BrIDGs). This program offers access to NIH contractors who will conduct preclinical studies with no cost to the investigator.

Equity Investments

Although grants have their place in funding a start-up, especially for technology development, they also have limitations. First, they take time to acquire.

A typical SBIR grant takes 9–12 months from date of submission to when the money is available. Added to that, the chances of getting the grant are dependent on the availability of federal funds, and generally fewer than one in four applications are funded, so there is a risk of having to resubmit, extending the time to get funding to years. Furthermore, the funding is tied to the objectives of the funding agency, which may not be completely aligned with the company's objectives. For example, a company whose focus is tissue engineering could receive SBIR funding to evaluate a hydrogel for drug delivery, an application slightly outside the main commercial focus of the company. Some of the data resulting from the SBIR funding (e.g., on toxicity) might be applicable to tissue engineering, but the rest of the data will not be relevant to the company's primary commercial focus. The second limitation of grant funding is that it can only go so far. Most grants will help develop a prototype or demonstrate feasibility but rarely are sufficient or intended for commercial activities such as clinical development or building production units. Finally and most important, grants rarely cover nontechnical expenses such as patent filing fees, regulatory consultants, or nontechnical personnel salaries, such as those of the CEO or the vice president of business development.

A common alternative to grants is the equity investment. As is the case for publicly traded companies listed on the stock market, an equity investment for a start-up involves the purchasing of shares of the company, the equity, for a specified price. At a later time, the shares can be sold for more than the original purchase price, thus realizing a profit for the investor. Equity investments come from many sources and at different stages in the company's growth. Different types of stage-appropriate capital are shown in table 2.5, with the general trend being smaller amounts of capital being deployed early in the company's history compared to later. This trend exists for two reasons: 1) the chances of failure are much higher at earlier stages, and investors are thus typically more risk-averse at this stage, investing smaller amounts; and 2) the capital requirements increase dramatically as the company grows and brings the product to market, and, related to point 1, the company becomes a less risky investment.

The first money invested into a start-up, preseed capital, is usually from those most closely associated with the new venture, namely the founders, as well as friends and family associated with the founder, investing personal money. The amount of money at this stage is small (up to several thousand) and is often used to pay for company-formation or patent-protection expenses. The money can be put into the company formally or informally. Informally, the founders can put money in as a loosely defined contribution

TABLE 2.5 Stages of equity funding for a typical start-up

STAGE	AMOUNT	SOURCE	USE AND ACTIVITIES
Preseed	$1K–50K	Friends Family Personal savings University venture fund	Company formation Legal expenses
Seed	$100K–500K	Angel Venture capital University venture fund	Technology development Hire CEO Complete the business plan
Series A/B	A: $1M–5M B: $6M–10M	Venture capital Corporate VC	Formal management team Company facility Product development Product launch (non-FDA)
Series D/C	$15M–50M	Venture capital Corporate VC Private equity	Product development Regulatory approval Scale-up Manufacturing Partnering
Mezzanine	$20M–50M	Private equity	Corporate growth Global sales effort Last private round before IPO

that does not result in a specified amount of ownership.[16] For example, each founder agrees to contribute $1,000, which will be put into the company checking account to pay for initial start-up expenses. A more formal arrangement involves cash in return for equity or a loan to be paid back at a later date (preferred). Founders who have put money into the company signal to others their commitment ("skin in the game"). People might be reluctant to invest in a company whose founders aren't willing to put several thousand dollars into the company themselves.

Investors making equity investments evaluate investment opportunities by weighing two factors: risk and reward. It is helpful to understand their perspective and way of thinking as one approaches them. Risk involves the factors that lead to failure, or at least prevent success. An investor is assessing risks in terms of their magnitude—that is, the amount of capital required to

16. Purchasing stock at this point is problematic in that it sets a value of the stock (price per share) which in turn sets a valuation of the company (number of shares × price per share).

overcome those risks, and determining which risks the investor can control and which they cannot. Risk comes in many forms and is relevant at different stages of a company's development. The different types of risk are shown in table 2.6.

Reward, or the "upside," is what shareholders receive when the company creates value and subsequently having a third party pay for that value. For example, a company might create tangible value by selling $10 million of product, up from $3 million the previous year, or create less tangible value by receiving approval from the FDA. In either case, the company has increased its value. If investors purchase equity (stock) prior to these value-creation events, then their investment has created a return—that is, they have seen a return on the investment, or ROI. (The actual return occurs when the start-up is acquired or has an IPO, where the investor receives cash for their now more-valuable shares.) Understanding an investor's return expectations is important in considering an investment. Two factors play into an investor's expectations. The first is the ROI. Do they expect to get two times their investment? Five times? The second is the time frame for the return. There is a time value of money from the investor's perspective. A return realized in two years is much better than the same return realized in ten years.

Equity investments beyond the preseed stage typically come from two types of investors: angel investors and venture capital (VC) firms.

Angel Investors

Angel investors (or angels) are high-net-worth individuals who invest their own money in start-ups either individually or as a group (angel network). Because their investments are relatively small compared to VC, and angel funds are often not committed capital funds, angels don't have the overhead and staff to carry out extensive due diligence.[17] As such, most of the work on due diligence is done by the investors themselves on a volunteer basis. While cost-efficient, this can increase the time between the first interaction with the angel and the investment decision. Angels are typically looking for a company that can get a product to the market in three or four years and be profitable shortly thereafter. They don't usually invest in capital-intensive companies because the amount of capital the company needs is often beyond their investment capabilities. These companies eventually need funding from VC firms, which can result in significant dilution for the angel investor. Consequently,

---

17. Committed capital funds are built around a commitment of capital by the partners up front and define the fund size. VCs use a portion of the committed capital to pay for overhead (such as partner salaries). Most angels and angel groups commit capital on a deal-by-deal basis.

university start-ups that require significant capital to get to a product (e.g., drugs, devices, diagnostics) will rarely have angel investors.

Venture Capital Firms

Venture capital firms make equity investments like angel investors, but they are distinct in several ways: 1) they are investing other people's money, 2) they employ full-time investment professionals who identify and vet investment opportunities, and 3) their evaluation of investment opportunities is more formal and at times more rigorous than angels'. But like angels, they spend a significant amount of time and effort working with the company's management to provide advice and connections, and, in some cases, they help set strategic direction.

A venture capital firm often makes a range of investments across the spectrum from the seed stage to much later stages in a company's development. Generally speaking, firms investing out of a fund of less than $100 million tend to invest in earlier-stage companies, whereas firms investing out of larger funds make investments in later-stage companies. Some of the larger funds will reserve a small amount of capital for a limited number of early-stage investments, typically for a hot new technology or a company started by a serial entrepreneur who has been successful in the past. Most successful VCs have multiple funds that are raised and deployed in succession, often denoted by roman numerals (Red Creek Fund I, II, III, etc.). The typical scenario is for a firm to raise a fund and then make investments out of that fund for six to eight years and getting returns ("harvesting") from those investments for up to ten years. In looking at a VC firm, one will often encounter several numbers. *Capital under management* refers to the aggregate amount of money the firm is managing, but it is often split among different funds (I, II, III, etc.). Since some of that money has already been invested, the more important number is the *current fund size* (e.g., Red Creek Fund IV) and how much of that has been invested ("deployed"). That number only comes from talking to one of the VC partners. The final and most important number is the typical *investment size* ("the bite size" or "investment chunk size"). This number can be fuzzy since it may refer to the initial investment or the total investment into the company over several investment rounds.

The business model of a venture firm involves limited partners (LPs), who invest in the VC fund in hopes that the firm has the experience, focus, and incentives to pick successful companies. Limited partners can range from those with large pension funds, to corporations, to individual investors. One often finds a mix of limited partners in a fund, and the mix may reflect the type of fund (e.g., life science or later stage). The VC will consider a number

TABLE 2.6 Types of start-up investment risk

TYPE OF RISK	DESCRIPTION
TECHNICAL RISK	Technical risk addresses the question, Will the product work? This is especially important for technology-based companies that need to bring a product to market and make it work with the features that command value. Technical risk ranges from software functioning properly, to instruments reliably working, to drugs being safe and effective. Investors find it difficult to mitigate technical risk since it can be hard to assess. Thus, many will set milestones or thresholds after which they will invest. Examples include preproduction prototype, validated assay, pilot scale production, first-in-human clinical trials, FDA approval.
IP RISK	IP risk initially involves the issuance of the patent and the associated claims. Many university start-ups are built on patent applications, not issued patents, so an investor must understand the risk of a patent being denied, a patent issued with limited claims, or a patent that has limited jurisdiction (e.g., U.S. only). Beyond this, there is the risk of freedom to operate: Does the company's patent allow the company to commercialize the IP relative to patents held by other companies? Investors mitigate IP risk by using experienced IP attorneys to assess the likelihood of patent issuance and a "freedom to operate" opinion. IP risk is also mitigated by the start-up filing additional patents to cover various applications or uses of the technology.
REGULATORY RISK	Regulatory risk relates to products that require regulatory approval (e.g., FDA) before they are offered for sale. Although it is related to technical risk, regulatory risk factors in clinical trial design, approvals or denials of other related products, and how clinical results are reported and argued before the regulatory body. Investors look to regulatory consultants to provide an analysis of the regulatory path and hurdles.
MARKET RISK	Market risk relates to, as one VC put it, "Will the dogs eat the dog food"—that is, will customers see the value of the product and purchase it in enough quantities to meet the company's financial needs. For technology-based products, this can be challenge when the product is a new way of solving a problem. Getting product adoption can take time, sometimes beyond the timeline of the investors. Market risk is driven not only by customer's need for the company's product but also by the competitive products that compete for the same customer. Investors mitigate market risk by reviewing market research data and assessing the customer's perception of the value of the product, the number of potential customers, the growth of the customer segment, and the competitive landscape.

TYPE OF RISK	DESCRIPTION
REIMBURSEMENT RISK	Reimbursement risk, considered a special case of market risk, relates to biomedical products where payments for the product come through a third-party payer (e.g., insurance company). Once considered a minor risk, reimbursement is not a given anymore with the advent of managed health care and accountable care organizations. As with regulatory risk, reimbursement consultants help investors and companies manage this risk.
MANAGEMENT RISK	Management risk relates to the people executing the business strategy. The company needs technical and business people who will make the right decisions as the company grows. More important, the management must have the experience to make key decisions when things don't go according toplan. Investors mitigate this type of risk by investing in companies with people who have the relevant industry experience and with a track record of successfully growing a company. Because the other types of risk are harder to assess, many investors will place a strong emphasis on the management team. Thus the adage, "People invest in people."
OPERATIONAL RISK	This area of risk covers many aspects of the business, from scaling up manufacturing of the product, to the appropriate business model, to the most effective distribution channel. Investors mitigate operational risk by understanding the business model and market the company is selling into.
PORTFOLIO RISK	This type of risk is outside of a single investment and relates to how the investor spreads risk among the portfolio companies. It is the cumulative risk of all of the investor's current and potential investments. Portfolio risk comes into play in a subtle way with regard to company risk. A company might make certain decisions that introduce additional, perhaps compounded risk, into an investor's portfolio. For example, a company might decide to pursue a second product opportunity in case the lead opportunity fails. What appears to be risk mitigation at the company level may compound risk for the investor on a portfolio basis.

of investment opportunities and after much deliberation and review (due diligence) make an investment in the start-up. At some point, perhaps after several rounds of investment, the start-up company has a "liquidity event" (an acquisition or an IPO), realizing a cash return to the VC for stock. The cash received by the VC for its stock is returned to the limited partners. If all goes well, the amount returned is significantly more than what was invested, the limited partner's ROI. The firm and its partners make money two ways. First, it receives a management fee (typically 2 percent of the fund size it manages), which is used to pay salaries and firm overhead. Second, it receives a portion of returns from a liquidity event, which is shared among the partners of the firm.

The general rule is that a VC investing out of a particular fund will make a number of investments over the life of the fund. For example, a $500 million fund will invest in perhaps 15–20 start-ups, with each company receiving around $25–30 million over the course of the investment. By contrast, a $100 million fund investing in the same number of companies would make a similar number of investments but less for each company, on the order of $5 million–7 million.[18] Thus, it makes sense for a smaller firm to commit $500,000 for a seed round of a company while setting aside larger amounts that it will eventually invest in future rounds of financing. If the firm is going to spend time to review the deal and engage in due diligence, then the investment size needs to match the fund size. In other words, it is hard for a $500 million fund to spend significant time on a deal that will be $100,000 of seed capital and maybe $5 million over the rounds of financing.

A venture firm, like any company, has a structured hierarchy. At the top, the partners, with titles like "partner," "general partner," and "managing director," run the firm. They find investment opportunities, work with the other partners to make decisions on investing, sit on the boards of invested companies, and share in the returns from those investments. Assisting them are "venture partners" who are either less experienced or part-time people with deep experience in an industry segment. They may source deals or provide significant input into the investment decision. Finally, "principals" and "associates" provide support to the partners by doing research, reviewing documents, and organizing the operations of the firm. Complementing the team may be a scientific advisory board composed of technical experts who

---

18. The number of investments a firm makes out-of-fund comes down to some probabilistic statistics. For a fund of a given size, too few investments decreases the probability of having a winner to cover the losses due to failed companies. Too many investments spread too little capital across the companies, not providing enough capital to make enough of the companies successful. The general rule of thumb is 12–20 investments to ensure enough success to cover the losses of the failed companies.

may be called upon to review the technology being commercialized or help identify science, technology, or industry trends that have implications for future investments.

Venture capital firms come in many flavors, each with a different focus in terms of industry, region, investment size, and company engagement. For many, the characteristics of the firm are driven by the background and experience of the general partners as well as the type of limited partner and the type of return they've been promised by the firm. The following are several common types of venture capital firms:

TRADITIONAL VENTURE FUNDS. With the ever-changing landscape of venture capital, it is hard to define a traditional venture capital firm, but some characteristics are common among these firms. Most of them are composed of investments by limited partners who can range from the general partners of the firm to wealthy (high net worth) individuals to other funds (e.g., pension funds) looking to diversify their investment portfolio. Most are located in and invest in a single geographical region, with the majority clustering around VC hotbeds like Boston and Silicon Valley. The reasons for the regional focus are that 1) the partner's management team and network of consultants and advisers tend to have a local reach, and 2) many partners like the convenience of short travel for visiting companies (e.g., board meetings). Firms will invest outside of their region when they co-invest (or "syndicate") with another firm, where the partner firm is located closer to the start-up. Some firms might invest across industries, while others focus on specific industry segments (IT, healthcare, cleantech). In addition to geographic reach and industry focus, firms might differentiate in terms of company stage; that is, early-stage versus late-stage start-ups. Finally, VC's will have different approaches regarding how they work with their portfolio companies. Some invest and participate on the board of directors; others will take a more active role in which their partners are part of the management team or lead the recruitment of management. The thing to remember here is that with the large diversity of firms, it is important for the start-up to do homework on each firm to determine the fit. Otherwise, a lot of time is wasted pursuing VCs that are unlikely to make an investment.

CORPORATE VENTURE CAPITAL FUNDS. Many corporations operate venture funds for making strategic investments and/or gaining access to early-stage innovations. Unlike a traditional VC fund with many limited partners, corporate venture capital firms have one limited partner, the parent company. Also, because they are looking at companies aligned with the mission of the corporate parent, they tend to invest nationally or globally. Although the fund is expected to provide a return, that expectation is balanced with enabling the commercial development of technologies and products strategically aligned with the parent company. As one corporate VC partner put it, "Our return is about a hundredth of the profitability of our parent company, so although we are expected to generate a return, the strategic focus is most important." Some operate in close partnership with the parent company, whereas others are much more independent, making investment decisions independent of the parent company management. They may invest alone but also will co-invest with traditional VCs. A list of corporate venture firms can be found at researchtorevenue.com.

Burrill and Company, a life science investment group, did an analysis of the effect of corporate venture firms co-investing with traditional firms in life science companies.[19] Looking at over 2,900 therapeutic start-ups during the period 2000–2011 (over 5,000 financing rounds), 286 (approximately 10 percent) received corporate venture capital investments. The companies that received corporate VC investments as part of a syndicate had a greater likelihood of a successful outcome than those receiving traditional VC funding. Forty-eight percent of the start-ups that received corporate VC investments entered into a partnership or collaboration, whereas 30 percent of the start-ups that didn't receive corporate investments did not. Likewise, 24 percent of corporate-VC-funded start-ups were acquired, while 14 percent of their noncorporate-funded counterparts were. Interestingly, only 9 percent of the companies acquired were acquired by the parent company of the corporate VC. Finally, 12 percent of the start-ups that received corporate investments went public, compared to the 8 percent of their noncorporate-funded counterparts that did.

PHILANTHROPIC VENTURE CAPITAL FUNDS. Another form of venture capital funding comes from foundations. A philanthropic venture fund is similar to a corporate fund in that the investment is strategically aligned with the foundation. Although they are less common than other venture funds, more and more foundations, especially those associated with life-threatening or orphan diseases, are making investments in companies

---

19. Burrill Report, June 2012, http://www.burrillreport.com/content/BR_June_2012.pdf (accessed 14 July 2015).

to bring a product to market. (One recent example is the Cystic Fibrosis Foundation, which invested $75 million in Vertex to develop and launch the CF drug Kalydeco.)[20] Although this development is encouraging, it remains to be seen how often foundations will take the risk to invest in early-stage start-ups. A list of philanthropies that make venture investments can be found at researchtorevenue.com.

UNIVERSITY VENTURE FUNDS. As mentioned above, universities are providing early-stage "gap funding" to help their start-ups reach a point of viability. In addition to grants, many are assembling formal venture-type funds that have an investment committee evaluating deals, and equity investments are made with the expectation of a return in seven to ten years. An excellent example is Partners Innovation Fund, which is associated with Partners Healthcare. The fund was established by Partners to invest solely in start-ups coming out of the research labs of Mass General and Brigham and Women's Hospitals. The main difference between this type of fund and a traditional venture capital fund is the return expectations. Since the university is backing the fund and the university is willing to take a higher risk than a private VC, the return expectations are lower. As such, some of these funds are organized to be "evergreen"—that is, any returns from investments go back into the fund and are not taken as profit for the university. This keeps capital available and the fund sustainable for the long run.

VC firms, no matter their type, should be considered more than a source of capital. Many are composed of experienced investors and entrepreneurs, business leaders in the industry, and scientific leaders in key areas. Each of these individuals has years of experience in translating cutting-edge ideas and innovations into products for building profitable companies. In addition, they each have a network of people that can add tremendous value to the start-up. Their experience and connections can, in some cases, be more valuable than the capital. VCs do have a reputation of being ruthless and cutthroat, but that arises from situations in which the start-up is not performing and the VCs need to take drastic action (e.g., fire the CEO), or when a VC is seeking a return on its investment in a time frame dramatically different from that expected by the management team and founders. For example, a company may have the option to be acquired now or continue to build value for a future acquisition or public offering. The VC may need to show a return

20. "Ivacaftor," Cystic Fibrosis Foundation website, http://www.cff.org/treatments/therapies/kalydeco/ (accessed 23 July 2014).

TABLE 2.7 Status of venture capital, 1993, 2003, and 2013

	1993	2003	2013
No. of VC firms in existence	370	951	874
No. of VC funds in existence	613	1,788	1,331
No. of professionals	5,217	14,777	5,891
No. of VC funds raising money annually	93	160	187
VC capital raised annually ($ billion)	4.5	9.1	16.8
VC capital under management ($ million)	29.3	263.9	192.9
Avg. VC capital under management per firm ($ million)	79.2	277.5	220.7
Avg. VC fund size to date ($ million)	40.2	94.4	110.3

Source: National Venture Capital Association.

now to help in the raising of another fund. Although waiting could increase the overall return, pursuing a shorter-term return may not be aligned with the desires of the founders and management team.

The venture capital industry has changed dramatically over the last several decades as a result of several economic cycles. The rise and bursting of the dot-com bubble at the turn of the century resulted in the industry's significant hypergrowth and then contraction after significant losses for these firms and their limited partners. In addition, the recession of 2008 resulted in additional losses and a further contraction of the industry. The result has been a decrease in the number of venture capital funds and less money invested by VCs (table 2.7).

What is the link between these macroeconomic cycles and venture investing? First, troubled economic times usually mean fewer opportunities for companies to go public, which is one of the main sources of liquidity for a VC. When this is the case, VCs are locked into keeping their current companies afloat until more favorable public markets emerge. In addition, economic contractions mean firms have a harder time raising new funds, since limited partners may not be in a position to invest (e.g., because they are more risk averse or their assets have decreased in value).

Equity, Valuation, and Dilution

To build a high-value start-up, the company must attract both management (people) and capital (cash). Since the start-up company has very little value at first, it must attract people and capital based on the hope that novel technology, combined with a great market opportunity, combined with hard work and good decision-making, fueled by investors capital, will create significant value for all. The management team is investing its time in hopes of a signifi-cant financial return. Likewise, investors are putting capital to work with certain return expectations, balanced by the risks described previously. The vehicle for realizing these financial returns is ownership (equity) in the com-pany such that when the company goes public or is acquired, the ownership stake is exchanged for cash (becomes liquid).

The company founders and management receive equity in the start-up at different times during the company's growth. Founders receive equity at company formation based on the value (perceived or otherwise) they have contributed to it prior to founding or will contribute going forward. Manage-ment that joins the start-up at or after founding will receive equity as part of the value they contribute to grow and increase the value of the company.[21] Investors receive equity in the start-up in exchange for their investments, which can be made by a single investor (angel), a single group (angel group or VC firm), or multiple co-investors (a syndicate of firms). In the case of the syndicate, there is usually one "lead" investor, who takes the primary role in evaluating and negotiating the terms of the investment.[22] Investments are made in a series of funding rounds (seed round, Series A, B, C, D, etc.) such that, ideally, each round of investment is made into a company whose value has increased substantially beyond the amount invested in the previous round (more on deviations from ideal below). The round is defined by a target investment amount made in return for a certain number of shares priced at a defined price per share. Sometimes within a series, the VC will "tranche" the investment, such that the capital is deployed after the start-up meets specific milestones. With each round, the company issues additional shares of stock to the investor, which dilute the current owners of stock (founders, management, and current investors). Ideally, the extent of dilution should be outweighed by the increase in the value of the company (i.e., after the investment, the owners own a smaller but more valuable piece of the pie).

The following scenario illustrates how dilution occurs over time: Velocity Systems is founded by Professors Smith and Jones, and 3 million shares are

---

21. Value is a slippery concept as it relates to equity. Sometimes equity is a form of compensa-tion; for example, the value of the person's time, which is given in lieu of a market-rate salary. Equity can also be used as an incentive for people to work hard and make their equity worth more. In many cases, equity is a mixture of both.

22. A common and often frustrating problem for entrepreneurs seeking venture investment is finding the lead investors. Many firms will say they like the opportunity but won't lead the investment. This is code for "we like the opportunity but we don't have the resources to do the work to lead the deal" or "we like the opportunity but we need to see others commit to the deal in a real way (i.e., lead the deal)."

issued to them as founders. They decide to split the company 60/40 based on their scientific contributions to the technology. They present at a local start-up showcase and attract an experienced entrepreneur with the background to head up the company. The new CEO receives 1 million shares that vest over four years. The CEO licenses the technology, and as part of the license agreement, the university receives 500,000 shares. It is recognized that additional employees (CFO, VPs) will need to be incentivized, so a stock option pool is established with 1 million shares. An early-stage VC likes the opportunity and invests in the seed round and in return receives 1.8 million shares. Velocity makes good progress and gets additional investments (Series A and C).

Table 2.8 shows the major events in this scenario and how the pie gets sliced thinner (dilution of ownership) with each event. Dilution is easy to quantify but only represents one part of the equation. The other aspect of dilution is the value of the company (company valuation) at each round of dilution. The value at each round is easy to compute, based on the price paid for the stock, but arriving at that stock price, and thus the company value, is complicated. Is the value of the company increased by 25 percent over four years with the addition of an experienced CEO? Is a license from the university worth one-tenth ownership of the company? Should the current shareholders give up one-third of the company in exchange for a $1.5 million investment? Most founders and company management have a healthy respect for dilution, but for some, the respect borders on fear. In general, dilution is one of the necessary evils of a start-up. A no-dilution scenario is great in theory but unrealistic in a growing company needing capital to develop and launch a product. The fear is that too much dilution results in less ownership, which can translate into less control, in the short term, and less potential financial return, in the long term. The idea of less control is usually illusory since real control is exerted by the founders' engagement, their hiring the right people, and their working with investors with a similar vision. The idea of less financial return is more real but harder to quantify since a very small piece of a very large (valuable) pie can be worth much more than a large slice of a small pie. More concrete examples of dilution and return are discussed in Chapter 4.

In general, the value of a company is determined by industry-specific metrics, comparable deals, and expectations for future growth. For example, a service company can be valued at two to three times its annual revenue. For start-ups, valuation of the company is harder to determine because there is usually no revenue to provide a basis for valuation (most future revenue figures are pure speculation and considered science fiction by investors) and because many of the risks in growing the business are hard to assess. Starting out, most investors have comparable deals from which they have established a

TABLE 2.8   Dilution-of-ownership scenario for Velocity Systems

EVENT	RESULTING OWNERSHIP
Founding of the company • 1,800,000 shares to Professor Smith • 1,200,000 shares to Professor Jones	Professor Smith, 60% Professor Jones, 40%
Hiring of a CEO • 1,000,000 shares issued to CEO	Professor Smith, 45% Professor Jones, 30% CEO, 25%
License agreement with university • 500,000 shares to university	Professor Smith, 40% Professor Jones, 27% CEO, 22% University, 11%
Seed round plus additional employees • 1,000,000 shares for additional employees • 1,833,330 shares to seed-round investors	Professor Smith, 24% Professor Jones, 16% CEO, 14% University, 7% Stock options, 14% Seed investor, 22%
Series A investment • 3,666,667 shares to Series A investors	Professor Smith, 16% Professor Jones, 11% CEO, 9% University, 5% Stock options, 9% Seed investor, 17% Series A investor, 33%
Series B investment • 5,500,000 shares to Series B investors	Professor Smith, 11% Professor Jones, 7% CEO, 6% University, 3% Stock options, 6% Seed investor, 11% Series A investor, 22% Series B investor, 34%

value and can point to that ("Most Internet start-ups are valued at $3 million based on deals done by firms X, Y, and Z"). Tension around valuation arises between the company founders/management and the investor because for a given amount of investment, the founders and management want a higher valuation (smaller amount of company sold, thus less dilution), whereas the investor wants a lower valuation to own more of the company. Table 2.9

TABLE 2.9 Valuation of Velocity Systems at investment rounds

EVENT	PREMONEY VALUATION	AMOUNT INVESTED	PRICE PER SHARE	SHARES ISSUED	POSTMONEY VALUATION
Founding	—	$3,000	$0.001	3,000,000	—
CEO hired	—	$1,000	$0.001	1,000,000	—
License signed	—	—	—	500,000	—
Option pool	—	—	—	1,000,000	—
Seed investment	$1.5M	$500,000	$0.27	1,833,333	$2.0M
Series A	$3.0M	$1.5M	$0.41	3,666,667	$4.5M
Series B	$6.0M	$3.0M	$0.55	5,500,000	$9.0M
Series C	15.0M	5.0M	$0.91	5,500,000	$20.0M

outlines the series of investments in Velocity Systems reflecting how valuation changes with each investment round. The table shows the "premoney valuation" of Velocity (the value of the company prior to its receiving any capital investment, the numbers of shares issued in return for the investment, and the "postmoney valuation" (the value of the company after investment) (premoney + investment = postmoney valuation). The following are descriptions of each event as the company grows.

Founding. When the company is founded, the founders each pay "par value" for their stock. The par value is an arbitrary value to signify that the founders paid for stock but that the stock is worth very little. The amount of money contributed by the founders at this point can vary significantly and is used to pay for incidentals (e.g., business cards, domain registration) and legal fees (incorporation, patents).

CEO hired. The CEO comes on board as a founder, paying par value for the stock, but the stock will vest. Vesting incentivizes the CEO to stay with the company over time. Instead of receiving all the stock on day one, the CEO will typically receive one-fourth at the end of the first year and then the 1/36th of the remaining stock each month for the following three years.[23] In addition

---

23. A four-year vesting schedule is typical, although some founders may reduce it to two or three years. Sometimes vesting is based on milestones (completing the business plan, closing financing, completing prototype). Although milestones look good on paper, difficulties arise in assessing whether a milestone was in fact completed (e.g., is this a finished business plan?) or whether a significant milestone was achieved that was not anticipated (e.g., a corporate partnership vs. a VC investment), or worse yet, whether the milestone was complete but not in the long-term interest of the company (e.g., compromising terms for a round of financing to reach the milestone).

to incentivizing the CEO to stay with the company for several years, the vesting also provides favorable tax advantages: the stock is given at a time when the company is worth little, thus the tax basis is small. Giving stock or stock options over time, as compared to vesting, increases the tax liability and the basis since the share price increases over time.

License and option pool. The shares here are issued without any investment. The university receives its shares as part of the license agreement. Shares from the option pool are distributed to employees at a "strike price" (typically the share price from the previous round) and then can be sold at the liquidity event, at which time it is hoped that the stock price is higher. The employee profits from the difference between the strike price and the sell price.[24]

Seed investment. The first capital infusion comes from the seed round and typically will be from one or two investors (angels or early-stage VCs). The negotiations start with the preinvestment value of the company, or premoney valuation, or simply "pre." The premoney valuation combined with the number of issued shares sets a stock price, which in turn determines the number of shares the investor buys for the given investment.

$$\text{stock price} = \frac{\text{premoney valuation}}{\text{number of issued shares}}$$

$$\text{investor shares purchased} = \frac{\text{investment}}{\text{stock price}}$$

So, for our example:

$$\text{stock price} = \frac{\$1,500,000}{5,500,000 \text{ shares}} = \$0.27 \text{ per share}$$

$$\text{investor shares purchased} = \frac{\$500,000}{\$0.27/\text{share}} = 1,833.33 \text{ shares}$$

The postmoney valuation is simply the premoney valuation plus the amount invested ($2 million "post" in this example).

---

24. Due to poor company performance or challenging market conditions, the stock price of the company can be lower than the strike price, making the options "underwater" (worthless), which reduces the incentive of the employee to stay with the company. New options at the lower strike price may be awarded to valuable employees.

As mentioned, determining the valuation of the company at this early stage if often difficult (no revenue; product still being developed), and the opinions regarding a company's value usually widely differ (founders see high valuation; investors see otherwise). One solution to this dilemma is to delay the valuation by having the investor invest in the company using a "convertible note" (a loan to the company that converts to equity at the valuation set at the first equity investment, e.g., Series A).

Series A, B, and C. Velocity uses the $500,000 to achieve certain milestones and remove some of the risk from the business. But eventually it needs additional capital before it can launch a product and become self-sustaining. The next rounds of financing proceed as before: a premoney valuation is established and the investors purchase stock at the new stock price. For these rounds, the seed investor is motivated to participate in the A round (and A round investors will want to participate in the B and C rounds) to keep seed investor's (and A round investor's) dilution to a minimum as well as stay engaged with the company (e.g., retain a board seat). The premoney valuation for these rounds is based on how the company has performed and general market conditions.

Flat and Down Rounds

If things are going well, the premoney of the current round of financing will be higher than the postmoney from the previous round (an "up round"), with the justification being that value has been created beyond the amount invested in the last round. This progression of increasing valuation with each financing round does not always occur. At times, the premoney valuation will be the same as the postmoney from the previous round (a "flat round") or, worse, the premoney will be lower than the previous postmoney (a "down round"). Flat or down rounds can be due to internal or external factors. For example, internally, the company might fail to meet certain milestones: product development might be delayed, the company might fail to meet certain revenue targets, or a change in business strategy sets back the product-development activities. External factors may involve eroding broader market conditions, which can make investors more cautious or limit their options for reaching a liquid exit, which in turn creates more scarce and more expensive capital. Many down rounds occurred after the tech bubble of 2000 and the recession of 2008; as public market values dropped and the number of possible IPOs decreased private venture financing values dropped.

Down rounds are painful for founders, management, and nonparticipating investors (i.e., investors in previous rounds not participating in the current round) alike, since a lower valuation (lower stock price) requires the com-

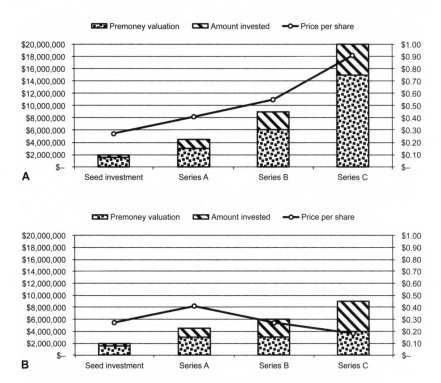

FIGURE 2.3 Premoney valuation, investment, and share price for a series of investments, showing up rounds (a) and down rounds (b) (assuming the same investments are made for each round)

pany to sell a greater number of shares in order to raise the same amount of money, thus creating more dilution. Figure 2.3a shows how premoney valuation and share price increase in an ideal scenario, that is, a series of up rounds, using the example in table 2.9. The increase in the premoney valuation in each round demonstrates the increase in company value, as perceived by the investors going into each round, and the increased value justified by the company meeting value-creating milestones (product development, launch, revenue, partnering, etc.). Figure 2.3b shows several rounds of investment in a less than ideal scenario. Here, the A series was a step up in valuation since everything went according to plan, but the B and C series were down rounds.

Exits and Returns

At the end of the day, equity investors (angels or VCs) are interested in only one thing: maximizing their financial return for their investment of money and time.[25] The only way for an investor and other shareholders to realize a return is for the start-up company to have a liquidity event, in which their shares are sold for cash. The two common liquidity events are acquisition by another company or going public through an IPO. Acquisition involves selling the company (its equity and assets) to an acquiring company in return for cash or a combination of cash and stock (usually publicly traded). A public offering provides an exchange of the privately held stock for publicly traded stock. This allows investors to sell their ownership, with certain restrictions, in the public markets. These types of successful "exits" provide money back to the investors (angels or VC) as a return on their financial investment and to the founders and management team for their investment of time.[26]

Although every investor expects each investment to be wildly successful, a typical set of outcomes for an equity investor may look like the following:
For every 10 investments,

- 4 companies fail
- 2 companies return the capital invested
- 2 or 3 companies return 2 to 5 times the investment
- 1 or 2 companies return over 10 times the investment

This mix of outcomes demonstrates how an investor views his/her investment portfolio as a numbers game; that is, one or two companies provide an exceptional return, enough to cover the losses of the failures of the other investments. As such, investors must not only choose investment wisely but have enough capital and time to create a statistical advantage.

Other Forms of Funding

With the contraction of the VC industry in recent years, start-ups have sought other avenues for investments.

Corporate Partnerships

The interaction of a start-up with a large corporate partner can occur on two levels. As mentioned, some corporations operate corporate venture funds

25. The other shareholders (founders and management) are also interested in their financial return, but that interest is blended with other factors, such as whether the product will be impactful, will meet an unmet need, or simply will beat the competition. Investors might be interested in these factors as well, but their first priority is a financial return.

26. An investor will not invest unless there is the opportunity to generate a return through an exit. A start-up without a clear exit strategy will be pejoratively labeled a "lifestyle" company. Lifestyle companies can be successful but often require other forms of funding to grow the company (personal funds, debt, bootstrapping).

that make investments in strategically aligned start-ups. The other form of interaction is a formal partnership between the company and the start-up.[27] Corporate partnering is increasingly popular for start-ups for several reasons. First, the competition for a smaller pool of venture capital dollars has increased and will likely increase further in future years. Second, many large corporations (e.g., pharmaceutical companies) have dismantled their R&D groups in favor of sourcing innovation from outside entities. The external acquisition of innovation provides greater flexibility in accessing leading-edge technology, especially in a rapidly changing areas such social media, nanotechology, or wearable devices. A corporate partnership with an early-stage start-up can take many forms. Some might involve sponsored research or technology development (i.e., funding for specific commercially relevant milestones), whereas others might involve in-kind services where the corporate partner may provide support in the form of clinical trials, engineering, or market research. They might also involve certain options as the product is developed. For example, a corporate partner might acquire the technology or the product for further development and eventual commercial sales (via sublicensing), or it might have the option to acquire the company. For a later-stage company, where the start-up has developed the product, the partnership may be a distribution agreement in which the partner leverages its sales, marketing, and distribution channels. The combination of components and options will depend on the expertise and resources of the start-up and the corporate partner, as well as the strategic fit of the start-up's products.

Robert Ackerman, founder and managing director of Allegis Capital, gives the following advice for a start-up working with a corporate partner:

SHARE EXPERIENCES AND GOALS. Like any good relationship, the more similarities between the two parties, the better. Both companies should have experience in the same areas and be good communicators. Both should also have good give-and-take skills, as well as mutual tolerance, because periodic disagreements are inevitable—and they need to be resolved amicably and successfully.

SEEK A SYNERGISTIC CULTURE. Large corporations tend to resist change. Entrepreneurs are precisely the opposite, priding themselves on being untethered, fast, and efficient. Predictably, partnerships between the two can create huge frustrations. Successfully combining the two cul-

27. These two forms of corporate interactions are not necessarily exclusive. Some corporate/start-up deals may involve both an investment and a partnering component. A third, more indirect interaction can be sponsored research by the corporate partner into the founder's lab, perhaps as part of an investment.

tures requires acknowledgment from both parties of what each type of company does well and what it does not. To promote collaboration, the start-up should have an inside "champion." Clearly, the start-up won't always win debates. If you don't think you can have fruitful conversations with a corporate partner, however, don't bother with this sort of partnership opportunity.

DEVELOP STRONG NEGOTIATION SKILLS. A corporation engages with a start-up for one of two reasons—to fill a technology product void or to secure an option on a potentially useful innovation. In other words, the corporation is looking out for its own interests. Start-up entrepreneurs need to do the same. A large corporation can easily overwhelm the resources of a much smaller strategic partner. And a large corporation can walk away from a strategic partnership with no more than a bruise. The consequences can be far more dire for the start-up. So a start-up must maximize its exit options to protect itself against the possibility of a dysfunctional partnership.

ENSURE ALIGNMENT OF INTERESTS. Strive to develop a partnership of equals, one in which both parties share commitments, milestones, and benchmarks. If a corporate partner asks for a start-up's financial records more than once or twice, don't do it, since this undermines the notion of a partnership of equals. Negotiations are impossible when a corporation holds all the cards.[28]

Debt

Funding a start-up through debt financing involves a loan to the start-up in return for a loan payback that provides a sufficient return for the loaner. Loans are ideal for companies with tangible assets (equipment, buildings, inventory) that can be used as collateral and/or with a track record of revenue. For these companies, traditional banks are a source of loans. Where a company needs to purchase capital equipment that will enable the short-term generation of revenue (e.g., a piece of lab equipment used for a service offering), an alternative is for the founders or management to use personal assets (house) as collateral.

For many university start-ups, however, lacking these tangible assets makes debt financing difficult. In these cases, debt financing is possible through banks that take on higher-risk loans. These "venture banks" (e.g., Silicon

28. Robert R. Ackerman Jr., "The Most Unlikely Place to Find Startup Funding," VB News website, venturebeat.com/2010/08/03/the-most-unlikely-place-to-find-start-up-funding/ (accessed 31 July 2013).

Valley Bank) provide debt to start-ups to purchase hard assets (servers, instruments, equipment). Venture debt is often provided in conjunction with venture capital since VCs may not be excited about funding the purchase of capital equipment. Given the due diligence conducted by VCs, venture banks offering debt see lower risk in this scenario. These lenders seek a return for the high risk of the loan by charging a higher than usual interest on the loan (12–25 percent), backloading the payment schedule with a balloon payment, taking multiple forms of collateral (intellectual property, capital equipment, buildings), and receiving equity in the company in the form of "warrant coverage" ("equity kicker").[29]

Bootstrapping

Most of our discussion of the funding of university start-ups has assumed that a technical innovation that provides some intellectual property is at the core of the company and that the company needs to acquire capital to develop, market, and sell a product around that innovation (Type I and II Start-ups). In some cases, though, the IP is a copyright to software or simply an idea for a service in which know-how or reputation is the core of the company. In these cases, the level of capital required to build the company is low. For example, a faculty member may license a copyright to software code from the university to start a company. Working nights and weekends, the faculty member may be able to build and launch software to a small set of customers. The revenue from those sales allows the employment of additional programmers, which generates additional sales, which lead to an office and equipment, and so on. The start-up has successfully "bootstrapped" itself into a viable company. Another example involves building a service company around a university capability. A faculty member might have expertise in providing a core service to university researchers (e.g., material characterization and testing). Through meetings and word of mouth, customers from the private industry contract through the university to gain access to this service and the faculty member's know-how. Eventually, the contracts may become large enough that the university is uncomfortable with the large industrial interaction, or the faculty member sees an attractive way to change careers and make money doing science. A spin-out can be accomplished by leveraging existing contracts or new contracts to bootstrap the company.[30]

29. A bank may receive 5–20 percent of the value of the loan as warrants. Warrants are similar to stock options in that they allow the holder to convert the warrant to equity at a predetermined time and share price. Most warrants are exercised at the time of acquisition or public offering.

30. An innovative approach here allows the company to use the university facility to provide the university with the core service while servicing industrial clients. This can free up enough cash to prepare the start-up for moving off campus (purchase of equipment, space, etc.).

Crowdfunding

An emerging source of funding is crowdfunding, made popular by sites like KickStarter.com and Indiegogo.com. These sites began as a means for people to raise money for projects, a film, or a nonprofit program, where people could donate to the projects. The scope of crowdfunding has expanded to include start-ups raising money for a specific product-development purpose. For example, if a company was developing a solar-powered car, it may raise money through crowdfunding to build a prototype and five production models. The donor could donate to the company to help with product development or make a larger donation and receive one of the early production models in return.

Recently, the U.S. government has enacted legislation to allow for *equity-based* crowdfunding, as distinct from the crowdfunding described above. Until recently, private companies (e.g., start-ups) could not solicit investments through public means, such as public meetings, websites, or social media. These companies had to have a "substantial and pre-existing relationship" with a potential investor, a relationship that required many face-to-face meetings with investors. With the passing of Title II of the Jumpstart Our Business Startups (JOBS) Act, these companies can now use a variety of means to advertise their companies and solicit investments. The only restriction is that they must verify that the investor is accredited—that is, he or she has either "an individual net worth or joint net worth with a spouse that exceeds $1 million at the time of the purchase, excluding the value (and any related indebtedness) of a primary residence, [or] an individual annual income that exceeded $200,000 in each of the two most recent years or a joint annual income with a spouse exceeding $300,000 for those years, and a reasonable expectation of the same income level in the current year."[31]

The U.S. government has proposed legislation for lifting the requirement of accredited investors for equity crowdfunding (Title III/IV of the JOBS Act). This legislation has been slow in coming as regulators develop ways to protect naïve investors from losing their entire savings on a high-risk start-up. One option being considered is limiting the individual's investment to a portion of his/her net income or net worth.

31. "Eliminating the Prohibition on General Solicitation and General Advertising in Certain Offerings," Fact Sheet, 10 July 2013, U.S. Securities and Exchange Commission, http://www.sec.gov/news/press/2013/2013-124-item1.htm (accessed 8 October 2014).

3

Key Steps to a Start-Up

Having covered many aspects of the entrepreneurial ecosystem, namely the university, money, and people, we now turn to the how-tos, the key steps in conceiving, launching, and building a successful university start-up. This chapter assumes a (Type I) start-up company is being formed around an innovative technology, protected by university-filed IP, and has multiple product options. It also assumes, as is generally the case, that capital will need to be raised in multiple rounds to get the product to a stage where it can either enter the market or be licensed by a partner. Finally, we assume the faculty members who developed the technology are motivated to commercialize the technology and will engage to the extent necessary for success.

Overview of Key Steps

A university start-up proceeds through a series of steps that follow a general timeline. Since not all start-ups are created equal, not all start-ups go through every step since some steps don't apply, and not all start-ups go through the steps in the order described. In addition, many steps are discrete and have a short timeline (e.g., incorporation of the company), whereas others are ongoing (e.g., writing and rewriting the business plan, fund-raising). Finally, some steps must follow others (e.g., incorporation before a license, a license before funding, funding before product development). Table 3.1 summarizes the key steps.

KEY STEP **Recognizing the Opportunity**

The first step in commercializing research is recognizing the utility of scientific research in solving a real-world problem in a way that can capture commercial value. Consider the following progression from science to products, as shown in figure 3.1. Scientific research is the source of discoveries and

TABLE 3.1 Key steps to a start-up

STEP	DESCRIPTION
Recognizing the opportunity	The first step in spinning out a company is recognizing the commercial opportunity that the academic research enables. This involves seeing a fit between a breakthrough technology and commercial need. Recognition of the opportunity can come from the faculty member (e.g., a medical researcher recognizing an unmet medical need), a colleague (e.g., an interdisciplinary collaborator seeing an application), or an external source (e.g., an entrepreneur seeing a gap in the market filled by the technology).
Disclosure to the university	Disclosure to the university involves a formal description of the invention, usually in the form of a prepublication, using an invention disclosure form. The disclosure begins the formal process of IP protection.
Filing for IP protection	The university technology transfer office (TTO) will make a determination on how to handle the IP, resulting in either the university filing for IP protection (patent, copyright) or releasing the IP to the inventor for his/her filing.
Recruiting advisers and mentors	The founders begin to gather advisers and mentors to help guide the early decisions around commercial opportunities, company formation, and the business strategy.
Developing the business case	A business case is developed for the technology that outlines the key features of the technology, the application, the utility, and the customer need. This provides the foundation of the business plan.
Forming the company	The decision to start the company is considered a go/no-go decision based on the business case and input from the TTO and advisers. Incorporation signifies the legal beginning of the start-up with the establishment of the board of directors and distribution of equity (ownership) among the founders and key employees.
Building the management team	A management team composed of a senior leader (CEO, president) and others (financial, business development, scientific) begins the formal development of the company (product development, fund-raising).
Licensing the intellectual property	In order for the start-up to develop and sell a product based on the university IP, the start-up must have a license from the university.

STEP	DESCRIPTION
Gathering market information	The target market for selling the product must be identified and characterized in terms of customer needs, product application, market size (number of customers), and growth rate.
Defining and refining the business model	Every business has a model or structure by which it develops and sells products.
Early-stage marketing	In preparation for raising money, attracting talent, and engaging partners, the basic marketing elements are put in place to position the company and its technology and products.
Writing the business plan	The business case is refined to lay out the business strategy of the company (product development, sales, marketing); assess the market size, growth, and competition; and develop the financials for the company that will drive the fund-raising effort.
Raising initial capital	The first money (preseed or seed capital) into the company will cover some legal fees, proof-of-concept experiments, technology development, and consulting fees. The source of funds can be grants (nondilutive) or investors (dilutive)
Finding space	With initial funding, the company will establish initial space to conduct experiments, house personnel, and hold meetings.
Raising growth capital	Capital is required for technology and product development, hiring the core management team, and producing the product. This funding usually occurs in multiple rounds based on the company's achieving value-enhancing milestones.
Developing the product	With the infusion of growth capital, formal product development can begin. For some products (e.g., those requiring FDA approval) the steps are defined. For others, "customer discovery" may be in order.
Establishing manufacturing	The product must be produced by the company or outsourced to a third party or by some combination.
Engaging the customer	As the product is developed, the company will begin to engage early customers or partners. The former will lead to sales and marketing of the product, and the latter will lead to partnerships for completing product development and/or for sales and distribution of the product.
The exit	For investors and other shareholders, the exit provides a cash return for the value created in building the company.

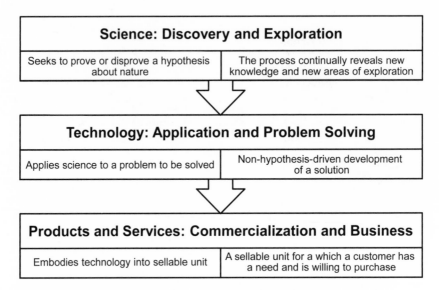

FIGURE 3.1 Progression of science to products

innovations that are then applied to solve a problem. These innovations, in turn, are embodied in a product or service around which a business can be built. One recognizes opportunity initially with understanding how science can be applied to solve a problem. One continues to recognize opportunity with understanding how widespread the problem is, how important it is to solve the problem, and how valuable the customer believes the solution is relative to other, competitive solutions.

When one considers the commercial potential of scientific research, a number of important aspects of the science and technology should be assessed:

UNIQUE PROPERTIES AND CAPABILITIES:

- Does the science or technology possess unique properties or novel capabilities compared to other approaches?
- Does it provide a substantial improvement in the way the problem is solved, or is the improvement incremental?
- Are these properties unique and novel enough that they can be protected, primarily through a patent, so that others can't copy?

MARKET NEED:

- Does the product solve a problem or meet an unmet need?
- Does the product solve a problem that someone cares about?

- Could the product solve a problem for a price someone is willing to pay?
- Are there a sufficient number of paying customers to support a business?

Not all of these questions can be answered at this early stage, but they are some of the most important considerations for a start-up and are the type of questions investors ask when making an investment decision. The first set of questions attempts to unlock the unique aspects of the technology and helps establish significant "differentiators" (unique features or benefits that set the product apart from competing products) between what is currently done and what could be done with the new product and whether these differentiators are significant enough to create a competitive advantage. In addition, the unique aspects of the technology need to be protectable, typically through patents. A patent will solidify the competitive advantage and create "barriers to entry" (impediments to keep the competition from copying your product). The second set of questions relates to the people who will use the product or technology to solve the problem. These people, the customers, are collectively considered "the market." The questions consider the market (customer) need as well as the size of the market. Collectively, these questions begin to frame the product opportunity enabled by the science and technology.

The unique, enabling features of the technology are at the core of a product opportunity. There are several ways to map out the relationship between technology, features, and applications. The technology might have a number of unique features that, when combined, can have a specific application. On the other hand, the technology might have a single feature that can have many different applications. Finally, some technologies have several enabling features, each of which can have a unique application. Figure 3.2 shows two examples of "opportunity mapping." For example, a novel hydrogel may have many exciting properties (fig. 3.2a). Each property might give rise to a distinct application, and those applications could be in related market areas (the two drug-delivery applications) or in a distinct market (bioremediation). In the second case (fig. 3.2b), a drug that inhibits an ion channel in cell might treat neuropathic pain but the therapeutic applications could be distinct and have implications for product development (e.g., will require clinical trials or regulatory approval).

At this early stage, it is important to consider all applications with the understanding that as one proceeds down the commercialization path, certain applications will be eliminated, others will be emphasized, and still others will be discovered. This application discovery and winnowing process is driven

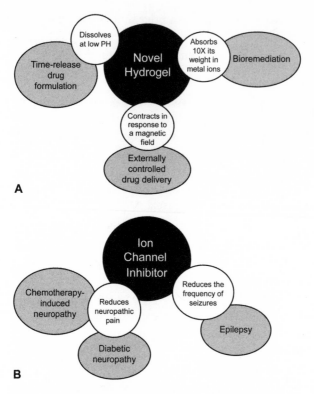

FIGURE 3.2 Product opportunity maps for a novel hydrogel (a)
and an ion channel inhibitor (b)

by a number of factors. The faculty member may emphasize a certain application because that is where their expertise lies.[1] The technical feasibility (will
it work?) and current state of technical development (how much feasibility
has been demonstrated?) will drive the selection of certain applications over
others. Having data in hand demonstrating one application can be worth
much more than the time and risk of getting funding to demonstrate another
feasible application. Finally, a number of market considerations need to be
assessed: size and growth of the market, current ways the problem is solved
today (competition), and the perceived value of solving the problem. This
illustrates a common early dilemma: Does one pursue the demonstrated and
feasible application, albeit for a small market or only an incremental improve-

---

1. This presents a dilemma in university technology commercialization. The faculty's scientific knowledge creates a bias that can preclude the recognition of an opportunity to apply
the technology outside the field of the faculty's expertise. For the entrepreneur considering
an opportunity outside the faculty member's field, expertise can be acquired but at the risk of
decreased faculty engagement.

ment, or does one step back and swing for the fences with a unproven application with a large and growing unmet customer need? There are no easy answers here. Clearly, few academic faculty have the experience to answer all of these questions, so it is important for them to reach out to commercialization champions, key opinion leaders, and entrepreneurs to begin assessing these opportunities.

Technology Push versus Market Pull

Identifying opportunities for commercializing technology underscores two distinct paradigms: "technology push" and "market pull." Understanding the difference between technology push and market pull is critical when evaluating product opportunities. Technology push can be thought of as a technology looking for an application: "I have a great hammer (technology), and I just need some nails (applications) to bang on." In this case, there is no clear market need, so one is left to look for applications that might fit the technology. As a business strategy, technology push comes under the mantra "if we build it, they will buy it." This strategy is risky and requires a specific approach to marketing the product, namely educating (i.e., evangelizing) the customer as to how this product can be applied to meet his/her needs, since the need was not initially expressed by the customer.

Market pull considers the defined market need first as expressed by the customer. At the opportunity-recognition stage, the market need for a product or a solution to a problem might be ill-defined or stated in general terms. The first step in defining the market need is defining the application: How can the technology be applied to solve this problem? Under the market pull business strategy, market need influences research, development, manufacturing, and marketing activities.

A trap one may fall into is being enamored with a revolutionary technology when the applications are not clear. It is tempting to think that the technology push approach is appropriate without doing the hard work to uncover the possible applications of the technology. A few truly revolutionary technologies have built their own markets (e.g., recombinant DNA, PCR, LEDs, lasers), but most technologies need to be explored in relation to a market need.

KEY STEP **Disclosure to the University**

Once a discovery or technology has been recognized as potentially commercially valuable, the first formal step toward commercialization is disclosure to the university (the TTO). Disclosing to the university raises the following questions:

Who owns an invention or discovery? Ownership of intellectual property is usually set forth in university policy. In general, an invention created in university facilities during the course of faculty research belongs to the university and not the faculty member. However, if an idea is conceived outside of the normal duties of the faculty member, the idea might belong to the inventor. One well-known university makes the distinction between a "supported invention" and an "incidental invention." Supported inventions are made with substantial support of the university (funding, facilities, space, people) and thus are owned by the university. Incidental inventions are made without university support, and thus ownership resides with the inventor. University ownership is further dictated by the source of funding that gives rise to the invention. Federal funding gives the university rights, more precisely, obligations under Bayh-Dole, to commercialize the technology. For privately funded research (e.g., by industry, foundations), the sponsored research agreement (the contract between the university and the sponsor) usually states how inventions arising from the research are handled. At minimum, industry usually has an option to license the technology arising from the research it sponsors.

A common area of confusion is the distinction between ownership and inventorship. The person or persons who make the discovery are the inventors (see below). Their names are listed on the patent as inventors. If the inventor was working out of his or her garage, then by default, the inventor owns the patent. In other words, the inventor was not under any obligation to share ownership of the invention with others. By contrast, a scientist employed by a company or university doing research funded by a third party (employer, university, federal government, industrial sponsor) who makes a discovery is in a different situation. In this case, the invention is under certain obligations—that is, the funder has certain rights to the invention. As such, the inventors are obligated to assign their invention to a third party (e.g., the university), giving the third party the right to develop the technology into a product or license the technology to another party (e.g., a start-up) for commercial development. As inventors, depending on the university, income coming to the university as part of licensing to a third party can flow back to the inventors.

What is the obligation to disclose an invention to the university? Some universities have no stated policy regarding the obligation to disclose an invention but encourage faculty to disclose potentially commercializable discoveries. Others state that faculty are obligated to disclose inventions to the university, but such a policy may have no teeth since the consequences of not disclosing are minimal. However, not disclosing an invention and attempting to commercialize the technology outside of the university can result in serious legal action. Beyond whether disclosure is an obligation, the more general question is, why disclose to the university? Some faculty don't want anything to do with commercialization, never make disclosures, and think putting the information in the public domain gives everyone an equal chance to pursue commercial applications for the technology. Faculty who disclose to the university early enough that a technology with commercial potential can be protected through patents or copyrights can both commercialize a technology and publish, as long as the patents are filed before publication (see below).

When should a disclosure be made? In terms of when to disclose, the earlier the better. By disclosing early, the TTO can assess the commercial viability of the technology, pass it by a few potential licensees, and have time to file a patent. A challenging scenario is a disclosure on the eve of a presentation or publication, which results in a scramble by the TTO to decide whether to file a provisional patent. As noted in Chapter 2, if the public disclosure is made prior to the filing of the provisional patent, a substantial loss in protection may occur.[2]

The disclosure form is typically completed by the faculty inventor(s) (see an example invention disclosure form at researchtorevenue.com). The form gathers the following information to help the TTO determine the appropriate course of action:

WHO ARE THE INVENTORS? The disclosure form usually asks who contributed to the research that led to invention. A legal determination will be made by the TTO and/or outside patent counsel as to who contributed to the "inventive step" and will be listed on the patent. The inventorship determination will also play out if the university receives licensing income for the invention (under Bayh-Dole the university is required to share a portion with inventors).

WHO FUNDED THE RESEARCH THAT GAVE RISE TO THE INVENTION? As mentioned, most university funding has certain intellectual property rights associated with it. Under Bayh-Dole, rights to inventions arising from

2. In the United States, if the public disclosure is made prior to filing the provisional application, all international rights are forfeited.

federally funded research reside with the university, whereas inventions from privately funded research will be handled by the terms of the sponsored research agreement.

WERE THERE OTHER OBLIGATIONS MADE RELATIVE TO THE INVENTION? Many faculty have relationships that extend beyond the walls of their laboratories. For example, it is common for faculty to consult with industry in their area of expertise. The consulting agreement may obligate any inventions made during the consulting agreement.[3] Those obligations can vary depending on the nature of the agreement and the extent of input the faculty member has in the invention. Obligations can also arise from other agreements, such as a sponsored research agreement, as mentioned.

HAVE ANY DISCLOSURES BEEN MADE OUTSIDE THE UNIVERSITY? The TTO needs to determine if any public disclosures have been made that would forfeit some intellectual property protection. In the event that the invention has been discussed in a publication or a presentation, the TTO will need to determine what was disclosed. Some key element might not have been disclosed, which could afford some patent protection. The presentation might have been given to a "private" audience and thus would not be considered a public disclosure.

DESCRIPTION OF THE INVENTION. The description will include features that make the invention unique or novel, as well has how useful the invention is. The TTO will use this information to determine whether to file the patent, and it will be the central part of the patent application (see below). Usually a manuscript of a publication in process is attached to the form to help describe the invention.

How do the inventors share in any monetary rewards for the invention? Through terms agreed to in the license agreement, a faculty-discovered innovation that is commercialized brings income back to the university. The

3. This type of obligation was at the heart of *Stanford v. Roche*, which was decided in 2011 by the Supreme Court. The case involved a Stanford research fellow who had assigned his inventions to Stanford as part of his employment agreement. The fellow visited a biotech to collaborate on a diagnostic test and, as part of the collaboration, signed an agreement obligating his inventions to the biotech, which was eventually acquired by Roche. After completing the collaboration, the biotech filed patents on the test, and, upon returning to Stanford, the fellow repeated the work with Stanford, filing patents on the test. The Supreme Court sided with Stanford, arguing that the fellow had no rights to assign since the original research had been federally funded and that the rights belonged to Stanford, under Bayh-Dole.

income is typically split between the university TTO and the inventors. In cases where the faculty-inventor is also a faculty-founder and owns equity in the start-up company, the distribution of licensing income might be different from that in cases where the inventor's IP is licensed to an established company. Some universities want to prevent "double-dipping"—that is, where a faculty member as the inventor receives income from the sale of the start-up via the university license but also receives cash from the liquidity event as a faculty founder.

KEY STEP Filing for Intellectual Property Protection

Once an invention has been disclosed to the university, the university's TTO makes a decision about whether to protect the intellectual property, when to begin the protection, and what form of protection is best. Most university TTOs will seek protection by filing a patent. (Copyrights protect a minority of university IP; for example, software code.) Unless there appears to be no commercial potential for the technology or it is clearly not patentable, most universities will file a provisional patent because it is relatively inexpensive (a few thousand dollars) and gives the inventor the freedom to publish; provides the university a year to gather more data for a more formal, nonprovisional patent; and allows the TTO to begin marketing the invention to potential licensees.[4] Figures from the Association of University Technology Managers indicate that slightly less than half of the reports of inventions result in provisional patent applications. Technologies for which patents are not filed are either abandoned or released to the university inventors.[5]

The TTO's decision to file a nonprovisional patent requires more deliberation because the costs associated with the filing can eventually reach hundreds of thousands of dollars. The decision primarily depends on the answer to two questions: 1) Does the invention have significant commercial potential? and 2) What is the likelihood a patent will be issued? Evaluating the invention for commercial potential requires the TTO to conduct market research, market the invention to potential licensees and assess the responses, and contact

---

4. The United States' recent change from a "first-to-invent" to a "first-to-file" country has changed some TTOs' patent strategy: Some may include much more information in the provisional patent, and in some cases claim language.

5. In cases where the university is releasing the invention *and* the invention was supported by federal (U.S.) dollars, the inventors must get a release from the federal government (i.e., the university has no rights to release the invention).

consultants or entrepreneurs for advice. To answer the latter question, the TTO, in collaboration with an IP attorney, will consider four points:

IS THE INVENTION PATENTABLE? The subject matter has to be patentable. Generally speaking, printed matter, scientific principles, abstract ideas, mathematical equations, and things of that nature are not patentable.

IS THE INVENTION NOVEL? Any aspects of the invention that were in the public domain prior to the filing of patent application will render the invention nonnovel.

IS THE INVENTION USEFUL? The invention must have a substantial, specific, and credible application. It cannot be a theoretical phenomena or idea.

IS THE INVENTION NONOBVIOUS? Here the determination is based on the difference between the "prior art" (i.e., information in the public domain) and the current invention and on whether anyone "skilled in the art" would have come up with the current invention or whether an inventive step was taken by the inventors.

Patentability is usually the easiest to discern. A number of recent Supreme Court cases have addressed the question of patentable subject matter. For example, in *Alice Corp v. CLS Bank International* the Court ruled that software algorithms are abstract ideas and thus not patentable. In *Association for Molecular Pathology v. Myriad Genetics*, the Court ruled on the patentability of genes. The case hinged on the nature of the DNA. The Court held "that a naturally occurring DNA segment is a product of nature and not patent eligible merely because it has been isolated, but that [synthetically created] cDNA is patent eligible because it is not naturally occurring."[6] The impact of the ruling is still being assessed. Novelty is typically assessed by reviewing the patent literature and publications, and determining whether the current inventors made any public disclosure (e.g., a poster at a public meeting). Utility is not usually an issue with most university patents since the research shows how the invention is used by way of examples. Finally, the nonobvious criteria is one of the most difficult to assess in advance since this opinion comes from the patent examiner.

The cost and timing of patent filings often create tensions between the faculty and TTO. In an industrial research setting, most patents for inventions are filed as late as possible for several reasons: First, more research can be done

6. "Opinion of the Court, *Association for Molecular Pathology v. Myriad Genetics*," http://www .supremecourt.gov/opinions/12pdf/12-398_1b7d.pdf (accessed 10 December 2014).

to determine the usefulness and market potential of the technology before incurring patent costs. Second, once the patent process is started, the clock is ticking. Patent life is typically 20 years, and each year of delay in getting the product to the market is a year of lost exclusivity. Finally, the pressure to publish is not as great. In the university, by contrast, with more pressure to publish, many patent applications are filed, and expenses incurred, when the technology is immature. Delay in patenting for further development and assessment is typically not an option since publications are essential for faculty members to get funding and tenure and for students to graduate and get jobs.

The typical stages of patent filing and protection are shown in table 3.2. Not all IP follows these steps, however, as in the following cases:

PUBLIC DISCLOSURE PRIOR TO FILING. If a public disclosure of the IP is made prior to filing a provisional patent (e.g., publishing of a paper, presenting a poster, making a presentation),[7] then patent rights will usually be limited to the Unites States. U.S. patent law allows one to make a public disclosure up to 12 months prior to filing a patent (provisional or nonprovisional).

LACK OF LICENSEE/LIMITED PATENT BUDGET. Most universities cannot afford to carry the patent costs associated with filing extensively in a wide range of countries without a licensee. If the IP has been marketed to potential licensees and there is no movement in getting a start-up launched and funded, the TTO may abandon the patent prior to the national phase, which is the point when the most significant patent filing expenses begin to accrue. An alternative would be to file in the United States only, which would greatly reduce the patent costs but would also limit the university's ability to license IP for developing a product that can be globally distributed (e.g., pharmaceuticals).

Elements of a Patent Application

A patent application is composed of the following elements:

SPECIFICATION. The specification is composed of several elements that together describe the invention. The level of description should be sufficient for someone "skilled in the art" (experienced in the field) to

7. A grant application and the review of publication are not considered public disclosure, since the information is not freely made available to the public. An abstract, lecture, or presentation can be a public disclosure, depending on the level of detail disclosed. For a disclosure to count as public, it must be "enabling"—i.e., it teaches someone skilled in the field to duplicate the invention.

TABLE 3.2 Stages of patent filing and protection

STEP	ELAPSED TIME	COST
Discovery	varies	0

A university researcher (faculty, student, staff) makes a discovery that has potential commercial application. The discovery is the invention and the researchers are the inventors.

Invention disclosure	varies	0

The inventor files an invention disclosure with the university, typically with technology transfer office (TTO).

Ownership	varies	0

The TTO makes a decision about who owns the invention by reviewing the means by which the invention was made (e.g., use of university resources), the sources of research funding, and any research agreements that may lay claim to the invention.

Decision to file	varies	0

The TTO, with input from advisers, committees, and outside legal counsel, makes a decision to file a patent application. The decision to file is based on the invention's patentability and licenseablity.

File provisional application	varies	$3K–5K

The TTO files a provisional patent application, which is a simplified, low-cost patent application that establishes the filing date (priority date) and provides 12 months for the TTO to decide whether to file a formal (nonprovisional) patent application.

At this time, the decision about inventorship is made by either the TTO or the TTO working with outside counsel (whose names will be on the patent and who will share in any income from licensing the patent).

File nonprovisional U.S. application and/or international application	12 months after provisional	$5K–20K

A nonprovisional application contains the formal descriptions, embodiments, and claim language that will be part of the final (issued) patent.

The decision to file a U.S. or an international application is based on:

1 If a public disclosure was made prior to filing the provisional, then no international protection.
2 Commercialization in markets outside the United States.
3 The need for additional time (up to 18 months) prior to entering patent prosecution.

STEP	ELAPSED TIME	COST
First office action and publication of the patent application	30 months after provisional filing	$3K–5K per office action

The U.S. Patent and Trade Office patent examiner issues the first office action (first response to the patent) 12–18 months after filing the nonprovisional application.

The patent application is made public 18 months after the nonprovisional or PCT application is filed (6 months if the application claims priority to a provisional).

National phase	12–30 months after provisional filing	$10K–100K, depending on how many countries

The patent application is filed in the individual countries where patent protection is sought.

Costs are associated with filing fees and translation to the language of the countries in question.

Allowance and issuance	3–5 years after provisional	$10K–50K total from start to finish

If the patent is allowed, it is issued. The patent term is 20 years from the nonprovisional patent application filing date (priority date).

reproduce the invention. The description also must include the "best mode" for creating the invention; failure to disclose the best way to produce the invention may result in a patent invalidation.

TITLE. Brief but technically accurate.

BACKGROUND. A description of the field of the invention and prior inventions and their shortcomings relative to the current invention.

SUMMARY. Overview of the current invention and what it can do, highlighting how it solves problems that prior inventions could not solve.

DETAILED DESCRIPTION. A thorough description of the invention, its method of production, structure, and operation.

DRAWINGS. Detailed drawings of the invention with labeled parts or chemical structures.

CLAIMS. The patent claims are the most important part of a patent application. They define the scope of the intellectual property protection provided by the patent. Claims establish a written boundary that excludes others from making or selling products that fall within it. Most of the discussion between a patent attorney and a patent examiner will focus on which claims to allow or modify, the lawyer wanting the broadest allowed, the examiner wanting the narrowest. In writing claims, attorneys will start with a set of independent claims and create a set of dependent claims based on the independent claims. For example, a novel polymer invention may have two sets of independent claims, one for the polymer composition and another for the method used to produce the polymer. The dependent claims set forth greater specificity of the independent claims. For example, the dependent claims of the polymer composition may describe various monomers or different ratios of monomers that can be used to make the polymer. Likewise the dependent claims for the method may describe different temperatures for synthesis or a different order of addition of the monomers and reagent. An extensive set of claims provides the broadest protection because even if certain claims are dropped during negotiations with the patent office other claims will still retain some protection. Furthermore, an extensive set of claims allows some flexibility in litigation: if certain broad claims are invalidated in court (e.g., prior art), the more-specific dependent claims may be still be valid.

An annotated example of a patent can be found at researchtorevenue.com.

Working with IP Counsel

Once the TTO makes the decision to file a patent, it will facilitate a series of meetings between the patent attorney and the inventors, with the tech transfer officer occasionally present.[8] The initial meetings with the attorney are abbreviated since the first filing is a provisional patent. As the one-year anniversary of the initial filing approaches, the TTO will decide whether to file the nonprovisional patent. At this point, more detailed meetings with the IP attorney will take place to draft the application. Most university-assigned patent attorneys have a technical background (e.g., Ph.D. in a scientific discipline) and can understand scientific concepts, but they are not experts in the field, as is the inventor. They need a full explanation of the invention, how it is made and used, and how it uniquely solves a problem. For the inventor, it is important to effectively communicate this information to the TTO (who will evaluate the commercial potential) and the patent attorney (who will consider patentability, prior art, etc.). The following are types of requests made of inventors during this process:

- Describe in a paragraph or two the invention and how it solves a problem.
- Compile a list of all prior art—i.e., aspects of the invention that are in the public domain from the inventor or from other disclosures.
- Prepare a list of the shortcomings of the prior art and discuss how the invention is different from the prior art.
- Describe exactly, in concrete language, what makes the invention different.
- Describe the unique advantages and value of the invention.
- Describe the value of the invention to customers—i.e., how is it cheaper, faster, or better than existing solutions.
- Compile a list all the likely inventors, even if you are unsure. The TTO and attorney will make the determination of ownership (better to be too inclusive than leave someone out).
- Compile a list of any pending patent applications or issued patents related to the invention.

8. TTOs may have in-house attorneys who write the patent, but most outsource this activity to outside counsel, especially counsel with specialized domain expertise (e.g., in chemical compound or gene patents).

The patent application will go through several drafts and revisions before it is filed. Once the nonprovisional patent is filed, there will be a long period of time (6–18 months) before the patent examiner will respond with an office action. This then triggers a request for additional information and a number of rounds of negotiation before a final determination on allowing or denying the patent application.

Software Protection

Novel software developed at a university may have significant commercial value. One option for protecting software is through the use of a copyright. Federal copyright laws, administered by the United States Patent and Trademark Office (USPTO), provide a certain level of protection to "original works of authorship" and cover "artistic expression" in the form of literary work, musical work, computer programs, video, photographs, sculpture, and so on. In contrast to a patent, which protects an idea, a copyright protects a piece of work. For university IP, copyrights play a role in protecting software by allowing the owner or licensee to make and distribute copies (suited for software distribution) as well as make derivative works (software updates). It prevents a third party from making exact copies of the licensee's work or from creating a work judged "substantially similar" to the licensee's works by an independent person looking at the two works. The biggest weakness of using a copyright to protect software is that two engineers, working independently to solve a problem, might come up with two unique solutions, each protectable by copyright and neither infringing on the other. In this case, neither would have a competitive advantage since neither has intellectual property that would exclude the other. Furthermore, litigation in this area has been difficult given that determining substantial similarity requires technical know-how. Few judges can assess computer codes or algorithms.

Patents, as opposed to using copyright, to protect software is evolving since protection by copyright may not be sufficient, and more rulings on software patents are favoring the use of patents for protection. In 1995, 396 U.S. patents contained the word "software." By 2010, the number had skyrocketed to over 6,000. Originally, software was considered a mathematical algorithm and therefore could not be patented. Increasingly, software is seen as a unique series of processes, a unique machine, or a combination of the two.

Confidential Information

The protection of university IP raises the issue of confidential information.[9] The concept of confidential information can be hard to grasp in a university setting, since its mission is knowledge discovery and information dissemination. Certainly any information publicly disclosed (e.g., through presentation, poster, or publication) is considered nonconfidential. Any information that has not been publicly disclosed and has been filed as part of a patent application is considered confidential until the public disclosure is made. Since it may contain information not disclosed publicly, the patent application is considered confidential until the application is published (18 months from filing the nonprovisional). Less clear-cut is whether trade secrets and know-how are considered confidential information. When in doubt, consult the TTO or university counsel.

The disclosure of confidential information to a third party is covered under a confidentiality disclosure agreement (CDA), sometimes called a nondisclosure agreement (NDA). These agreements are made between the university and the third party to allow sharing of information, usually one way, from university to a third party.[10] A point of confusion arises as faculty founders begin to talk to third parties (e.g., advisers, management) about starting a company. Until the company has licensed the technology from the university, any confidential disclosure needs to be handled by the TTO using a CDA between the university and the third party. To keep things simple, it is best to disclose only public information such as publications to third parties. For initial discussions, this is usually sufficient. Once the company has been incorporated and a license has been signed, it has an obligation to the university not to disclose university confidential information (e.g., pending patent applications). Any additional company confidential information (business plan, financials, etc.) can be disclosed to a third party under a CDA between the company and third party.[11]

9. Other types of confidential information not related to IP exist within a university (e.g., patient data and student records).

10. For practical reasons, two-way agreements are often signed in case the third party needs to disclose information to the university. This is most often the case with industry-sponsored research where the university might receive information from the corporate sponsor as part of the collaboration.

11. In some cases, a three-way disclosure can be signed between the university, the start-up company, and a third party (e.g., a potential corporate partner). Note: Rarely will an investor sign a CDA.

KEY STEP Recruiting Advisers and Mentors

With a potential commercial opportunity identified, some buy-in from the university to protect the IP, and a faculty interested in starting a company, the next step is recruiting people to help develop the rationale for starting a company and its associated path for bringing a product to market.[12] To this end, it is extremely important to seek the advice and opinions of others. Advisers and mentors come in all shapes and sizes but usually have relevant experience that complements that of the faculty and will help guide the formulation of the business strategy, including technology development, product development, regulatory approval, fund-raising, IP licensing, sales and marketing, and business development. Recruiting a group of advisers and mentors serves several purposes. The first and most obvious is to get advice on building a successful company whose mission is commercializing the technology. Advisers can provide counsel on a variety of topics, depending on their background and the company's needs. Second, gathering advisers and mentors is a way to begin identifying potential board members and management for the company. After several meetings, the founders will likely be able to identify the people who are excited about the technology, have the ability to join the company, and have the skills, experience, and expertise relevant to the company. If advisers are spending time helping to develop the business case, and they are adding value, then that is a sure sign of their interest. Once several advisers have been identified through a series of one-on-one meetings, it can be beneficial to bring the group together to further discuss the opportunity. The sharing of ideas in a structured meeting can be very fruitful.[13] At this stage, a group of advisers can be called a "board of advisers" or "business advisory board." The group has no corporate governance (since no company exists yet) but can add a level of legitimacy to the company as it forms and becomes known to others. After the company forms, it is a good idea to give these advisers some small portion of equity as compensation for their time, but be selective: Reward those who can make a real contribution.

12. The assumption here is that the commercial opportunity is best pursued as a start-up rather than through licensing to an established company. As discussed in Chapter 1, technologies suitable for a start-up have certain qualities: they are revolutionary and applicable across multiple problems or markets; they have strong IP protection; and there is significant tacit knowledge residing with the inventor.

13. The key to this type of meeting is to provide enough depth of the science so everyone is on the same page, to describe the business opportunity, and then to pose several questions to help structure the discussion (e.g., What are the options for fund-raising? What markets appear to be the best fit for the technology?).

Finding advisers can be a challenge, especially for faculty who do not have strong connections with the business and entrepreneurial community. Although advisers can be drawn from outside the community, having them local provides greater access. Personal recommendations and introductions are the best way to find advisers because the recommender will provide a level of screening in terms of fit, personality, and appropriateness. And if you meet with someone and are not able to help out, then ask that person to recommend others. The following are other potential sources for advisers:

- University TTOs usually have a list of people they know who can be advisers: for example, former CEOs of university start-ups, business people who have retired to the area, or entrepreneurs-in-residence.
- Faculty members who have started companies in the past have connections to the local business and investor community. If the university has a business school, the school often works with local entrepreneurs as adjunct lecturers or business plan judges who can act as advisers.
- Seminars, forums, and other networking events for industry segments (e.g., life science, IT, social).
- Social media groups such as LinkedIn.

Once people have been identified, the first practical step in recruiting advisers is being sure you are able to effectively communicate the science and the opportunity to them. The product might not be fully envisioned and the business model is yet to be developed, but the exciting, enabling aspects of the technology should be encapsulated in terms a broad audience can understand. In some cases a publication can suffice, especially when combined with a literature review, but often one needs to put together a summary or a set of slides (see page 135) that convey the opportunity to those with less technical training or outside the field. Next, arrange face-to-face meetings with potential advisers (don't forget to pay for their coffee or lunch). Another option is to gather a group of advisers for a roundtable discussion of the technology.

There is no substitute for good advice, but a few caveats are necessary about seeking and taking the advice of others.

YOU GET WHAT YOU PAY FOR. Buying someone a cup of coffee in exchange for advice is different from paying for a few hours of an attorney's time. Advice gleaned in the former case could be just as good as that acquired in the latter, but paying for advice usually guarantees better advice.

EVERYONE HAS OPINIONS. The somewhat black-and-white world of research and technology can be quite different from the grayer world of business. You can pose the same question to five different people, each of whom has good experience, and get five different answers, and most of the answers are likely to start with "That depends . . ."

MAJOR IN THE MAJORS, AND MINOR IN THE MINORS. Seek advice for the big decisions that have long-term consequences and are harder to undo. Deciding which product application has greatest commercial potential, for example, is much more important than the company logo.

KEY STEP Developing the Business Case

The business case frames the opportunity for developing a product around the university technology and lays out the rationale for starting a company. It differs from the business plan, which demonstrates the steps necessary to create and grow a successful business, in that it is smaller in scope and less formal. In addition, the objective of the business case is to collect enough information about the market (customer need, market size) to develop a compelling argument for starting (or not starting) the company. The business case is a way for the founders (academic founders along with any external founders) to establish that an opportunity actually exists based on the enabling features of the technology combined with preliminary market research into customer need rather than on conjecture and infatuation with the technology. The business case is also written for the university TTO, who may need to be convinced to support patent costs while the company is forming. The business case should support a "go/no-go" decision about forming the company prior to the founders making further decisions like incorporating the company, licensing the technology, or raising capital. In addition, the business case will provide the core for building the business plan.

In building the business case, the following five elements need to be addressed:

1. What is the product? Customers buy products, not technologies. Technology enables products. The first step in building the business case is developing a clear vision of the product. Imagine you had to make a sales call to sell the product. How would you describe the product to the customer? What types of ideal features and benefits would you mention? How would the product be used? What problem would be solved? What application would be addressed? The product vision is just that: a vision. It may not be the final product, but it is the ideal product to be developed from or enabled by the technology.

2. What is the need for the product? Assessing the need in the market is the most important aspect of building the business case, and the approach will differ according to the type of technology and product. How does one assess the need for the product? Some information can be garnered from web searches or reading market reports, but by far the best method to identify the need is by developing a product hypothesis and testing that hypothesis with several customers. This may take several iterations and require exploring several markets. At this point, the number of interviews does not need to be extensive, as compared to the business plan, but having a conversation with someone who experiences the need will provide significant insight into the market opportunity.

The following steps will help you gather market information from potential customers:

- DEVELOP A CLEAR PRODUCT VISION. A vague product definition will lead to vague responses. The product vision can be communicated by a nonconfidential one-pager that briefly describes the product, its application, and its unique features and benefits.
- IDENTIFY POTENTIAL CUSTOMERS. Use a wide array of sources to locate potential customers: tech transfer office, colleagues, advisers, friends, family.
- INITIAL CONTACT. E-mail potential customers the one-pager with the intent of arranging a face-to-face meeting or phone call.
- INTERVIEWS. The conversation with the contact should cover three topics:
  - The problem, in order to get confirmation that the contact agrees the problem is as stated.
  - Current products that the contact may be using to solve the problem to get confirmation that the list of current solutions is complete.
  - The proposed product concept in order to get feedback on how the contact reacts to the product.

3. How large is the market? The next most important aspect of the business case is assessing how many customers with the articulated need exist. For example, supposing a start-up has developed a novel microscope for imaging cancer cells with an estimated selling price of $75,000, its market size analysis would look like this:

Number of research universities in the United States and Europe (major markets)	2,000
Percentage of research universities with medical schools	20 percent
Number of medical centers in the United States and Europe (not university affiliated)	300
Total number of medical centers and medical schools	700
Percentage of medical centers/schools with significant cancer research effort	30 percent
Number of medical centers/schools with significant cancer research	210
Average number of cancer researchers per medical center/school	25
Average number of imaging microscopes per investigator lab	2
Total number of imaging microscopes in the market	10,500
Annual growth in imaging microscope market	8 percent
Number of new imaging microscopes purchased each year	840
Percentage of imaging microscopes replaced each year	15 percent
Number of replacement imaging microscopes	1,575
Total microscopes purchased each year	2,514
Market size estimate (microscopes × $75,000)	$181 million

Another approach determines the market size by aggregating a number of revenue figures from leading companies in the market. Using our example above, one would look at the current manufacturers of imaging microscopes and obtain revenue figures for each. If the market is dominated by publicly traded companies, the information will be more readily available than if the market is highly fragmented and dominated by privately held companies. By adding up the larger players' revenue for imaging microscopes, another market size figure can be obtained. Having two market size estimates helps triangulate on an actual figure, especially if the two approaches produce similar numbers.

Both of these approaches are based on assumptions about certain aspects of the market: "Average number of imaging microscopes per investigator lab" or "the percentage of revenue of company X is attributable to imaging microscopes." As such, the assumptions need to be clearly stated to the reader and, if possible, backed up by a reference or citation. Some of these assumptions are best guesses, as is the case with how many imaging microscopes need to be replaced each year.

In cases where the assumptions have a significant number of guesses, it might be useful to cast the market size as a range, looking at a best case and a worst case. In our example, the percentage of replacement microscopes could range from 2 percent (worst case) to 15 percent (best case). This approach will also allow for some crude modeling. If the market size assumptions are in a spreadsheet, then they can be tested with different numbers: What if the market growth is only 4 percent? What if number of microscopes per lab is actually four instead of two per lab? Market size estimates can also be found in market research reports. These reports, done by market research firms, are used by many businesses to assess markets for future growth or to gauge the competition. They can save significant time and help to further triangulate a market size but can cost thousands of dollars and the quality can vary. In using market research reports, be sure the market definition of the report aligns with the market definition for your product. A scientific instrument market size is going to be much larger than a microscope market size, which is going to be larger than an imaging microscope market size.

A question related to market size is market growth rate. Investors like large, growing markets. Market size and growth rates will come out of the market research efforts described below.

4. What competitive products exist? The success of a product relies not only on how well the features and benefits meet the needs of the customers but also on how those features, benefits, and price are perceived by the customer relative to comparable products. Understanding competitive products at this stage provides insight into the market dynamics and how much of the market can be captured. One should not view competitors as "the enemies." The existence of companies selling similar products in one's target market can validate the market. For an investor, attacking this market is less risky than going into a market with no other players. On the other hand, a large number of competitors signals a crowded market, one to be avoided. Competitors can also represent potential partners or acquirers. A large player in the market may be looking to increase its market share or see that a start-up's product is different enough to capture a closely related market segment.

5. What are the risks? The types of risks investors face in funding a successful start-up company are discussed in Chapter 2 (see table 2.6). In terms of the business case, founders need to focus on several types of risk: technical and regulatory risk (Will it work?) and market risk (Will the customers buy it?). They might not be easily assessed at this point, but outlining the major risks associated with the product will provide a framework for better understanding the hurdles ahead.

TECHNICAL AND REGULATORY RISK. It is difficult to fully assess the technical and regulatory risks for bringing technology-based products to market. This type of risk can be simplified into thinking about whether the product will work. Will it be safe and effective for patients? Will the coating last more than five minutes? Will the test diagnose the disease reliably? Will the instrument be reproducible? Predicting the success or failure of a product at this stage can be a challenge. Often, the best you can do is to map out the major technical hurdles or milestones with enough granularity to provide some understanding of the path to market. For example, a polymer coating might need to be optimized through a series of chemical syntheses, formulated in different ways, and tested on different substrates to find the best polymer. Then more extensive testing may be required using "real-world" conditions. A rough timeline of each of these steps identifies the major hurdles and the time frame in which to achieve the milestones. For a regulated product, the steps are more defined, but the studies vary by type of product (drug, device, diagnostic) and disease indication.

MARKET RISK. Market risk captures whether customers will see the value of the product and purchase it at a price and at quantities that will make a profitable business. It is assessed as part of the preliminary market research described above, primarily through talking to potential customers. Assuming you have identified the right customers and have adequately described the features and benefits to them, it's not hard to gauge whether they "get it"; they get excited about how the product can solve their problem or meet their needs.

A more structured approach to developing the business case is often referred to as a "technology assessment." One methodology, originally developed by NASA and refined by the University of Texas, Austin, and the IC² Institute, is called a QuickLook Report. A QuickLook involves the following steps: 1) identifying potential markets, 2) identifying end-users and customers, 3) contacting experts and companies, and 4) identifying barriers and opportunities. The detailed sections of a QuickLook are provided at researchtorevenue.com.

KEY STEP **Forming the Company**

Timing

One of the questions most often asked is, "When should we start the company." The timing of company formation depends on the completion of a number of activities. The following are usually in place at the time of a start-up's incorporation:

THE BUSINESS RATIONALE. Whether it's a formal technology assessment, a business plan, or a business case that answers the questions posed in the previous section, there must be a business rationale for starting the business.

PROTECTABLE IP. The university must have filed the appropriate IP to protect the innovation. At minimum, provisional patents should be filed. It is also important to understand the extent of university commitment in terms of paying patent costs (e.g., international filings).

THE FOUNDING TEAM. There needs to be a group of people who are committed to the founding of the company and engaging in activities for the next one to two years to help establish and grow the business. At minimum, the group includes the faculty founders, but often nonuniversity people, such as a business leader or entrepreneurs, are part of the group. The level of commitment is likely different among the founders, but they all share the vision of building a company around a compelling technology.[14]

COMPANY ACTIVITIES. Practically, there needs to be something for the company to do once formed. Simply forming the company and distributing equity is not sufficient. The company needs to be formed to carry out certain corporate activities (e.g., applying for SBIR grants, negotiating a license, raising capital, hiring employees, etc.).

In some cases the company is formed without the above in place. For example, the technology around which the company is to be built might require further development or "de-risking" in order for the founders to fully

---

14. The issue of who is a founder and who is not a founder often arises. The founders are typically those who receive equity at incorporation of the company. Is a graduate student who made a key discovery and receives equity but has been out of the lab for years a founder? Is a former adviser who gets equity a founder? Is a faculty member who gets equity at incorporation but quickly gets busy and cannot be part of the company a founder? These may be distinctions without a difference.

develop the business rationale or attract a management team. A common way to develop technology is to seek grants or raise capital from friends and family. Many grants, particularly SBIR grants, are awarded only to companies that have already been formed. In other situations, the business case might need much further development (e.g., extensive market research or a detailed review of the IP landscape). Since there is rarely money to pay people to spend time engaged in these activities, issuing equity can help compensate and/or incentivize the founders and early management team. And only after a company is formed is there equity to distribute to people for these activities.

Can you start a company too soon? There are two downsides to incorporating a company too early:

LOSS OF ENTHUSIASM. Signing the articles of incorporation and receiving stock certificates create excitement and buzz. It is important to build on that enthusiasm by making further progress. If the company remains idle for too long, it can lose the initial momentum generated by the incorporation, leading to founder malaise.

SHIFT IN BUSINESS FOCUS. If the company is founded before the product vision or business strategy has been fully contemplated, the initial distribution of equity to the founders may not reflect the new strategy. The technology and know-how contributed by a cofounder may not be relevant to the new company direction.

Company Name

Outside of equity, no subject can polarize founders more than the naming of the company. Some don't care; others consider it a hill to die on. Here are a couple of pointers in naming the company:

- Don't make it personal. Don't name it after the founder. Anderson Pharmaceuticals won't get investors too excited.
- Make sure it's pronounceable. Syzcitika Optics, for example, is a mouthful, and you will end up having to spell it every time you introduce it on the phone.
- Avoid acronyms. Don't, for example use the first letters of the founders or the technology: Microscopic Interrogation of Nanostructures In Drug Applications (MINIDA).
- It shouldn't have more than three syllables. BioCantiNovaPlex is way too long, and people will end up calling it BioCant.
- Avoid the negative: BioCant never could.

- It should have a unique web presence. The name and the URL need to be unique. The general rule is not to create "confusion in the marketplace" with your name. Ebuy, MacroSoft, and Appel are probably going to get you into trouble, even if your business in unrelated to Ebay, Microsoft, or Apple. A similar name in two distinct fields is usually ok: Cisco (networks) and Sysco (food service). A common practice is to find a name you like and add another name to the end to get the URL. Purex.com is taken (laundry detergent) but purexpharma.com, purex biosciences.com or purexsytems.com may be available and won't be confused with a laundry detergent.
- Use general terms. Naming a company too specifically at first can require a name change in the event that the company changes focus. Mohave MosFETs, for example, won't make sense when the company no longer makes MosFETS. Mohave Components or Mohave Materials gives the company more options down the road.

A naming matrix is available at researchtorevenue.com.

Corporate Attorney

One of the first and most helpful external parties to be engaged is a corporate attorney, who will handle incorporation, stock certificates, by-laws, and other documentation. Most corporate attorneys that work with start-ups are well-connected in the region; they will know most of the investors through deals they have done, as well as entrepreneurs and consultants. Since this will be a very close working relationship, it is advisable to talk to other founders to get recommendations and meet with several attorneys before deciding on one. Although the attorney's experience working with start-ups is important, how well you interact with the attorney is equally important. Most law firms have a starter package that provides the key incorporation documents, makes the appropriate filings (state and federal), and allocates a set number of hours of legal advice in return for equity, typically a single-digit percentage.

A word of caution to those who take a do-it-yourself approach: There are very inexpensive ways to incorporate a company, but a law firm not only provides years of experience in setting up a company the right way from the start; it also will provide excellent advice when it comes to key decisions around hiring the first employees, licensing the technology, or negotiating an investor's term sheet. Don't be penny-wise and pound-foolish by not having strong legal counsel. Extraordinary legal fees have been spent on undoing legal messes caused by the inexperienced.

Corporate Structure

Once the law firm has been chosen, it can help founders set up the corporate structure. The purpose of a corporate entity is several fold. First, ownership in the corporation can be split up and shared among multiple groups, either distributed to individuals (founders, management) or sold to investors for capital. Second, the corporation limits the liability of the owners, which means the owners' personal assets are protected from lawsuits and settlements (e.g., bankruptcy) against the company. Table 3.3 provides a brief overview of the three main types of corporate structures. The rule of thumb for deciding on a corporate structure is this: if the company expects to have significant external investment from a venture capital firm, then the C-corporation is usually required. If the company expects to have little or no outside investment (e.g., only angel investors, grants) and will be turning a profit soon, an LLC would be preferable. One alternative is to incorporate as an LLC, given its simplicity, and then convert to a C-corporation at a later date, if and when it's necessary.

Corporate Governance

At the time of incorporation, the incorporator, typically the corporate lawyer, files the articles of incorporation, adopts the initial by-laws, and appoints a board of directors, usually the founders. The board has an organizational meeting to take care of initial corporate matters: authorization of shares, issuance of founders' stock, appointment of officers (the founders), establishment of a stock option plan, and indemnification agreements between the company and its directors and officers. A number of documents are used to establish the rules of corporate governance (examples of each can be found at researchtorevenue.com):

> ARTICLES OF INCORPORATION. This brief document is filed with the state in which the company is being incorporated (usually Delaware).[15] It identifies the names and addresses of the corporation and its founders, the purpose of the corporation, the registered agent, and the number of shares of stock the corporation is authorized to issue and the value of each share.

---

15. There are number of reasons to incorporate in Delaware. First, the state's corporation law encompasses the most advanced and flexible business formation statutes in the United States. Second, Delaware's Court of Chancery uses judges instead of juries for hearing cases, which reduces the risk of a company getting a wildcard jury. Third, since judges are used, decisions

TABLE 3.3 Comparison of three types of corporate entities

	C-CORPORATION	S-CORPORATION	LIMITED LIABILITY CORPORATION (LLC)
Owners	Stockholder	Stockholder	Member
Form of ownership	Stock	Stock	Units or membership interests
Class of stock	Multiple	Single	Multiple
Number of shareholders	Unlimited	100	Unlimited
Taxation	"Double taxation" • corporate tax • tax on shareholder dividends	Pass through of profits and losses to owners	Pass through of profits and losses to owners
Governance	Board of directors	Board of directors	Managers
Issuing stock options	Simple	Simple	Complex
Case law	Extensive	Extensive	Developing
Use of federal tax incentives	Yes	No	No
Preferred by VC investors	Yes	No	No
Conversion to a C-Corp		Yes	Yes

BY-LAWS. The by-laws lay out the rules of the corporation and how it will be governed. It specifies aspects of the board of directors' activities (e.g., meetings, voting), and the titles and responsibilities of officers. For an LLC, an operating agreement replaces the by-laws.

STOCK PURCHASE AGREEMENT. If not covered in the by-laws, a separate stock agreement will be signed for anyone issued stock. It outlines the vesting schedule, if any, and restrictions in selling or transferring the stock to another person.

---

are issued as written opinions that the start-up company can rely on. Finally, Delaware does not require director or officer names to be listed in the formation documents, affording a certain level of privacy.

INDEMNIFICATION AGREEMENT. An agreement between the directors or officers and the company to indemnify the former (hold them harmless) in the event of lawsuit or claim against the company.

In addition to these, other agreements might be put in place, depending on who is founding the company and the role they will play and on the stage of development at founding. For example, the company and the founders might sign a confidentiality agreement (CDA) to keep company information confidential. (This is more important once the license agreement is signed and the company wants to keep confidential information beyond the business strategy.) In some cases, an invention assignment agreement is put in place, perhaps as part of a consulting agreement, between the faculty founders and the company. This will assign any inventions the faculty member or any other employee or consultant discovers as part of their company involvement.[16]

Board of Directors

A start-up is governed by the company's board of directors (or a similar name in an LLC). The board is responsible for making key strategic, high-level decisions in the governing of the company, including hiring and firing of the CEO and other senior management, setting of compensation, approving the budget, accepting investment, issuing stock. These issues are presented to the board as a proposal by the chairman of the board, discussed, and then voted on by the board. In general, the board deals with oversight and company governance, whereas the management team is responsible for corporate execution. As such, some decisions are left to the CEO (e.g., signing a lease, hiring a VP of business development), who will keep the board informed. Other decisions, like selling the company or amending the corporate by-laws, may require approval by a majority of the shareholders, as outlined in the corporate by-laws. At the early stage, some founders don't see the need for the formality of a board (regular meetings, taking minutes, etc.), but the discipline is good and the board will help decide on and record details that may be important later (like issuance of stock).

Technically, the board is formally elected by the shareholders, but in reality, at company formation, the founders, who own a majority of stock, become the de facto board. At the early stage, before a management team is assembled, the board (founders) manage the company. It is advisable to keep the size of

---

16. Assignment agreements between the faculty founder and the company can get tricky and hard to enforce since the faculty members cannot assign inventions that fall within the scope of their research at the university, especially if the research is federally funded.

the board small at first and aim for an odd number to avoid stalemate. For example, a start-up may initially have a board with two scientific cofounders and the corporate attorney. When a CEO is hired, he or she usually joins the board and the attorney might become a "board observer" (no voting rights). The board will grow in two ways. External directors (not part of the management team or significant shareholders) can be brought on for their expertise, experience, and connections. Second, as part of their investment in the company, some investors expect to have a board seat. As the board grows, some members will rotate off (e.g., early founders who are no longer active with the company) or take an observer role (e.g., an early investor).

Equity Distribution

As part of the incorporation of the company, equity (ownership in the form of shares of stock) is distributed among the founders. Typically, the company will authorize a pool of stock from which shares are issued. When the company calculates the percentage of ownership for each shareholder, it counts the shares issued to the shareholder out of the total shares issued, or outstanding, not the total authorized.[17] There are two basic approaches to splitting "founders shares."[18] One is to simply take all of the authorized shares and divide them among the founders according to agreed upon percentages. As future employees and investors are issued equity, the company authorizes additional shares and founders' percentage of ownership is diluted. The other approach is to set aside shares at founding as stock or stock options for key employees or perhaps a CEO if one is not on board at founding. Either approach is fine. Some founders prefer the former approach because it is simpler, whereas some prefer the latter approach because it provides the perception of nondilution as additional shares are issued to new shareholders (in a sense this approach "predilutes" the founders).

Shares of stock (or stock options) issued usually have some restrictions associated with them. The two most common restrictions have to do with vesting and selling stock. The purpose of vesting is to incentivize shareholders to stay engaged (employed) with the company over an extended period of time and to prevent employees from joining a start-up, getting their shares, and leaving shortly thereafter. Vesting of equity involves the company issu-

17. Authorized shares are the total number of shares the company is allowed to issue to others. Outstanding shares are the number of shares issued to others.

18. There is no class of founders' shares or founders' stock. Founders are given shares of common stock at founding. The other class of shares is "preferred stock," given to investors as part of their investment.

ing the full amount of unvested stock to the shareholder at once, and then, as the shares vest over time, according to a schedule, the shareholder owns them. On a typical vesting schedule, one-fourth of the equity vests at the 12-month anniversary of issuance, and then the remaining three-fourths vest at a monthly rate of 1/36th over 36 months (or 1/24th over 24 months). The one-year "cliff" often serves as a trial period for an employee. If employees do not work out for some reason, then they will not own a significant portion of the company when they are let go.[19] As for the restriction on selling or transferring stock, usually companies want to retain control over who their shareholders are so they often don't allow the stock to be transferred or sold to another individual without permission.

When founders distribute equity among themselves, they need to keep the following in mind:

EQUITY FOR PAST CONTRIBUTIONS. A certain portion of equity should be distributed to individuals in recognition for their past contributions that led to the founding of the company. Past contributions include the scientific discoveries they made that led to the intellectual property, the time they spent in bringing the moving parts together for founding (e.g., attending meetings, preparing documents) or developing the business case (e.g., conducting market research or IP review), and the funding they brought in to discover and develop the technology.[20] This equity is often given vested and is usually split among the faculty/scientific founders and perhaps a business person who has engaged early, although the latter's contributions are minor at this point. Dividing equity among different scientific founders can be difficult since assessing the relative contribution of each founder is hard, especially since one cannot predict what the final product will be. Unless there is a compelling argument for giving different amounts to each founder, splitting the equity evenly is often the easiest.

EQUITY FOR FUTURE CONTRIBUTIONS. Equity is also distributed for contributions and value added after the founding. These contributions will be both scientific and business-related and might be contributed as time or money. Examples include further development of the technology

19. The exception is where equity is being given to the management team during the early days when the company has no money and the equity is in lieu of salary. In these situations, the equity may be split, with some given each month as compensation and an additional amount given as incentive.

20. There is a temptation to add up the contributions to date (i.e., hours spent, research funding received), but these are difficult to quantify and equate to equity.

within the founder's lab; fund-raising (developing the pitch deck, writing SBIR grants, engaging investors); general scientific knowledge and advice about applications, competition, and decisions around product development; guiding the company; and hiring employees. Because this equity is intended for future contributions, it is often vested.

The majority of faculty founders' equity will be for past contributions with no vesting, but a portion may recognize future contributions and be tied to a vesting schedule. Most of a nonscientific founder's or the early management team's equity will be tied to a vesting schedule.

One of founders' major concerns relative to equity distribution during the early stages of company development is retaining control of the company. In general, founders make a much larger issue out of control than it really is. It is important for founders to be able to steer the company according to their vision, but control can be exercised in many ways (e.g., being an active member of the board, organizing a strong scientific advisory board, being engaged with the management team, being active on the board of directors). Therefore, a faculty founder needs to ask several questions: 1) How important is my control of the company? 2) Is control through ownership really control as compared to control through engaging in strategic or scientific decision-making? 3) What types of decisions am I better suited to make about the company's direction than the nonscientific founders (e.g., business management)? and 4) Given that a founder's ownership is usually diluted to a minority position, at what point am I ready to take the minority position?

Faculty Role in the Company

Faculty founders typically play a significant role in successful start-ups, at least initially. However, their role can vary greatly and will change with time. In general, the faculty founder provides essential scientific and technical insight during the early stages. As stated earlier, most start-ups are built around technology that is not well codified (i.e., technology relying on the tacit knowledge of the faculty), so it is important that the faculty member play a role in the company during the formative years. That role can range from consultant to chair of the SAB, from board member to CSO, and to even CEO. The role of consultant is the least formal, and the individual in that role may or may not have a formal contract with the start-up. If there is a contract, it can outline the scope of the consultant's time commitment to the company, setting expectations for both parties. Rarely does the faculty member earn a consulting fee, but he or she can either defer a fee until the start-up is sufficiently funded or take equity in exchange for the consulting services. As head of the SAB, the faculty founder can recruit key advisers to the company and hold meetings to review the science, technology, and product development. Most founders start out as members of the start-up's BOD to provide early guidance and decision-making for the company (e.g., hiring a CEO). If there are a number of faculty founders, only a few will serve on the board, just to streamline meetings and decision-making. On occasion, the faculty founder will leave the university and become the CSO or, more rarely, the CEO.[21]

KEY STEP Building the Management Team

Arguably the most important aspect of launching a university start-up is bringing on board the right people. Faculty founders can provide some early management, but time constraints and lack of experience limit their effectiveness. Advisers and mentors play a role, but they may not have the interest to devote significant time to the endeavor. A management team consisting of people with the right skills and incentivized in the right way will develop the business strategy, raise funds, and then execute the strategy. This team begins to form as the company forms. Some of the advisers may take on management roles, or a business person may engage with the faculty founders early in the process. At this stage, prior to any significant fund-raising, most companies face this "chicken and egg" problem with regard to management: You cannot attract talented business and scientific people to join because there is no money, and there is no money because talented people have not joined. There is no easy solution here, but a start-up that achieves key technical milestones or gathers early market information (e.g., customer feedback) can greatly improve its chances of attracting high-quality management. In some cases, key advisers will remain involved with the company and then come on board once there is funding. In other cases, an experienced business person may join as CEO and take deferred compensation or equity in lieu of a salary (see compensation options below).

---

21. It is rare but possible for a faculty member to quit and become CEO of the start-up. Many faculty founders, needing to have someone at the helm, list themselves as CEO or interim CEO in the early days of the company. Investors and entrepreneurs understand that early-stage companies often have no CEO and are comfortable with the founders simply taking the title of "founder."

Positions and Titles

When formed, the management team will be comprised of the following:

CHIEF EXECUTIVE OFFICER. The CEO is hired, guided, and fired by the board of directors. As captain of the ship, the CEO needs to have the experience to guide the company through both calm waters and stormy seas. A CEO will have the following qualities:

- Experienced in the industry. He or she should have worked and preferably started a company in a relevant industry.
- Experienced in fund-raising. Raising capital for a company is difficult and is not getting any easier. Fund-raising experience helps in deciding when and how much capital to raise and provides the connections with the investors.
- Easy to work with. While the start-up needs someone who is confident and decisive, abrasive people can be hard to work with. Investors and partners may not make it past the first meeting if the CEO is extremely aggressive or combative.
- Positive but realistic. Starting companies is hard work and it takes an optimistic approach to weather the tough times. A CEO needs to have a positive, "can-do" attitude, but he or she also needs to be realistic enough to know what is doable. In other words, a CEO needs to be a realistic Pollyanna.
- Part of an extensive network. A CEO needs to have worked with enough people to draw on them for advice, as potential members of the management team, and as future investors.

CHIEF SCIENTIFIC OFFICER OR CHIEF TECHNOLOGY OFFICER. The CSO or CTO, reporting to the CEO, is in charge of the "big picture" of the science or technology around which the company is based. He or she must have domain expertise in the field in which the company is operating, and it will have been acquired from either heading up research and development for another company or doing academic research. It is the faculty founder with the latter experience (if he or she decides to leave academia) who will most often find a role as a CSO/CTO. For a small company, the CSO/CTO will cover a wide range of duties, from overseeing research and development (e.g., clinical development) to working with the university faculty founder to better understand the many applications of the technology or to translate the vision of the faculty member into product opportunities. As the company grows, a VP of R&D might be hired to oversee product development. For clinical products, a chief medical officer (CMO) might be hired to oversee clinical trials and report to the CSO/CTO or the CEO. For a start-up relying heavily on science and technology for its products, a CSO/CTO is usually the first key hire after the CEO, especially if the CEO does not have the technical expertise.

CHIEF FINANCIAL OFFICER. As the name implies, the CFO oversees the finances of the company. Rarely does a start-up need a CFO during the early days when most of the financials relate to bookkeeping and simple accounting, which can be outsourced to a CPA firm. The need for a CFO becomes greater when the company starts to raise significant amounts of capital, but even then, only a part-time or "fractional" CFO may be needed. As the funding rounds progress (Series B, C, D) a full-time CFO is usually required, and if the company is contemplating going public, a CFO is mandatory.

CHIEF BUSINESS OFFICER. Of the three "chiefs" the CBO is the least common as a title, but the function for many companies is essential. Whether one is called the CBO or the more common VP of business development or VP of sales and marketing, the main duty of this position is the same: generate revenue. On the business development ("biz dev") side, this means doing deals with partners to facilitate commercialization, be it licensing of the company's technology, jointly developing the product, or funding company research. A sales and marketing executive will be in charge of developing a marketing strategy for the product and building a sales force for selling the product. If a university start-up's strategy is to partner for developing the product, the founders will want to bring on a business development person early, if the CEO does not have the bandwidth or expertise/contacts to fill this role.

In the early days of a start-up, there might be only one chief, the president or CEO, with several VPs reporting to him/her. For example, a VP of R&D and a VP of business development working with the CEO is a good team to start raising money and building the company. These people may be promoted to CSO or CBO later, or another person may be hired.

These positions cover most of the needs of the company: leadership, technical, financial, business development. When considering bringing additional people into the company, founders should think about the following points:

THE NEEDS OF THE COMPANY WILL CHANGE OVER TIME. As the company grows, the talent and experience needed by the company will change.

For example, in the early stages, the company needs a CEO who can assemble a compelling business plan and raise seed-stage capital. Over the years, the company might need a CEO who can manage a large number of employees and make strategic decisions about sales and marketing. Some companies consider the CEO who is hired at the beginning a "Starter CEO," and some entrepreneurs like to see themselves that way as well. In this case, they come on board at founding and work three to five years to get the company to a place where it needs a different type of CEO. In an opposite case where the company grows beyond the skills of the CEO, the CEO will need to be replaced, which is a stressful but necessary action.

ORDER OF ADDITION. The traditional way to build a management team is to hire a CEO who will then hire the rest of the management team. Another approach would be to bring on board a technical person (CSO, VP R&D) who can shape the vision of the product and contribute to its early development by writing grants or working with the faculty founder to conduct key studies. This approach will help clarify what the product is, what its application will be, what the market for it is, and how much funding will be necessary to get it to the market, all of which will make it easier to identify the skills and experience needed in a CEO. This approach may also reduce the technical risk and thus increase the caliber of person one can attract.

INVOLVEMENT OF THE BOARD. The management team is critical to the success of the company, and the early hires can make or break a company. As such, the board of directors, as skeletal as it may be in the early days, should work together to critically evaluate each hire in terms of experience, skills, and personal fit. In lieu of a formal BOD, advisers and mentors can help evaluate potential management team members.

DIFFERENT PEOPLE WILL BE ATTRACTED OVER TIME. As the company grows from a high-risk start-up (no funding, no management team, no revenue) to a more stable enterprise, different types of people will be attracted to the company. Some refer to this as the "stray cat theorem." When a company is just getting started, the only people who are willing to take a risk are stray cats, people who like to wander from job to job and don't like the confines of big corporations. Stray cats are essential for a start-up because of the skills they bring (e.g., technical/scientific) as well as their willingness and flexibility to take on many of the tasks needed by the start-up. However, they often leave the start-up as it becomes more "corporate" (e.g., wearing of ID badges, performance reviews, etc.). By contrast, a more developed company will attract skilled people looking for a more stable company.

PEOPLE LIKE TO BE PROMOTED, NOT DEMOTED. With all of these titles and little salary to offer the first employees, it is tempting to make up for the lack of compensation by giving them the "Chief" titles. As mentioned, a company will change and additional, likely more-experienced, management will be hired. With everyone as a chief, there may be no room at the top to hire more-qualified individuals without demoting someone else. One solution is to start people off one or two notches down.[22] For example, a scientific or technical leader could be named vice president of research and development or director of product development with the understanding that a "C-suite" position will need to be filled in the future and that he or she will be considered for the job. Likewise, a business development person could come in as VP or director of business development and move up to CBO later. This approach also allows the company to take a risk with less-experienced but motivated people who have the potential to develop into a position.

TITLES DO MAKE A DIFFERENCE. Although taking the approach of starting people down a notch or two gives room for promotion, too many notches down or a title without enough cache (e.g., associate director) may be limiting. A person working with vendors, partners, and investors needs an appropriate title in order to be taken seriously as part of the senior management team.

SERIAL ENTREPRENEURS. High value is often placed on "serial entrepreneurs," or people who have started, and (presumably) built and successfully exited from, multiple companies. However, when considering hiring this kind of entrepreneur, it is important to understand the nature of those successes and the role the entrepreneur played. Success can be the result of good timing, the right combination of factors (internal and external), or just plain luck. It is also important to understand that it is very difficult for entrepreneurs to replicate what they did before. Thus bringing someone in with the expectation that he or she has the golden touch is unwise. However, an experienced entrepreneur who has

22. This strategy may not work with a CEO. Many people will not take on the top position without that title even though they may have to be replaced later (e.g., during a financing round). An alternative is to give that person the title of president with the understanding that he or she can be promoted to CEO at some milestone (e.g., raising $1 million in equity financing).

learned from his/her successes and failures can be invaluable (in fact, entrepreneurs who have failed are sometimes even more valuable those who have been successful).

Employment Agreement and Compensation

People brought in to manage the company can start informally as business advisers, with or without receiving equity, or they can be formally hired. Since these early hires are so critical and things change so much in the early days (e.g., funding, product focus, management team), it is important to outline both parties' expectations through a contract or letter. In addition to the employment letter, the employee usually signs an agreement that covers the conditions and general terms of his/her employment, including confidential information, inventions (disclosing and assigning all inventions to the company), and noncompetes (not taking a job with a competitor for a period of time after leaving the company). The latter of these conditions is the most contentious since the noncompete clause can severely limit a person's ability to find a job after leaving the start-up. The compromise can be to narrow the scope of the activity (e.g., from "website development" to "website development for companies in the apparel industry").

All employees need some form of compensation to engage in the work of the company. The compensation rewards them for carrying out their duties (salary) and for the risk they are taking in hopes of future wealth (stock and stock options).

An example of an employment letter that outlines salary, equity, benefits (if any), and job responsibilities can be found at researchtorevenue.com.

Salary

Since many start-ups have very little cash for paying employees, the following are some salary alternatives:

DEFERRED SALARY. The company can establish a salary for the employee that is usually below market rate (i.e., salary one would receive in an established company) and defer it until the company has raised enough capital or is generating sufficient revenue. If the deferral is for an extended period of time, however, it may saddle the company with a significant debt to the employee. The company can mitigate this situation by either setting a cap on the total accrual or converting some percentage of the accrued compensation to equity at the next financing.

PART-TIME. If the employee has the means to generate income through another job (e.g., as a contractor or consultant), then she/he might be able to work part-time for the start-up for equity only. The challenge here is ensuring that the employee is devoting the hours and mind-share to the start-up.

"EAT WHAT YOU KILL." In cases where the company has an opportunity to sell product or enter into partnering or out-licensing agreements, compensation can be tied to cash an employee brings in as part of an agreement. For example, a partnering agreement in which the parties jointly develop a product might stipulate that the employee, who would be developing the agreement, would be compensated with a percentage of up-front fees and milestone payments. The risk here is placing the employee in a position where he or she might work to increase the value of the compensation (e.g., up-front fees) while compromising other important aspects of the agreement (e.g., royalty on sales, marketing rights).

GRANTS. Grants from foundations or the federal government can be a substantial source of income for technical employees since they serve as principle investigators on the grant.

Equity

The other side of the compensation coin is equity, or compensating employees with company ownership in hopes of an "upside," or that when the equity is sold in the future it will be worth much more than it is today. Employees who own a part of the company will be motivated to work hard toward the same goal of making the company more valuable. How much equity to give an employee depends on a number of factors:

ROLE AND RESPONSIBILITIES. Usually the amount of equity employees receive depends on their position in the company. Employees in more senior positions, who generally have more responsibility and ability to add value to the company, will receive more equity than those in lower-level positions. For example, a CEO will usually receive more equity than a CSO, who will receive more equity than a VP of product development.

SALARY AND RISK. Most employees are working for less-than-market rates in hopes of future returns. In return for putting their salary and time at risk (the start-up may fail), the employee receives equity. Employees who take the most risk, usually by joining the company earliest in its development or forfeiting the most salary, should receive the most equity.

FUTURE VALUE AND DILUTION. The estimated future exit value of the company (how much it will be acquired for or the value at IPO) and how much an employee's equity will be diluted up to that point is another factor in how much equity is given. This figure will determine roughly a) how much salary the employee will have lost by working below market until exit and b) how much "upside" he or she will have at exit.

Stock Options

An alternative to issuing stock is the stock option. Stock options are granted under an incentive stock option (ISO) plan or an employee stock option plan (ESOP). As with the issued stock, the options have a vesting schedule and restricted transferability. But unlike stock, the employee does not purchase the shares at the time they are granted. Employees are allowed to buy the shares ("exercise the option") at a specific price (the "exercise price" or "strike price"). Whether a company should grant restricted shares or stock options depends on a number of factors related to the value of the company and personal tax implications. Generally, stock is granted to the founders and early management when the company has little or no value. Options are preferred once the company increases in value since employees do not have to purchase the shares up front. In either form, owning equity is an incentive for employees to add value to the company so that when the company is acquired or goes public, the shares are worth significantly more than the purchase price or the strike price.

The Investor's View on Management

Angels and venture capitalists have invested in many companies over the years and understand the importance of the management team for a science-based company. Bruce Booth, of Atlas Ventures, a life science VC firm, posted on his blog some key lessons he and his partners have learned about the management team. Although his comments relate to biotech start-ups, they are applicable to any science-based company. He writes,

[There] is an axiom in venture: getting the right group of early entrepreneurs and executives around the table is critical. But this is often not easy in early-stage biotech companies.

Different management teams are often required at different stages of a biotech, and the reality is that many seed- and early-stage deals don't need a CEO. They are science-driven companies that need great Chief Scientific Officers to build the fundamentals of the story, and a BD [business development] executive to help build the broader vision. It's upon that progress with which a company can recruit a great CEO. Putting a founding CSO in as the CEO early on often creates unnecessary conflict in the future: having the conversation about a perceived "demotion" to CSO when hiring the future CEO is uncomfortable and avoidable. Same goes for putting the lead BD entrepreneur in as CEO early on to "fill the role." Keeping the role vacant in the beginning prevents future discomfort, or at least minimizes it.

Making management changes quickly is almost always the right answer. We have historically not moved fast enough to make senior management changes even when we knew it wasn't working. Trusting one's instincts is important: if it feels like its not working, it probably isn't. And the team working in the company probably sees the same thing from their view of the executives. Further, if real management questions are present at the closing of a new investment it's unlikely to improve: it's often worth being explicit about this with the existing team before the closing to lay out expectations and possible action plans. Closing the deal and then firing the CEO immediately after doesn't feel like the high road.

Don't hire for the resume, hire for real talent. Lots of folks in biotech have good resumes, were part of stories with great drugs or great exits but didn't actually shape them (or at least nowhere near as much as they think they shaped them). We've certainly hired our fair share of great paper-resume CEOs that didn't translate into excellent leaders and operators in our start-ups. Checking the specifics of their actual contributions in the past is an important part of reference checking and recruiting. Some of the disconnect between paper and practice is that the transition from large to small companies is hard despite great past roles; others is that their past success was more luck than skill and repeating luck is a challenge.[23]

---

23. "Lessons Learned: Reflections on Early-Stage Biotech Venture Investing," *Life Sci VC* (blog), 8 February 2013, http://lifescivc.com/2013/02/lessons-learned-reflections-on-early-stage-biotech-venture-investing/ (accessed 11 February 2013).

In summary, people can be the greatest asset for creating a successful start-up. The chemistry is extremely important for the team to be effective. Given the small number of people involved in the early days of a start-up, a new person can add or detract from good chemistry. Don't rush into the decision to bring people into the company; set up ways to "date" first before making a more formal decision. One smart way to date is to have a potential management team member help as an adviser or consultant. It might not be his or her ideal situation, but it will give good insight into whether the person is a good fit for the company and the rest of the team. On the flip side, a real rock star who appears to be a perfect fit might not put up with the dating and the company may need to bring that person on board pronto.

KEY STEP **Licensing the Intellectual Property**

For a start-up to commercialize a product based on university-developed technology, where that technology is protected intellectual property, it must have the right to do so. That commercial right is granted to the company by the university through a license agreement. In return for those rights, the company agrees to compensate the university. The agreement outlines the compensation as well as the rights and responsibilities of both the company and the university.

Most universities work from a template license that is used as a starting point for negotiating the license. The completeness or flexibility of the starting point varies among universities. The following are terms of a license agreement that are usually negotiated (example language is shown in italics; explanations of the terms highlighted follow the sample language)[24]:

GRANT OF LICENSE (defines what is being granted as part of the license)

The University hereby grants to Licensee and its Affiliates to the extent of the LICENSED TERRITORY *an* EXCLUSIVE RIGHT *and license to use The University Technology in the* LICENSED FIELD, *with the right to sublicense as set forth in Article 6, provided that each such sublicense is granted concurrently with the grant of a license to Patent Rights, if any, subject to all the terms and conditions of this License Agreement. Licensee may only grant a sublicense to The*

---

24. Because of how license agreements are structured and the ease of changing a term in a single location, most licenses will have a list of definitions at the beginning. For example, the License Field is defined first (e.g., aerospace applications), thus referring back to the definition wherever it is used in the agreement. See the example license agreement in the companion content.

University Technology concurrent with a sublicense of Patent Rights to the same sublicensee.

The University hereby grants to Licensee and its Affiliates to the extent of the Licensed Territory an exclusive license under the Patent Rights to make, have made, use, offer for sale and sell Licensed Products in the Licensed Field, with the right to sublicense as set forth in Article 6, subject to all the terms and conditions of this License Agreement.

Licensed territory. The territory defines the geographical region in which the product can be sold. The default is the location of the university (United States, Europe, etc.). Ideally, the territory should be worldwide.

Exclusivity. One of the most important aspects of the license is whether the license is exclusive or nonexclusive, namely whether the university licenses the technology to a single entity (exclusive) or multiple entities (nonexclusive). In most cases, the start-up should have an exclusive license; otherwise potential investors or partners will almost always perceive the risk of competition as too high.

Licensed field. The licensed fields are defined as the markets and industries in which and applications for which the company can sell the product. For example, the field for a drug may be a defined therapeutic indication (e.g., cancer). Ideally, the start-up wants "all fields" since the company focus may change with time (e.g., the therapeutic may fail in cancer or be more effective in inflammation). The university is going to limit the field as much as possible since another application (i.e., therapeutic indication) that is not anticipated or outside the company's mission or capability could be licensed to another company. Thus, the license might be exclusive but only exclusive for a restricted field of use. The start-up can renegotiate a restricted licensed field, but another licensee may have taken that field in the interim.

CONSIDERATION (what the university receives for granting the license)

Within ten (10) days of the Effective Date, Licensee shall pay to The University a non-refundable LICENSE ISSUE FEE *in the amount of _____ dollars ($).*

As further consideration for the rights granted to Licensee under this License Agreement, Licensee will issue to The University [or its foundation] that number of SHARES OF COMMON STOCK *[see equity and antidilution, below] of Licensee equal to _____ percent (_____%) of the total number of issued and outstanding Equity Securities of Licensee on the Effective Date. If at any time after the Effective Date, and before the* TRIGGER FINANCING *[see equity and antidilution, below], Licensee issues any Equity Securities, then in such event, Licensee shall issue additional shares of common stock to The University such that immediately after such issuance, the total number of shares issued to The University constitutes _____ percent (_____%) of the total number of Equity Securities on a fully diluted basis. The issuance of common stock to The University shall be made in accordance with that certain Shareholder Agreement by and between The University and Licensee dated _____, 20_____.*

Beginning on the Effective Date and continuing for the life of this License Agreement, Licensee will pay The University a RUNNING ROYALTY *of _____ percent (_____%) of all Net Sales of Licensed Products.*

If in any calendar year during the term of this License Agreement, the total amounts payable under the running royalties are less than the minimum amount indicated in the attached schedule corresponding to such calendar year, Licensee shall pay The University the difference between the amounts payable for such calendar year and said MINIMUM AMOUNT *within thirty (30) days after the end of such calendar year.*

License issue fee. The university usually charges an up-front licensing fee with the justification that they need to pay for past and ongoing patent costs. Since many start-ups have little capital, some universities will reduce this fee and increase either the equity amount or the royalty rate.

Equity and antidilution. Most universities take some equity as part of the license. The amount varies widely, but the typical range is 5–20 percent. Equity is one of the greatest sticking points of negotiation because of the difficulty in assigning a value to the equity. Universities take equity to share in the upside if the company is successful. It also provides some risk protection in the event the company significantly changes directions. For example, if the university-derived technology ends up not being used in a commercial product (e.g., it doesn't work, there's a shift in product focus, etc.) but it provides a springboard or impetus for other, nonuniversity technology that is commercialized, the university wants to share in some of that value creation. In the second section of considerations above, there is an antidilution clause that prevents the university's equity percentage from being diluted through the issuance of additional equity. The clause stipulates that dilution of the university's ownership will be triggered only after a significant amount of capital is raised (see "trigger financing," above). This protects the university from being diluted if the company issues large amounts of equity with no investment (e.g., equity to employees). For example, if a company raises $500,000 in a seed round, and the trigger financing is $1 million, then the company must issue additional equity to "true up" the university, keeping its percentage ownership the same as it was prior to dilution.

Royalty and minimums. The company usually pays the university a percentage of any sales of products ("royalty rate") that use the licensed technology. The royalty rates can range from the low single digits upward, depending on the state of development of the asset and the amount of capital required to get the product to market. Another aspect of the license agreement to consider is a "royalty stacking" clause. In some cases, a product requires IP from multiple sources to bring the product to market. For example, a recombinant therapeutic protein may require licenses for the gene, the vector, the expression systems, and the purification protocol. Each license could have a royalty on the sale of the product, and the "stacking" of those royalties would be prohibitively high. Royalty stacking provisions attempt to provide some relief from multiple royalty rates. In some cases, the product introduction is delayed or sales are less than expected. In this event, the university requires a minimum amount to be paid each year, according to a schedule.

DILIGENCE (incentives for timely product development)

Licensee shall use its best efforts and due diligence to proceed earnestly and assiduously with the research, development and commercialization, including manufacture and sale, of Licensed Products during the period of this License Agreement. In particular, Licensee will meet all obligations under the performance milestones set forth in Appendix B, which is attached hereto, and shall pay to The University the following payments for each Licensed Product within thirty (30) days after reaching each payment milestone.

Because it can take years to get a technology-based product to market, the university will not receive any royalty income for a long time after licensing. Meanwhile, value is being created as the product is developed. In recognition of the value created, the license agreement has diligence milestones, some of which may have an associated payment to the university (see page 37). In addition, these milestones are usually time-based so as to measure progress or lack thereof. Time-based milestones give the university the option to revoke a license in the event the company has not progressed toward commercialization.

SUBLICENSING (the ability to partner)

Licensee may sublicense any or all of the rights licensed hereunder, excluding the right to sublicense further unless prior written consent has been received by Licensee from The University, provided that Licensee notifies The University in writing and provides The University with a copy of each sublicense agreement and each amendment thereto within thirty (30) days after their execution.

In respect to sublicenses granted by Licensee under this Article 6, Licensee shall pay to The University an amount in royalties equal to the amount Licensee would have been required to pay The University had such sublicense sales been made directly by Licensee. In addition, if Licensee receives any payment other than royalties, including any fees, minimum royalties, milestone or other payments in consideration for any rights granted under a sublicense agreement, and then Licensee shall pay The University _____ percent (_____%) of such payment.

Sublicensing allows the company to license the university technology to a third party. The license will be negotiated between the company and the third party and contain many of the same general terms as the university license. For some types of IP (e.g., pharmaceuticals), sublicensing plays a major role since the cost of bringing the product to market is beyond the reach of a start-up and its investors. The university license agreement usually calls for some amount of income derived from the sublicense to flow back to the university. Sometimes the university will apply different rates to different types of sublicensing income (e.g., royalty- vs. nonroyalty-based income).

PATENT COSTS AND PROSECUTION (keeping the patents in force)

Licensee shall bear the cost of all patent expenses incurred following the Effective Date and associated with the preparation, filing, prosecuting, issuance and maintenance of U.S. Patent applications and U.S. Patents included within the Patent Rights. Such filings and prosecution shall be by counsel of The University's choosing and shall be in the name of The University. The University shall keep Licensee advised as to the prosecution of such applications by forwarding to Licensee copies of all official correspondence (including, but not limited to, applications, Office Actions, responses, etc.) relating thereto. Licensee shall have the right to comment and advise The University as to the conduct of such prosecution and maintenance, provided, however, that The University shall have the right to make the final decisions for all matters associated with such prosecution and maintenance.

As regards prosecution and maintenance of foreign patent applications corresponding to the U.S. Patent applications described above, Licensee shall designate in writing that country or those countries, if any, in which Licensee desires such corresponding patent application(s) to be filed. Licensee shall pay all costs and legal fees associated with the preparation, filing, prosecuting, issuance and maintenance of such designated foreign patent applications and foreign patents. All such applications shall be in The University's name.

In addition to the up-front payments and royalties, the company is responsible for patent costs, both domestic and foreign. For a start-up company, patent expenses are one of the most problematic areas because many companies lack the capital to pay for them, especially those associated with foreign filings. Even grants to the company (e.g., SBIRs) limit the amount of money that can be spent on patents. Some universities recognize the problem and have come up with creative ways to make this work. Some departments are willing to help defray these costs for their faculty founder, with the expectation of being reimbursed at a later date. Some TTOs will set up a payment schedule in which the company pays a minimum monthly payment for a period of time (e.g., 12 months), followed by a "balloon" or "catchup" payment, along with assuming all ongoing patent costs. This arrangement buys the start-up some time to raise capital without a significant amount of debt on the books.

It is important to remember that most of the terms of a license are negotiable, but rarely can one term be changed without affecting another. For example, a lower up-front payment might be offset by more equity or a larger royalty rate. Furthermore, once a license agreement has been signed, it is not uncommon for it to be renegotiated as the company moves forward.

Another approach to licensing the technology is the option agreement. This can be useful when the founding team needs to conduct due diligence on the IP without the risk of the IP being licensed to another party. Option agreements give the start-up team time to incorporate, bring on additional team members, and get funding. The option is usually exclusive for a fixed period of time (e.g., six months) and can be renewed (e.g., another six months). Options may require a fee, which may or may not be applied to subsequent licensing fees.

A sample license agreement can be found at researchtorevenue.com.

Additional IP

After licensing technology from a university, the company will often include additional components to ensure success. For example, additional IP may need to be licensed because of improvements or derivations from the original

IP made over time. As the company begins to develop technology on its own accord, through SBIR grants or seed-stage investments, additional IP is often developed. In some cases, the company's IP diverges significantly from the university's IP and, in extreme cases, can result in the company abandoning the university license in favor of its own IP. A third source of IP might come from third parties; for example, other universities or companies with IP for license. Until the product trajectory has been firmly established, the company should acquire as much IP as possible both to exclude competitors and to demonstrate to investors that it has many options for product development.

Freedom to Operate

In licensing a technology to develop a product, the founder must also assess the freedom to operate (FTO)—that is, whether the inventor's patent infringes on another party's patent. For example, if a prior patent claims A and B but the university patent claims A, B, and C, then the start-up may need a license from the owner of the first patent in order to sell a product based on the invention. One of the biggest misconceptions about patents is that they grant a company the right to commercialize the product described in the patent. However, a patent only prevents someone else from "making, using, or selling" the product described.

When assessing the FTO, the first thing the founding team needs to do is to examine the "patent landscape," or search patent databases to identify patents that may have claims that overlap with the current patent. The search often can be done using online resources, but interpreting the results usually requires the help of an IP attorney. The next step is to have a formal FTO opinion prepared by a legal firm. An FTO provides detailed analysis of the patent and nonpatent literature in terms of potential risks of infringement. Because this is a legal opinion and can be used for patent litigation, it is extensive and expensive ($50,000 to hundreds of thousands). TTOs rarely invest in an FTO, leaving that option for the licensee. Many investors will require an FTO, prior to investing, if there appears to be significant IP risk.

KEY STEP Gathering Market Information

As the company begins to develop its business strategy and prepare a formal business plan, it is essential that it collect as much market information as possible. Information about customers, markets, and market size will help bolster the rationale for the business.

Primary Market Research

Preliminary primary market research was begun in developing the business case (described previously) and is continued here with more in-depth interviews of potential customers. These interviews provide a chance to drill down in some detail to understand the customer's needs. These conversations have three objectives: 1) to understand the customer's problem or unmet need or the market gap that currently exist, 2) to understand the current solutions used to address the problem, and 3) to get a response from the customer as to the perceived desirability of your product in solving the problem. Before you talk to potential customers, you need two things: a clear definition of the customer and a concise description of the proposed product. If you ask the wrong customer, you'll get unusable answers, and likewise, if you ask the right customer about an ill-defined product concept, the responses will be of little value.

Interviews allow the most flexibility in getting information. A skilled interviewer or interviewers armed with a well-thought-out set of questions can gather a wealth of information from the right customer. In particular, interviews allow for understanding of nuanced issues such as a customer need versus a want (i.e., does the product sound necessary or "nice to have"). They also permit a deeper exploration of certain topics that are hard to access using surveys or focus groups (see below). For example, an interview can yield a complete picture of the current products used to solve this problem (competitive landscape) or the way doctors are treating the disease (current standard of medical care). A comment or response can be more fully explored and different paths can be taken with different people, depending on their background, receptivity, and experience with the problem. Also people tend to be more forthcoming with information one-on-one, especially when they are giving their opinions or don't want to share information with a larger group.

One of the barriers to conducting interviews is creating the initial list of potential customers to interview. Many times you have to start with friends, family, colleagues, and advisers to get introductions or referrals. The typical first step is to send to people who might know a potential customer an e-mail that includes a description of what you would like to accomplish (e.g., an interview to better understand how they solve a certain problem). It is important not to appear as though you are selling a product; emphasize that your goal is to gather information and gain insight. Have your contacts forward the e-mail to the potential customer(s) with a request asking if you could schedule a follow-up phone call. The interview can be conducted either by phone or in person, the latter being preferred by far, if feasible.

Once you have identified potential customers, it is critical that you ask the right questions. The best practice is to start by presenting the problem to the potential customer to assess 1) whether the customer understands the problem to be addressed (i.e., this might be the wrong customer) and 2) whether the customer agrees that this indeed is the problem. Through this conversation, you must be open to the fact that the problem, as originally framed, may not be the most significant problem from the customer's perspective. This may have implications for product development. Next, ask about the current (competitive) solutions for solving the problem, assuming the problem has been articulated correctly. This provides the opportunity to check assumptions about how the problem is currently solved and facilitates identifying competitive approaches. Finally, describe the product and how it will solve the problem. Then solicit a reaction from the customer. It is often the case that the interviewer does not adequately listen during the first stages of the interview because they think they fully understand the problem, which they usually don't, and their enthusiasm for the product prompts them to immediately talk about their solution.

The following are typical questions for an interview:

QUESTIONS RELATED TO THE PROBLEM:

- As stated, is this your current problem?
- How would you restate the problem?
- Are there really multiple problems that need to be solved?
- How would you rank the problems?
- How significant is the problem? Can you quantify it in terms of time, money, or quality of life?
- How many other people (within your organization and beyond) have the same problem?

QUESTIONS RELATED TO CURRENT SOLUTIONS:

- How are you solving this problem today?
- Are you satisfied with the solution?
- How are others solving this problem?

QUESTIONS RELATED TO THE PROPOSED SOLUTION:

- What are your first impressions with the proposed product?
- What features do you think it lacks?
- Would solving the problem in this way create other problems?

- If this product existed today, would you use it? Why?
- If this product existed today, would you buy it?
- What would be too much to pay for this product?

It is also important to gather information about interviewees—for example, what position do they hold in the organization, what does their typical day look like, what journals do they read, and what trade shows do they attend,

These interviews should be followed up by soliciting names of additional individuals who might provide similar insights. It is also worthwhile to consider bringing on contacts who are especially insightful or get very excited about the product as advisers or early product testers. It is unlikely that enough in-depth interviews can be done to provide any quantitative assessment that can be included in the business plan. However, it can be helpful to provide a list of the potential customers who were contacted (including the name of the organization and the title of the person interviewed) and include a few quotes to help build the case that a problem exists, that current solutions are inadequate, and that the proposed solution will be significantly better.

Once the questions become more standard and some of the responses more reproducible, primary market research can expand to include focus groups and online surveys. A focus group can be thought of as a large-scale group interview. Here, a group of potential customers are assembled to hear about your proposed product. It is important to pitch the group as a way to help your company better understand the needs in the marketplace, as opposed to pitching them to buy a product. The advantage of this approach is that the group dynamic can elicit responses not seen in a one-on-one interview. For example, several members may discuss the problem in detail, providing more depth or nuance about the nature of the problem. Or they might compare notes on competitive products and how the product solves the problem. The downside is that group interactions may limit input from people because they are shy or they don't want to be forthright in front of a group.

Surveys are typically web-based tools for gathering information from large groups of people. Surveys have the advantage of being able to reach a wide audience, both geographically and demographically at a low cost. Although good in theory, they suffer a number of limitations: 1) most start-ups don't have large e-mail lists for sending the survey, and purchased e-mail lists tend to be general and not targeted to specific market segments, and 2) the response rate of e-mail surveys is very low, yielding small and often biased samples from which to draw conclusions.

Secondary Market Research

Secondary market research looks at the market on a more macro level, examining market sizes, growth, and drivers. Market size can be estimated several ways, as described in the "Developing the Business Case" section (page 98). Growth rates are harder to assess and can come from market research reports. Market research reports can be found for a variety of markets. These reports, written by market research firms, are compiled from both public information and interviews with key opinion leaders. They can cost thousands of dollars, but, if they are done well and directly address the relevant market, they are well worth it. (On the other hand, some reports are a waste of money.) In addition to market size and growth rate, secondary market research will help to define the major market drivers that are at play. Market drivers are forces that are shaping the market today and will have an impact in the future; perhaps creating a greater or lesser need for the start-up's products. Market drivers can include demographic changes (e.g., the aging population), regulations that will force changed behavior (e.g., air pollution compliance), and technology shifts (e.g., adoption of smart phones).

A list of market research resources can be found at researchtorevenue.com.

Mapping Markets and Customers

Through market research, you begin to develop a better understanding of the product's application, the customer's needs, the competition, and the product features, which can help drive product adoption. At this point it is important to begin developing a market landscape that will provide a context for your product opportunity. Two different approaches are considered here. First, the market map arranges products and solutions according to different market dimensions—that is, features of products that distinguish them from other products. This diagram shows different products or product categories in the market according to two independent dimensions. The size of the bubble for each category denotes the product's relative market size, and its position on the map shows the alignment of that product category with the features. As an example, take the case of a start-up that is developing a novel ceramic material that can be used for audio speakers, providing high fidelity in a compact size. Figure 3.3a is a map of the market for speakers along the dimensions of fidelity and size.[25] The map conveys a large amount of information but

25. There are some who argue that it is best to choose two dimensions that will show the product opportunity in the upper right quadrant, or high in both dimensions. This may provide a perceptual edge, but showing a clear gap in the market is much more important.

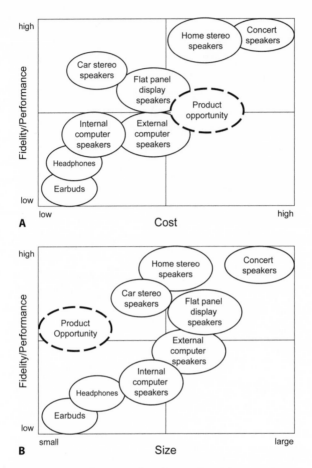

FIGURE 3.3 Market maps showing market drivers: cost vs. performance (a) and size vs. performance (b)

easily distinguishes the product opportunity from other product categories in the market. There might be multiple features at play in the market, so it is important to explore different features to see how the market maps out. For example, cost may be a large driver so that in mapping cost versus fidelity, a different map emerges and the opportunity shifts (fig. 3.3b).[26]

The second approach drills a bit deeper than the market map. Here, one can show the importance of these different features to different customer segments. This type of analysis uses information gleaned from interviews about what features and benefits are important to customers. Using our example of

26. For the scientifically oriented person, these maps might seem crude and nonquantitative. One could spend hours arguing about where these bubbles should be, but the point of the maps is to simply demonstrate visually a product differentiation in the current market.

TABLE 3.4 Customer segment chart for compact high-fidelity speakers

SEGMENT	COST	SIZE	PERFORMANCE	RELIABILITY
Teens/young adults	+++	+++	+	+
Older adults	++	+	+++	++
Stereophiles/musicians	+++	+	+++	++
Military	+	++	+	+++

the novel speaker material and focusing on one product category, headphones and earbuds, the customer segments can be mapped out to different market drivers, as shown in table 3.4. The table shows the results of the responses to the question, How important are the following to you in buying headphones or earbuds: cost, size, performance, reliability? The number of pluses relates to how important the feature is to that segment (since the source of the data is an interview, numbers are rarely presented, thus the one, two, or three pluses). This exercise is useful because it forces founders to explore all of the possible market segments, comparing different market segments to arrive at their target market segment.

A final aspect of market research is the competitive analysis, wherein a start-up's product is compared to competitive products using many of the product features discussed previously and usually displayed in a table. Competitive analysis is fully explored as part of writing the business plan (page 140).

KEY STEP Defining and Refining the Business Model

The business model, as discussed in Chapter 2, is the mechanism by which the company will capture value, or, more simply, make money. For some companies, the business model choice is driven by the type of product. For example, a company developing a therapeutic will likely choose a partnering model, given the amount of capital and expertise required to bring the drug to market. A software company, on the other hand, needs much less capital and could pursue the software as a service (SaaS) model. A new trend is to consider the business model and other business elements, such as customer input, much earlier. Entrepreneurs Eric Ries (author of *The Lean Startup*)[27] and Steve Blank (*Four Steps to Epiphany*) advocate business-model development and customer-driven product development early in the start-up process. In

27. Eric Ries, *The Lean Startup: How Today's Entrepreneurs Use Continuous Innovation to Create Radically Successful Businesses* (New York: Crown Business, 2011).

addition, they advise using an approach that involves testing a minimal viable product (MVP) with customers and then modifying the product and reconfiguring the business model based on market feedback.

For some start-ups, the business model will not be the same over the life of the company. A morphing business model may be the best strategy for getting a complex technology to market. For example, consider a series of monoclonal antibodies that can detect a range of water pollutants at low concentrations. In its initial embodiment, the analysis of water samples using the antibodies is not robust and requires sophisticated instrumentation and highly trained scientists. The first business model incarnation could involve a service business where samples are sent to the company for analysis and the results are returned to the customer. After further refinement of the technology (more robust and reproducible) and receiving the initial feedback from the market, the company could shift to selling instruments to test labs where the labs do the analysis. This would represent a change from a service business model to a scientific equipment and reagent sales model. With further product development, a kit that allows the test to be done in the field without sophisticated instruments could be launched. This hypothetical example shows three different business models and the shifts the company could make, taking up each model. In reality, changing business models can be difficult. The potential advantages in increased revenue will have to far outweigh the disadvantages with regard to company infrastructure changes. For example, moving from a scientific instrument sales model to selling kits requires a change in sales and marketing infrastructure as well as the possible dismantling of the manufacturing operation if that model is completely abandoned. A more realistic scenario is for the company to have multiple business models addressing multiple markets. The advantage is keeping two revenue streams intact while expanding market reach.

One approach to developing and mapping out the business model involves using a business model canvas, a chart that identifies key partners, activities, and resources, value propositions, and customer segments and relationships, as well as channels to reach those customers and the cost structure and revenue streams inherent in the model.[28] The elements of the business canvas can be grouped into the following:

CUSTOMERCENTRIC ELEMENTS. The canvas starts with *customer segments*, the customers and organizations for which the company is creating value and represent the users as well as paying customers. The bundle

28. Alexander Osterwalder and Yves Pigneur, *Business Model Generation* (Self-published, 2009), www.businessmodelgeneration.com (accessed 14 July 2015).

of products and services that create value for the customer are the *value propositions* and deliver value to each customer segment. Products and services can be delivered to the customer via *channels* (also called touch points or modes of selling). As part of the transaction with the customer (delivering the product or service via the channel), *customer relationships* are established. Finally, the *revenue streams* describe the pricing strategy for customers buying products and services

INFRASTRUCTURE ELEMENTS. The internal elements of the business model include the *key resources* for creating the products and services (e.g., capital, manufacturing, distribution channels). The *key activities* are the activities that use the key resources to create the products and services for the customer segments. Few companies have all the resources at their disposal, so *key partners* are needed to supply certain resources and activities. Finally, knowing key resources, activities, and partners will help define the *cost structure* of the products and services.

Examples of the business canvas can be found at researchtorevenue.com.

KEY STEP **Early-Stage Marketing**

The idea of marketing at this early stage may seem odd, especially since there are no products to sell. However, attracting the best management team, investors, and partners is critical, and effective marketing of the company will enhance the appeal of the company. The role of marketing at this stage may fall on the founders, many of whom are faculty. Although they might not call what they do "marketing," most faculty are engaged in marketing. They promote their ideas to funding agencies to gain support; they promote their science to colleagues at conferences and publications to establish their reputation; they promote their lab and their expertise through websites; and they promote their students to others to help them secure academic positions. This level of promotion may not compare to the slick ads and websites of corporate America but the idea behind it is very similar: convincing others to consider their ideas, approach, and "products."

An important concept to keep in mind when marketing is to "transmit on the frequency of the person receiving the information," or, more simply, "know your audience." For university start-ups, this can be critical since you need to tailor the level of detail, the amount of data, and complexity of the explanation to fit the person receiving the information. In addition, there are a number of ways to communicate, or "channels" on which to transmit, this

TABLE 3.5 Communication tools for early-stage marketing

CHANNEL	TOOLS				
Internet	Website	Video	Social media	E-mail	
Written	Executive summary	Intro deck	Reading deck	Business plan deck	Business plan document
Presentation	Intro pitch	Detailed pitch			
Meeting	Elevator pitch	two-pager graphic			

information. Table 3.5 shows various channels of communication and the tools used for each. For example, the Internet is an effective communication channel for either posting a website, developing social media (e.g., a blog, Twitter, Facebook), or reaching out via e-mail (e.g., a newsletter). A number of written pieces need to be developed (as discussed in key steps below) to promote the company, technology, and products. These can range from a complete business plan to an executive summary. Finally, face-to-face meetings require tools ranging from the elevator pitch to an hour-long company pitch for an investor meeting. The elevator pitch is particularly important since it may be the only chance to connect with someone.

Marketing at the early stage of a company's development is less about creating demand for the products as it is about establishing the image of the company and encapsulating the technology and products in an easy-to-understand way. Marketing a university start-up can be thought of as having three levels. At the first level, the company is marketed. Since the company at this point is fairly immature, the marketing is built around the founder's vision of the company and expressed via the company name, logo, and website. At the second level, the technology that is being embodied in the product is marketed. Since products have not been developed at this point, the technology will be a placeholder for them. This allows the founder to talk about the broad features of the technology (how it works) and how they will give rise to the product (how the technology is applied to solve a customer problem). This approach is especially useful for platform technology companies where the technology can be presented as the core of a series of products. At the third level, to come later, the product is marketed.

For the early-stage marketing effort, the following elements should be developed (assuming the company has a name at this point).

Company Logo

A company logo at this stage might not seem important, but it can give a company a polished look and feel. An effective logo will enhance the image of the company, but a bad logo can send the wrong message. An effective logo is simple and elegant and one that can be easily recognized and reproduced in different formats.[29] A safe approach to the logo is using a "bug," a small graphic that is used next to the name of the company, which is set in an appealing font. An ineffective logo is one where the letters in the company's name are contorted into a logo, or is so complex that it will be difficult to see, particularly on slides in a slide presentation. One of the most cost-effective ways to get a starter logo is through crowdsourcing or a design contest. Here, founders post information about the company and a description of the type of look and feel desired (e.g., formal, casual, colors, etc.). Often, designers from around the world will submit logo ideas that then can be winnowed down by the company to a winner, who wins a fee ($100–1,000). A number of web-based companies facilitate this type of logo development (e.g., logo tournament.com, designcontest.com, 99designs.com). Examples of effective and not-so-effective logos can be found at researchtorevenue.com.

Company Website

There are different philosophies about whether to launch a website. Some start-ups like to be able to send prospective management and advisers to a place that provides detailed information about the technology, the current management/advisers, and the intended product. Others want to stay in "stealth mode" until there is something to talk about (investments, partnerships, products to sell). A company will take the stealth approach when there is concern about publicly identifying the opportunity that others could copy. In general, a company with well-protected IP is taking less risk in building an early website than one whose IP is not. Finally, the website should not be made until the resources and talent have been identified to launch a professionally designed site. There is nothing more damaging to a company than a homemade site with broken links, misaligned graphics, and typos. In creating a starter site, keep several things in mind.

First, keep it simple. The following elements should be sufficient:

---

29. Think how the logo will look embroidered on a shirt in low resolution. That's how simple the logo should be.

- HOME PAGE: A bold image with a description of the company or the company's mission.
- "TEAM" OR "ABOUT" PAGE: A list of founders, management, advisers. In the early days, a simple list of people involved without titles is sufficient; as the management team is formed, the BOD is named, and the SAB is assembled, more details can be added.
- TECHNOLOGY PAGE: A simple explanation of the technology (using the technology name) with the key enabling features. Links to publications and/or a short slide presentation will provide the viewer further details. Videos are good, but they need to be short (less than three minutes) and to look professional.
- CONTACT PAGE: Contact information.

Additional pages to be added over time include a Product page and a Company News page.

Second, the site needs to be easy to update. The site should be built using a format such as WordPress, where the founders and management can easily change content as needed without having to work through a website designer. Finally, because the content can be easily updated, it should be updated regularly. Subtle things like when a two-year-old copyright date is at the bottom of the home page or when the latest company news is over a year old will send the message that the company is dead or stalled. It is better to have no company news than to have old company news.

With a logo chosen and a website up and running, letterhead stationery and business cards should be printed and a PowerPoint template created. Again, a professionally designed look goes a long way in portraying an image of confidence, competence, and success.

Technology and Product Names

In addition to the company name, the technology and products need to be developed as part of the marketing effort. A name gives the technology a sense of identity and makes it real. For example, after the technology is explained (in a piece for marketing or on a website), rather than saying "the technology enables great flexibility in surgical instruments," you can use the name: "Flex-Fit Technology enables great flexibility . . ." Likewise, even though a product might be years from market, it should also have a name. For example, "The OmniProbe 2000 is two-times lighter . . ." sounds more convincing than "Our proposed product is half the weight . . ." The link between the technology and the product then can be conveyed more effectively; for example, "The novel OmniProbe incorporates NewCo's proprietary FlexFit technology, producing a surgical probe with 10 times more maneuverability" or "NewCo's OmniProbe, powered by FlexFit technology will increase maneuverability 10-fold."

The Executive Summary and the Two-Pager

The executive summary (also called a one-pager) is a one-page overview of the company that succinctly outlines the following:

- Problem (unmet need, customer pain, market gap)
- Solution (technology, products)
- Implementation (go-to-market strategy, business model)
- People (founders, management team)

This is usually sent to potential customers, team members, investors, etc., via e-mail or as a handout for them to take with them after you've met with them. Rather than packing information into the single page using a tiny font and small figures, consider this as a high-level summary, where your audience can be given a phone number or directed to a website for further information.

The two-pager is a graphic-rich document (printed front and back) in a plastic sleeve. This stays with you for that coffee shop meeting with an adviser or possible team member. Pulling this out of a briefcase is easier than opening a tablet or laptop. One side might have a key piece of data that explains the technology or a schematic of the prototype. The second side might have information on the business itself (e.g., market size, growth rate), a diagram showing the business model (i.e., the flow of money in exchange for services), or a market map, as described previously, that shows the viewer where your product fits relative to others.

The Elevator Pitch

The elevator pitch, in a sense, is a verbal version of the executive summary. It is a short pitch given without any notes at a moment's notice,[30] used during a one-on-one encounter to quickly and succinctly explain the business. The purpose is to get the listener interested enough to want more information ("tell me more" or "send me your executive summary"). The elevator pitch has the following attributes:

30. The phrase "elevator pitch" comes from the situation in which you step onto an elevator with a key potential investor and you have from the time the door closes until the time the door opens at the investor's floor to pitch the company, usually 60 seconds.

SHORT. The pitch should be no longer than 60 seconds or between 150 to 250 words.

CLEAR AND CONCISE. Speak without using jargon or acronyms and deliver your message efficiently.

VISUAL IMAGERY. Paint a picture with words to help the listener rapidly grasp the company's mission, product, and strategy.

THE HOOK. Come up with an opening statement or question that piques the potential customer's, team member's, or investor's interest (e.g., "There are more than 10,000 babies born each year with . . ." or "Have you ever wondered why less than 2 percent of people . . . ?")

THE ASK. End the pitch with a request, for either a follow-up meeting, a business card, or a referral.

An elevator pitch might look something like this:

Imagine a world where flat tires are things of the past. No more getting out of the car in the rain or snow or sweating in your business suit to change a tire. No more having to wait for AAA to provide help. Nova-Tech will revolutionize the way people think about flat tires with its FlatPal products. FlatPal uses our proprietary AirSense technology to continuously monitor the air pressure in your tire, adding air over time for a slow leak or rapidly adding air for a flat. For severe flats, FlatPal will dispense a tire sealant to plug holes. All of this happens under automatic control. Being wireless-enabled, FlatPal will send a text or e-mail with any change in air pressure. Imagine getting a text that your car in the airport parking lot has a flat and has been automatically fixed. The company will first target the passenger vehicle market to establish a beachhead and then turn to taxis and cabs as its second market, and, finally, targeting the trucking industry. I was hoping you could introduce me to Tim Smith, head of R&D at General Motors to get his thoughts on our business.

KEY STEP Writing the Business Plan

Using the information gathered from the previous three steps (market research, product mapping, and business model), and combining it with product-development plans, sales and marketing plans, and financial estimates, the writing of the business plan should be initiated. The business plan captures the various elements of the business strategy and business execution and builds on the business case, described above. Whereas the business case was the rationale for starting the business and used to attract advisers and the management team, the business plan serves two purposes: 1) it establishes a roadmap for the business so that everyone is "singing from the same song sheet" but with enough detail that the road map can be implemented, and 2) it provides enough detail for a potential investor to fully understand the opportunity and how the company will capture value around that opportunity (and how the investor will get a return on investment from those activities).

The business plan has changed dramatically over the last decade. Traditionally, a company would put together an extensive, 30–50-page plan and send the plan to investors for their review. Today's business plan has changed in several important ways. First, the "lean start-up," described by Ries and Blank, takes a more customer-centric, business-hypothesis-driven approach. Instead of starting with a business plan, the person wanting to start a business establishes a hypothesis for a product or business model, develops a lean version (the MVP), and tests that hypothesis with customers. Insights gained from those tests allows rapid iteration of the product and business model. Those insights may lead to a less formal business plan, instead generating more of a report of marketing efforts. Second, entrepreneurship and commercialization have grown dramatically over the last several decades as the start-up culture has become more mainstream. At the same time, the pool of risk capital (VCs and angels) has shrunk because of the economic downturns of 2000 and 2008. With more start-ups chasing less money, investors have less time to review each start-up opportunity in detail. As such, entrepreneurs are preparing not only a business plan but also documents that provide an efficient way to communicate the opportunity and the flexibility to alter them for different circumstances. Table 3.6 shows these documents.

The following is an example of a scenario in which these documents can be used to maximum effect.

1 Through a chance encounter, you bump into a business associate at a coffee shop. Using the two-pager, you walk her/him through the business.
2 The associate follows up with an introduction to a potential investor using the one-pager.
3 The investor is interested and wants more information, so you send him/her the business plan reading deck.
4 You telephone the investor to introduce yourself and present the company pitch deck.

TABLE 3.6 The elements of the business plan and derivative documents

DOCUMENT	DESCRIPTION	USE
Business plan	20–50-page document with text and figures outlining the various aspects of the business in extensive detail	1 Internal document for planning the business 2 External document for investors once they've decided to dig deeper into the opportunity
Business plan reading deck	10–30 slides (depending on appendices); a distillation of the business plan	For an investor or partner to review the opportunity in less than 30 minutes
Company pitch deck	10–20 slides with limited text and rich graphical elements, videos, and animation. Prezi is a common alternative to PowerPoint.	Pitching the company to investors or during a business plan competition
Executive summary	A one-page overview of the company describing the problem, the solution, and the team	Many uses, from recruiting other team members to making a first introduction to an investor

5 After the meeting, you resend the reading deck with extensive appendixes for potential distribution to the investor's partners and/or perhaps other investors he/she has recommended.

6 You arrange a face-to-face meeting with the investor and his/her colleagues where the pitch deck, with some minor tweaks based on the first meeting, is used, followed by a Q&A.

7 The investors want to go further with some due diligence, so you send them a full business plan.

Although recent trends have lessened the importance of the business plan, there is no doubt that writing it is extremely useful. The discipline of having to thoughtfully consider every aspect of the business will help you create a comprehensive framework for the business, as well as identify gaps in the strategy.

There is no one right way to organize a business plan, and the elements of the plan will be different for different companies. The plan is roughly divided into two parts. The first part (Company Overview, Technology and Products, and Market and Customers) covers the "What" of the business. It describes many aspects of the company and lays out the market opportunity and rationale for the business and its products. The second part (Strategy and Implementation, The Team: Management and Advisers, and Financial Plan) covers the "How," of the business. It explains how the company will build the business, deliver value to the marketplace, and provide a return to the shareholders.

Executive Summary

Like an abstract for a publication, the executive summary provides a succinct overview of the business. This executive summary might be the same as the one developed earlier but likely will have more detail since it summarizes the business plan. Since most investors won't make it past the executive summary, it needs to be well written, clear, and, most of all, compelling. In short, it needs to grab readers' attention, encouraging them to read further. It should be one or two pages, max, and be able to stand alone so that it can be sent prior to sending the full plan.

Company Overview

If the executive summary is the abstract, this section is the introduction to the business, giving the reader an overview of the company, the nature of the business and perfunctory information like its location and contact information, the legal form of the business, the number of employees, and the company history.

Market and Customers

Assuming the reader has made it through the executive summary and company overview with continued interest, a description of the market creates a compelling case for the business opportunity. It outlines the need in the market, the size and growth of that market, trends and market drivers, and the competition. This section sets up the next section, Technology and Products, as the solution to the market need. Most of the information in this section was gathered previously but will be refined and articulated to make a strong case.

Market Need and Customer Pain

This is the linchpin of the entire business plan. If the reader cannot be convinced that 1) a significant problem exists in the market, and 2) the problem is not adequately solved today then it is unlikely the solution described in the Technology and Products section will be compelling enough to attract support. The market need can be framed in a several different ways:

PROVIDING A SOLUTION. A customer might have a problem, and your product solves that problem like never before. This approach can vary depending on the customer, problem, and product. The customer might be solving the problem using a costly solution (in time or money), and your product will reduce those costs. The customer also might have somehow gotten around the problem or might not have even considered that he/she has a problem and your product will allow him/her to both see and solve the problem.

UNMET MEDICAL NEED. In the healthcare space, many diseases exist for which there is no adequate diagnostic test or treatment. A new product that either can treat patients better than they are currently being treated (e.g., a drug that has fewer side effects than the current one) or can provide a new way of treating patients (e.g., a diagnostic test predicting a disease) would have obvious value.

CREATING A NEED. In some cases, there is not a clearly definable need in the market, but the product will create a new need. For example, Apple recognized the value of an easier way of purchasing and listening to music on a portable player (iTunes/iPod) even though the need was not demonstrated by the existing market. Likewise, the need for wireless headsets (Bluetooth) would not have been considered a source of significant customer pain before they were introduced. There is a tendency among founders of university start-ups to quickly take a "we are going to create a new market" approach instead of doing the work to identify the need or to verify that the groundbreaking technology will generate market demand.

There are two important points to remember when developing this part of the business plan. First, the more quantitative the language, the better; for example, "The product will reduce costs by half"; "the product will increase throughput tenfold"; "the product will reduce waste by 30 percent." Second, don't confuse application with the need: It is not enough to say that you have developed a fiber optic sensor that will be used by a wastewater treatment technician to measure dissolved oxygen in the treatment plant effluent. You must also determine whether there is a current problem in measuring dissolved oxygen in plant effluent and that is not being currently solved. Measuring dissolved oxygen in plant effluent is a feature; the benefit would be remote monitoring, improved ruggedness, or greater precision.

TABLE 3.7 Market segment chart for three products

PRODUCT	TARGET CUSTOMER	MARKET SEGMENT	MARKET	INDUSTRY
Chocolate sports recovery drink	Women triathletes under 30	Triathletes	Endurance sports	Sports and fitness
Drug-eluting stent	Cardiovascular surgeon	Surgeons	Medical device	Healthcare
Cloud-based software for storing patient records	IT director in a hospital with at least 1,000 records	Hospital information managers	Healthcare information technology	Healthcare

Target Market and Customer Profile

Starting with the customer interviews, you need to build out a typical customer profile. Describe the typical customer in as much detail as possible. These customers all share a similar need to solve the same problem and together make up a market segment. Multiple market segments make up a market, and multiple markets can be aggregated into an industry. The distinction between markets and market segments can be arbitrary, and the levels of granularity numerous. Examples of these different levels are shown in table 3.7. One way to think about these distinctions is to consider the characteristics of the groups and how they organize themselves. For example, if you held a focus group with potential customers, would they have enough in common to cogently discuss the problems and solutions? A group of cardiologists would have less to say about a drug-eluting stent (and might be predisposed to pessimism) than a group of heart surgeons who would actually use the stent. Customers and market segments are specific enough to have their own journals and specialized conferences. Market segments and markets usually have enough in common to organize around conferences, trade shows, and industry groups.

Market Size and Growth

With an articulated need and a clearly defined target customer and market, you now need to build the case that the market size is large enough to support and sustain the business. Extending the work done previously to develop the business case and gather market information, a more refined market size estimate may need to be established. Given these are only estimates, it is important to convince the reader that the assumptions being made are credible.

This means stating the assumptions explicitly and providing some rationale for the assumptions. Using the example of the microscope market discussed previously (page 100), the assumptions are stated for estimates for each step. Going further, one could discuss the source of the numbers or why a certain percentage was chosen, even if these figures are guesses at this point (e.g., why the 15 percent replacement rate for microscopes).

Investors like investing in businesses that address large and rapidly growing markets. The question then becomes, How big is big and what is a rapidly growing market? As a general rule of thumb, most investors don't get excited about a market size under $50 million. On the other hand, showing a market size of $10 billion might call into question how the market was defined (e.g., should it be more narrowly defined?) and whether the company is able to address such a large market. In terms of growth rates, any figure over 10 percent is good, but, again, it has to be substantiated with the factors driving this growth. This level of detail not only will make the numbers more believable but will demonstrate the company's deep market knowledge. In general, large markets grow much slower than small markets. Current market size is usually easier to estimate than the expected future market size and the related growth rate.

Competitive Analysis

Competitive analysis explores all the ways a customer currently solves the problem your product will address. It is important to recognize two types of competitors: primary and secondary. A primary competitor is a company that offers a product that meets the market need or solves a problem in a similar way that your product does. Your product may provide a faster or cheaper way, but the methods are similar. A secondary competitor solves the problem in a different way than you do.

For direct competition, a good exercise is to create a table in which the features and benefits of your product are compared to the competition's. The table will provide an overview of the competition and should be backed up with extensive detail, usually a profile of each company and its product (this can be presented in the go-to-market section where each competitor is discussed relative to the company's products). The differences between the two products can be qualitative or quantitative. It is important to make the analysis believable and realistic. Few people will believe your product is superior to the competition in every area. The message should be that, overall, and especially on the features and benefits that matter to most customers, your

TABLE 3.8   A competitive analysis on a database product

	OMNIDATA™	COMPETITOR 1	COMPETITOR 2
Cost per year (one license)	$500	$1,250	$250
Lifetime cost of product	$2,500	$6,500	$1,200
Number of users per license	10	1	12
Number of records	Unlimited	10,000	50,000
Ease of integration	+++	+++	+
Ease of upgrade	+++	++	+
Ease of customization	++	+++	++

product has a significant competitive advantage. Table 3.8 shows a competitive analysis for a fictional database product.

Several common mistakes are made in thinking about competition. The rookie mistake is to state that there is "no competition." This naïve statement is a red flag to the reader. Even if there is no primary competition, there probably is secondary competition. Another common mistake is not seeing the potential of competitors as partners. In our ultracompetitive world, we often only think about how we can beat the competition, steal market share and customers, and perhaps drive them out of business. When closely examined, competitive products might turn out to be complementary or synergistic. If your company's product is in direct competition with another company's, the competitor's acquisition of your product/company can help expand its product offering. If your business strategy is to partner, your product and technology should be positioned to be attractive for the partner. In this case, the partner becomes the customer. For example, you may be creating a device that will be greatly enhanced by incorporating it into another product. It is important to understand the business of each of your potential partners, including its customers, its competition, and its market dynamics. Therefore, after you compile the list of competitors, you might also select a few of the competitors to talk to about how they may play a role in a partnership or to include in the exit section of the business plan (e.g., acquisition by the competitor).

Barriers to Adoption

Many university start-ups are based on a cutting-edge technology that gives rise to a novel product. That's the good news. The bad news is the novelty of the product may limit the number of customers who are willing to take the risk to buy it. The extent of market penetration or product adoption is driven by a number of factors. For the business plan, it will be important to enumerate any barriers to product adoption that exist and how to address them.[31]

Barriers to adoption are the reasons that keep customers from buying the product. A start-up must overcome competition to be successful, but even if a product has limited competition, customers will not automatically purchase it, especially a technology-based product. Customers need to be convinced that the value of a new product is commensurate with the cost of the product, both in terms of time and money. There are a number of reasons why a customer won't buy a technology-based product, including:

LOW LEARNING CURVE. Some products are technically complex and require a certain expertise to use. If that expertise is highly specialized, then only a few people can use the product, which will limit adoption. Or, if the time it will take to be trained to be able to use the product is perceived as excessive, the customer might turn away.

LOW PERCEIVED VALUE. Customers perceive value in a product prior to purchasing it. If the perceived value of the product is low, even though its actual value after it is purchased is high, the adoption will be low.

LACK OF CONFIDENCE. For new products based on an unproven technology, customers may lack the confidence that the product will deliver the value promised.

Before you begin preparing this section of the business plan, we recommend reading *Crossing the Chasm*, by Geoffrey Moore.[32] This book outlines the barriers to adoption of technology-based products as well as a strategy for overcoming those barriers. Moore takes the basic principles of the product adoption curve (a bell curve that shows the rate of adoption of a new product) and explains why it is difficult to move along the curve with disruptive products. The curve, shown in figure 3.4, is divided into segments corresponding to different types of customers. The first customers to buy disruptive products are innovators, followed in order by early adopters, early majority, later majority, and, finally, laggards. He argues that most start-ups succeed in selling technology-based products to innovators and early adopters but often fail

31. One might perceive describing barriers to adoption as painting a negative picture of the market opportunity. To the contrary, the company should be entering the market with both eyes wide open, and investors will want to know up front not only the risks associated with the opportunity but also, more important, how the company is going to mitigate those risks (i.e., overcome the barriers to adoption).

32. Geoffrey A. Moore, *Crossing the Chasm: Marketing and Selling Disruptive Products to Mainstream Customers* (New York: HarperCollins, 2006).

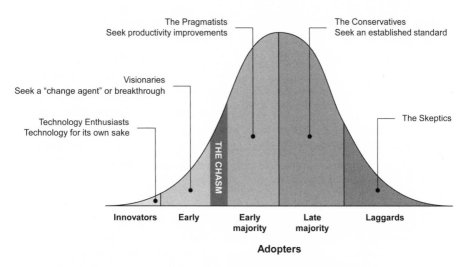

FIGURE 3.4 The product-adoption curve with the chasm between early adopters and early majority customers. Adapted from Moore, *Crossing the Chasm*.

in selling to the early- and late-majority customers (the largest segment of the market). These companies are unable to "cross the chasm" between early adopters and early-majority customers for several reasons. First, for disruptive products, most customers will reference others before buying. That is, if they get a strong recommendation from someone they trust, they are more likely to purchase. In general, early adopters are visionaries enamored with the technology at the core of the product and the exciting features it enables, undeterred by the risks of the product or its imperfections. Early-majority customers, by contrast, are pragmatists focused on solving a specific problem and are not willing to take a risk on an unproven product. As such, the early majority rarely will seek a referral or trust the recommendation from an early adopter. This disconnect between these two customer groups results in the chasm. Successfully crossing the chasm opens the market to a substantial customer base since the early and late majority are similar enough that one can seek and trust references from the other. Moore proposes the easiest way to cross the chasm is to start small by focusing on a niche market segment, developing the product to address the needs of that market segment, and assemble an effective sales force to sell into the market. In doing so, the market niche can be dominated, creating a significant number of customers who can be references and providing the market leadership that can be leveraged into other, larger markets.

Technology and Products

Technology Description

This section gives the nontechnical reader some understanding of the unique features of the technology around which the company and products are being built. As the section progresses, the technical detail increases so that a person who works in the field can start to assess the technology. It's best to start at the most basic level so the reader understands how the technology works (imagine you're explaining it to a fifth grader—really!) and how it could be used. For example, if the technology is a novel biomarker for a disease, provide context for the disease, such as how prevalent the disease is and how it's being diagnosed today, and explain the general role of biomarkers in medicine. Cartoons, illustrations, images, and graphics are very important in describing the technology. As mentioned in the discussion on developing the business case, it is important to emphasize the key enabling features of the technology. What can the technology do that no other can? How is this technology different from any other technology today? The next step is to provide limited data to emphasize the unique features of the technology. The most useful device at this stage is often a head-to-head comparison to another technology or product highlighting a significant difference (e.g., three times more sensitive, twice as effective with half the dose, etc.). The level of detail in these analyses should convince the reader of the substantial advantages of the technology. Details around experimental protocol can be captured in table legends, footnotes, or an appendix. If the data has been published in a top-tier journal, be sure to emphasize this point since it provides a certain level of scientific and technical validation. Progress to the technical details, citing relevant publications where the technical reader can go to further explore the technology.

Intellectual Property

One of the most important assets of a university start-up is its IP. This section should describe the scope of IP coverage and the current status (e.g., filings, office actions, allowances, university expenses to date, etc.). Describe the scope of the IP protection in general terms unless the patent has published, in which case including the significant claims can be helpful. (For patents that have not been published, treat the contents of the patent as proprietary.)[33] In

---

33. Investors rarely sign NDAs, so the intellectual property section should not disclose confidential information, such as details of an unpublished patent. Listing the patents and the topic

addition, outline plans for increasing the strength of the patent portfolio by describing future patent filings (in general, nonproprietary terms) as well as additional IP to be licensed into the company. If any potentially conflicting patents have surfaced from office actions or patent searches, it is best to get that disclosed here rather than wait for an investor to find them through his/ her due diligence.

This section should also outline the terms of the license the start-up has, or will have, with the university. A summary of key terms should include the subject matter (patents), exclusivity, scope (geographic, fields of use), royalty rates, sublicensing terms, milestone payments, and the university's equity and any nondilution clauses.

Product Opportunities

With a firm foundation of the technology and its key benefits established, the next section should set forth a vision of the product (or products) and drive home how it meets a significant customer need.[34] Map these opportunities in ways that embody key features of the technology, as described on page 132. Describe the product in as much detail as possible, keeping in mind that customers buy products, not technologies. A mock-up of the product, if appropriate, can help the reader visualize the product, making it more real. The most important aspect of the product vision is describing the problem or need the customer has and how this product will solve that problem. Go beyond describing the application. Here it is important not only to bring in the features of product that are enabled by the technology but also to cast those features as benefits to the customer. If working with a platform technology, describe the many products and markets they will serve. Exploring the different applications and markets at this stage can lay the groundwork for considering a pivot later (i.e., change strategic direction to pursue a different market). However, although broad applicability is good to show, make sure there is a clear first target application.

---

and general areas of coverage is fine. Much has been written on why investors, especially venture capitalists, don't sign NDAs. One explanation is that at any one point, investors might be looking at a number of competitive deals, and if they fund one, an unfunded entrepreneur may claim his idea was stolen. NDAs can also take time and money to execute and track and in general are difficult to enforce. Keep extremely confidential information (chemical structures, proprietary processes, unpublished patents) out of the plan but make note of them in general terms. If investors want more information, they can ask for it.

34. In some cases, the technology is the product (e.g., a drug that reduces inflammation), in which case the technology and product sections are combined.

Strategy and Implementation

Up to this point, the focus of the business plan has been on the "what": what is the technology, what is the product, what is the application, what is the market size, etc. The remainder of the business plan focuses on the "how": the strategy and timeline for developing, manufacturing, and marketing the product; the capital required to bring the product to market; the growth and profitability of the company over time; and the management team that will make the key decisions to build and grow the successful business. The business plan typically includes the following sections, with different emphases depending on the particular technology, products, and markets.

Business Model

The business model, sometimes referred to as the revenue model, describes how the company will market the product and what the transaction with the customer looks like. As discussed in Chapter 2 and the key step section "Defining and Refining the Business Model," there are a number of different business models from which to choose, and the model choice is a strategic one based on the resources of the company, customer requirements, the speed required to reach the market, and the other vendors or partners who can be part of the model. In this section, discuss the business model using the relevant elements described previously. If it's not clear what the business model will be, this section is where options are discussed and what key data will go into choosing the best business model. As was discussed, a changing business model can be a viable option if it supports the product strategy.

Product Strategy

This information supplied in the product strategy section outlines what specific markets the company will initially target, the corresponding products to be introduced, and the timeline for introduction. (This information could also go under the Technology and Products part of the business plan.) For a single product (e.g., a therapeutic), the product strategy will be fairly simple since there will likely be one broad market and the product might have several applications (e.g., colon cancer, pancreatic cancer). The strategy might also outline a family of products and describe how those products will be launched. In keeping with the current trend of the lean start-up, a minimal viable product might be introduced and then further developed into a more feature-filled product based on market feedback. The product strategy could also involve multiple markets. For example, one strategy would involve introducing a product into a small, niche market to gain important feedback and establish a foothold (see "The Sales Cycle and Product Adoption" section, below). From there, one would launch into a much broader market.

Technology- and Product-Development Plan, Timeline, and Milestones

Once a strategy has been developed, more granularity is required to lay out a plan going forward. Be it a home sensor, database software, or pharmaceutical compound, the product goes through a series of development stages. Each stage ends with a specific milestone that is measureable. The completion of prototype testing can be a milestone, but completion with a less than 1 percent failure rate by a certain date is better. Choosing these milestones and the time to reach them is critical because investors see each milestone as a significant "value inflection point" (i.e., a measurable event that increases the value of the company). Failure to reach a milestone can cause angst among investors and board members, resulting in them asking hard questions of management and making unpopular decisions (e.g., firing the CEO). So pick the milestones carefully, trying to make them reasonable and achievable in the stated time frame.

Part of the product-development plan will be outlining the costs associated with achieving each milestone (e.g., the cost to treat 30 mice with the drug, the cost to build 10 beta units to put into the hands of early customers, or the cost to convert wireframes into a working e-commerce website). These figures need to be as detailed as possible. Experienced management and consultants are critical for estimating these figures. The timeline, the milestones, and the funding required to meet those milestones form the foundation of a financial plan, as described below.

A common mistake as it relates to the product strategy and the product-development plan is the lack of focus. It has often been said of start-up companies, especially those with multiple product opportunities (e.g., arising from a platform technology), that they often fail because of indigestion, not starvation. In other words, they try to take on too many product opportunities, leading to diffuse activities that never bring any single product forward. Companies that have laser focus on a specific product and market opportunity have a better chance to succeed. Additional product opportunities that build on the first product should be outlined with estimated costs and timelines, and product opportunities that address different markets can be described in general terms to demonstrate options going forward if significant funding occurs or if the initial product fails.

Manufacturing Plan

The manufacturing plan dovetails with the product-development plan and should outline all aspects of manufacturing the product. It can take many different forms depending on the company strategy. It may include a plan to outsource the manufacturing (e.g., using a contract manufacturer to produce the beta units and the first units for sale) or to manufacture the product exclusively in-house. Or a hybrid model may make more strategic sense: outsourcing the manufacturing initially and over time, once revenues and profits allow for bank loans to build the manufacturing infrastructure, bringing the manufacturing in-house. The manufacturing plan should back up the financial plan in terms of the manufacturing costs (cost of goods sold, or COGS). If key suppliers are needed, they should be listed along with alternative suppliers in the event the key supplier is unavailable. Admittedly, at this stage, details of manufacturing may be few, at best. An acceptable approach is to discuss the different manufacturing options that will be considered once the company reaches the point of needing manufacturing.[35]

Go-to-Market Strategy

The go-to-market strategy is the action plan that will focus on sales and marketing efforts and how those efforts will translate into revenue.

Marketing and Sales Plans

An essential part of the implementation plan is the sales and marketing strategy.[36] This section considers the product features and benefits, the barriers to adoption, and the competitive landscape, described earlier, in outlining the strategy and tactics for creating demand for the product, which will translate into revenue.

MARKETING PLAN. The marketing plan describes how the company will create demand for the product. This plan should be broken down into

---

35. If the plan is exclusively focused on partnering to bring the product to market, which would include manufacturing, then this section can be omitted.

36. There is often overlap in and thus confusion between sales and marketing, so remember the old adage, "Marketing creates the appeal; sales close the deal."

strategic marketing and *tactical marketing*. The strategic marketing plan describes how the company image, product branding and positioning, and product design will be used to sell the product. Product names, taglines, and even website color choices can be strategic decisions. The tactical marketing plan is more down in the trenches. This describes the actions that will implement the strategy, including choosing what trade shows to attend; developing publications, white papers, newsletters, or applications notes; establishing relationships with key opinion leaders; and implementing advertising and social media campaigns.

SALES PLAN. As with the marketing plan, the sales plan should address both the strategic and tactical approaches. Strategic issues to be considered include pricing and discount strategy relative to the competition and the development of different sales channels (direct sales, distributors, etc.). Sales tactics include the ramping up of the sales force, territory design, compensation, and sales processes (e.g., demos, beta units, etc.). A specialized area of sales is business development. For some products (e.g., therapeutics) that require more strategic transactions (e.g., licensing, partnering), a business development plan is more relevant than a sales plan.

More details on sales, marketing, and business development can be found in the key step section "Engaging the Customer," below.

Market Share, Penetration, and Revenue Estimates

The sales and marketing plans will demonstrate how the company will penetrate the market, capture a percentage of the market (market share), and generate revenue. These estimates should be justified with reasonable assumptions since they will form the basis of a financial plan. A common mistake is to estimate a huge market and a modest market share ("If we capture just 1 percent of this $200 billion market, we're looking at projected revenues of $2 billion."). Most savvy investors will see market size inflation here. On the other extreme, estimating that you will capture a large percentage of any market will seem unrealistic ("If we capture half of the $200 million market in five years, we'll be a dominant player."). Predicting that you will have the sales force and manufacturing capacity, not to mention the ability to influence market adoption, that would be required to capture half a market in five years will seem overly ambitious to a smart investor. A good approach here is to take an operational estimate of market capture—that is, simulate how the company will capture market share based on company operations. One can make realistic estimates of the number of potential customers ("leads"), the number of customer interactions (i.e., through website visits, sales calls, etc.) over a period of time, the percentage of interactions that lead to a sale ("conversion rate"), and the time it takes to close the sale after the interaction ("sales cycle"). For example, if the product is being sold over the Internet, then estimates of site traffic over time can be developed (leads), how many visitors buy after visiting (conversion rate), how many visits or how much time before purchase (sales cycle). With these numbers, one can begin to calculate how rapidly a sales force can be hired and trained to begin generating revenue. These bottom-up estimates provide much greater credibility than statements like "if we only capture 1 percent of the market . . ."

The Team: Management and Advisers

This section describes the people who have gathered around this new opportunity. Investors are always looking for ways to reduce their risk, and they can readily assess whether the right people are involved in the company by looking for experience (Has this person done this job before and was he/she successful?) and skills (Does this person have the domain expertise to add value?) and through the intangibles (first impressions, interactions, social skills, etc.). In short, investors are looking for the people who can be trusted to execute effectively on the business plan but, more important, make the right decisions when the plan needs to be changed. It is often said that people invest in people, not companies or technologies and this is most true for a start-up.

Depending on the stage of the company, the team can vary from a few to many. Investors understand the fluidity of the situation, so it is wise not to oversell someone's involvement at this stage. In other words, if you've had coffee with a key opinion leader and they've given advice, don't pretend that they are an adviser until you ask them formally and they accept. At this stage, it is best to put people into the proper categories. It helps the investors understand the players and their involvement. Management are those people who have committed to managing and launching the company, even if on an interim or part-time basis. As such, they will have some level of ownership that is commensurate with their background and level of commitment. So investors have some idea of the roles and responsibilities of management team members, it is helpful if members have been given titles. As mentioned earlier, titles are important, but don't hand them out like candy. If an individual has the obvious experience and background to be the CSO, for example, then he/she should have that title. A very early-stage company with a CEO, CSO, CFO, CBO and so on may look a little top heavy at this stage. Not all these positions have to be filled, and it is reasonable to list the position followed by "TBH" (to be hired). For management team members on board, a paragraph-long biography is sufficient along with a current LinkedIn profile. If you have a board of directors and a scientific advisory board, list them here as well (if a website has been launched for the company, make sure the same information is in both places).

A frequent conundrum is how to list the faculty founder (or founders). It is important to signal to investors the founder's role in the company, and this can be done by showing him/her as chair of the SAB or board member. Often faculty founders list themselves as CEO or CSO, which, as discussed before, is not appropriate unless they are planning to leave their academic posts upon a successful round of funding. The best way to handle this is to assign interim titles, which clearly signal individuals' intention to step aside when the position is filled. If there are multiple faculty founders, it is fine to list them on their own founders or list them as advisers with the title "founder." The role of the founder(s) will become clear to the investors during the first several meetings (e.g., if they don't show up versus if they lead the scientific section of the presentation).

The Financial Plan

The financial plan, broadly, shows how the company will make and spend money over time. For technology-based start-ups, the revenue will likely be zero for the first several years other than perhaps "income" from grants or partnerships. Investors are trying to answer the following questions:

- How much is the company looking to raise this round and subsequent rounds?
- Does that amount fit with the amount I typically invest in a company?
- Are the expenses, in general, appropriate for what the company is trying to accomplish (e.g., too much for R&D, not enough for marketing)?
- Does the amount of money the company wants to raise get it to important, value-inflection milestones in a reasonable amount of time?
- How much money does the company need to raise and how long will it take to get to liquidity?

Investors want to create value with their investment and they want that value to translate to some liquidity or exit event that will turn that increased value into cash, their return. As such, they are looking critically at what value-creating milestones their investment will enable. The list below shows examples of milestones versus value-creating milestones:

MILESTONES	VALUE-CREATING MILESTONES
Hiring of the tenth employee	Hiring of a chief technology officer
Building a working prototype	Delivering a prototype to a beta customer
Filing a patent application	Have a patent issue
Hiring a VP of business development	Signing a $5 million partnership deal
Completing a market survey of customers	Identifying a beachhead market from a customer survey
Demonstrating preclinical safety and efficacy	Obtaining approval for an investigational new drug application from the FDA
Establishing production	Shipping the first product
Selling $1 million of product	Becoming cash-flow positive

Thus, in developing the financial plan, closely link the investment with the value-creating milestones.

For some investors, the assumptions for the financial plan are more important than the actual numbers. The assumptions need to be clearly stated (e.g., the estimated cost of the product is X, market size is X and will grow at Y percent over Z years, the number of customers is X, the cost of the Phase I clinical trial is X, etc.). Because there are so many assumptions, it is best to show those assumptions explicitly and build those assumptions into the financial model (the spreadsheet).

There are three documents companies use to show the various financial aspects of the business. The *balance sheet* shows the company's assets (what it owns) and its liabilities (what it owes) as of a certain date (e.g., end of a calendar year). The *income statement* shows the income the company expects to receive (e.g., grants, revenue) and the expenses it will have (e.g., payroll, equipment, rent) each year. The *cash-flow statement* shows the flow of cash into the company and the flow of cash out of the company on a month-to-month or quarter-to-quarter basis.[37] For the business plan, since the company has little or no financial results to report, all financial statements are pro forma (i.e., based on financial assumptions). Of the three financial statements, the income statement is the most important to develop initially. If there has been any sig-

---

37. For an easy-to-understand book explaining these financial statements, see Chuck Kremer and Ron Rizzuto, *Managing by the Numbers: A Commonsense Guide to Understanding and Using Your Company's Financials* (Cambridge, Mass.: Perseus, 2000).

nificant investment in the company or the company has taken on significant debt, a balance sheet may be necessary to show the equity of the investors (in lieu of a balance sheet, a capitalization or "cap" table can be shown, see tables 3.11 and 3.12). A cash-flow statement can be a very important statement for companies since it can help predict where the company will be tight on cash or where the company may have extra cash to reinvest in capital equipment or infrastructure. For start-ups that are prerevenue, a cash-flow statement is not necessary. However, as we'll see below, a pseudo cash-flow statement can be appended to the bottom of an income statement to show where the company needs investment and how much.

The Income Statement

Let's look at an example income statement and dissect it line by line. We'll consider an example of a company making a product (a sensor) and show the pro forma numbers for year three, where the company anticipates selling $2 million of product (table 3.9). There are several points to note about this table. First, the statement is read from top to bottom, starting with the company's income (revenue/sales) at the top, subtracting costs and expenses, resulting in the "bottom line," the profit. The statement is divided into two major sections: the top section shows how much gross profit the company will make (sales of product minus the cost of producing that product); the second section shows how much net profit the company will have after paying all other expenses associated with running the company (e.g., research and development expenses). In the top section, the company income is shown as sales of the product. For some companies, income may be more than sales; for example, it may have income from grants or service contracts. These sources of income may be lumped together as revenue.

Although informative, this example income statement could be improved. For instance, it would be important to know how may units the $2 million in sales represents. From that number, the management team (and the savvy investor) would be able to assess some of the fundamental assumptions of the business plan by asking the following questions:

- Are there enough sales people to sell that many units in a year?
- Is there enough manufacturing capacity (e.g., employees, space) to deliver that many units?
- With that many units and the growth rate predicted, should the manufacturing be outsourced?

TABLE 3.9 Example of a year-three income statement for a start-up

INCOME STATEMENT	YEAR 3	DESCRIPTION
Sales	$2 million	The amount customers paid for the product sold (often referred to as revenue)
Cost of goods sold (COGS)	$900,000	The cost of making the product—namely, parts, raw materials, and direct labor (sometimes referred to as cost of sales, COS)
Gross profit	$1,100,000	The profit, or "margin," taking into account the cost of producing the product (sales minus COGS) (sometimes referred to as gross margin)
GM %	55%	Gross (profit) margin as a percentage of sales
Operating expenses		These are all the expenses *not* associated with producing the product
Research and development	$300,000	Expenses associated with developing new products or making revisions to the current product; include salaries for product-development engineers and any equipment or supplies required (e.g., parts for prototypes)
Sales and marketing	$200,000	Expenses associated with promoting and selling the product; salary and commission for sales reps, marketing personnel, tradeshows, advertising, website
General and administrative	$350,000	A broad category that includes senior management salary (CEO, VPs), rent, utilities, insurance, legal fees, office equipment
Total operating expenses	$850,000	
Operating income	$250,000	Gross profit minus operating expenses (sometimes referred to as operating profit)
Nonoperating expenses/income	−$25,000	Taxes, interest income
Net income	$225,000	(sometimes referred to as net profit)

- Are there enough service people to service the units sold (e.g., repair failed units, answer application questions)?
- Is there enough cash to purchase the raw materials prior to getting paid for those units?

A further improvement would be expressing key financial numbers as a percentage of sales. These figures would show what percentage of the incoming cash is associated with the various costs. For example, the cost of producing the product (COGS) equals 45 percent of each sales dollar ($900,000 ÷ 2,000,000 = 45 percent), resulting in a gross margin (GM) of 55 percent of sales. Investors often look closely at the GM percentage and compare it to that of other companies in similar industries. Some industries have a "rule of thumb" GM percentage: retail, 5–15 percent; manufacturing, 30–60 percent; and software, 75–90 percent. The percentage of sales represented by the other expenses shown in the table are as follows:

Research and Development   15 percent

Sales and Marketing   10 percent

General and Administrative   17.5 percent

Since these numbers are best guesses, it is good to know what investors are usually looking for as reasonable. For example, at a large, research-intensive corporation, R&D expenses might amount to 10 percent of sales. But for a start-up, a higher number is expected since a larger investment will be needed to develop the product (of course in the early years, the percentage is extremely high since sales are low). As the product is further developed and eventually launched, sales and marketing expenses will ramp up the company operations to pursue customers. A typical figure for sales and marketing expenses may be 30 percent of revenue. Thus, the figure given above might be criticized as too low.

A complete income statement for our example company is shown in table 3.10. There are several things to note about it. First, the table shows that the company loses money in the first three years while operating on little or no sales. A line for the cumulative losses (net income [cumulative]) over time shows the amount of total loss for the company before the company becomes profitable. This number (approximately $1.5 million) represents the estimate for what the company needs as an investment to reach profitability.[38] Second, below the income statement is a pseudo cash-flow statement (cash

38. Two terms, which are often used interchangeably, are associated with a company's profitability: "cash-flow positive" and "break even." Cash-flow positive refers to the monthly cash flows of the company. In other words, for each month, did the company earn more than it spent (i.e.,

balance) to show the timing of the investment and its effect on the cash flow of the company. This is particularly useful for scenario planning, especially when multiple rounds of investment will be required. Third, the margins (gross profit percentage) increase over time as production becomes more efficient (less labor required), the cost of parts goes down (the company is now buying in quantity), and the prices go up (once the company drops the "early-adopter discount"). Fourth, R&D expenses rise over time, based on a product-development plan that shows a series of products being developed. Fifth, sales and marketing expenses rise sharply over time as the company hires more sales people, attends more trade shows, and places more ads. And, finally, general and administrative costs are mostly flat since the majority of the executives were hired early to manage the company.

A narrative, such as the one above, describing the numbers and their trends should be included as part of the financial plan so that investors will see that the management has a rationale for the numbers (i.e., they aren't just made up) and investors won't have an unmanageable number of questions for the company.

For a live presentation, one would never use the income statement shown in table 3.10 since it has too much detail. It would be relegated to the reading deck or an appendix. An alternative is a profit and loss chart showing some of the key numbers (fig. 3.5). This allows one to quickly see the extent of investment needed and the projected upside (revenue) that an investment could generate.

For some companies, the prospect of revenue may be many years away, or the strategy is to partner with a larger company prior to launching the product. For example, a company developing a drug may not see sales of the product for years. Its business strategy may be to pursue venture capital for preclinical development, pursue a pharma partner for development through Phase II, and then either license the drug or sell the company. In these cases, the financial projections will focus on expenses required to meet key milestones (e.g., IND application, completion of first-in-human trials).

The Capitalization Table

The capitalization or "cap" table shows the investment and ownership positions of the company. There are a number of ways to represent company

---

make profit)? Break even refers to the point were the cumulative cash flows reach zero. For a start-up, the amount of negative cash flows each month (losses) must be paid for either by debt or by investment. Once the cumulative cash flows equal the investment (or debt), the company has reached break even.

TABLE 3.10 Complete pro forma income statement

INCOME STATEMENT

	YEAR 1		YEAR 2		YEAR 3		YEAR 4		YEAR 5	
Units	—		5		16		27		50	
Unit price			$100		$125		$130		$150	
Sales	—		$500	100%	$2,000	100%	$3,510	100%	$7,500	100%
COGS	—		$400	80%	$1,100	55%	$1,575	45%	$2,200	29%
GROSS PROFIT	—		$100	20%	$900	45%	$1,935	55%	$5,300	71%
OPERATING EXPENSES										
Research and development	$200		$250	50%	$300	15%	$350	10%	$400	5%
Sales and marketing	$150		$200	40%	$500	25%	$800	23%	$1,000	13%
General and administrative	$250		$300	60%	$350	18%	$350	10%	$350	5%
Operating income	$(600)		$(650)	−130%	$(250)	−13%	$435	12%	$3,550	47%
Nonoperating income/exp	—		$(25)		$(25)		$(25)		$(25)	
NET INCOME	$(600)		$(625)	−125%	$(225)	−11%	$460	13%	$3,575	48%
Net income (cumulative)	$(600)		$(1,225)		$(1,450)		$(990)		$2,585	
CASH BALANCE										
Beginning balance	—		$(600)		$(1,225)		$(1,450)		$(990)	
Investment	—									
Ending balance	$(600)		$(1,225)		$(1,450)		$(990)		$2,585	

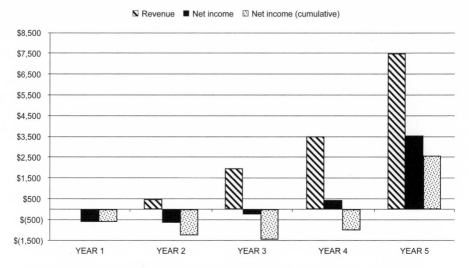

FIGURE 3.5 Profit and loss chart (based on income statement shown in table 3.10)

ownership. A pie chart will show the amount each investor owns. For a business plan, however, a more sophisticated format is needed to show the ownership of the company, the investment at each round, the price per share for each round, and the resulting ownership after each round. For a company with no investment, the cap table is fairly simple (table 3.11). Using our example company from above, if the company had raised $1.5 million but was seeking additional capital for expanding overseas or developing a new product, its cap table would reflect those investments (table 3.12). This table shows two rounds of investment, the amount invested in each round ($500,000 in the first, $1 million in the second), the price paid per share in each round, the shares issued for the round, and the resulting ownership percentages after each round. It also shows the hiring of the management team during the first round of investment. The cap table spreadsheet can be found at researchtorevenue.com.

KEY STEP **Raising Initial Capital**

Although funding through the founder's lab may help to further develop the technology, at some point the company must seek the capital to start commercialization activities and carry out the plans being developed as part of the business plan. As described in Chapter 2, this funding comes in two basic

TABLE 3.11 Capitalization for a company with no investments

FOUNDING	AMOUNT RAISED ($)	SHARES	% OWNERSHIP (FOUNDING)
Price per share ($)	—	—	—
Founder 1	—	1,000,000	30.8
Founder 2	—	1,000,000	30.8
Founder 3	—	1,000,000	30.8
University	—	250,000	7.7
Total after founding	—	3,250,000	100.0

forms: dilutive and nondilutive. Dilutive capital comes from investors (venture capitalists, angel investors) and is invested into the company in return for equity, thus diluting the equity of the owners of the company. Nondilutive capital does not involve sharing in ownership and comes in the form of grants.

The type and amount of capital required at any given stage will vary over time as the company grows.

Preseed Capital

Preseed capital helps fund activities associated with organizing and forming the company. The expenses at this stage run in the $5,000–50,000 range and include legal fees for incorporation and setting up the corporate documents (e.g., the operating agreement, stock certificates, etc.), fees to the university for licensing or patent reimbursement, and consulting fees to advisers to get early information for the business plan (e.g., market research, regulatory path). This money can come from the founders (e.g., each puts in $5,000 to get the company started), friends or family members, or local/university start-up funds ("company inception grants").

Seed Capital

When the company needs to begin early operations, the next level of financing is seed capital.[39] This capital allows the company to do pivotal studies or reach a milestone that will demonstrate some level of commercial potential, which will answer the "go/no go" questions for both the investors and the found-

39. The distinctions between preseed, seed, series A, and so on are somewhat arbitrary.

TABLE 3.12 Capitalization for a company with investments

		AMOUNT RAISED ($)	SHARES	% OWNERSHIP (FOUNDING)	% OWNERSHIP (FIRST ROUND)	% OWNERSHIP (SECOND ROUND)
Founding, price per share $0	Founder 1	—	1,000,000	30.8	14.8	10
	Founder 2	—	1,000,000	30.8	14.8	10
	Founder 3	—	1,000,000	30.8	14.8	10
	University	—	250,000	7.7	3.7	3
	Subtotal	—	3,250,000	100.0	48.1	33
	Total after founding	—	3,250,000	100.0		
	Postmoney valuation —					
First round, price per share $0.20	CEO	—	800,000	—	11.9	8
	VP business development	—	200,000	—	3.0	2
	Investor	500,000	2,500,000	—	37.0	26
	Subtotal	500,000	3,500,000	—	51.9	36
	Total after first round	500,000	6,750,000	—	100.0	
	Postmoney valuation $1,350,000					
Second round, price per share $0.35	Investor	1,000,000	2,857,143	—	—	30
	Subtotal	1,000,000	2,857,143	—	—	30
	Total after second round	1,500,000	9,607,143	—	—	100
	Postmoney valuation $3,362,500					

ers. The studies may involve building a working benchtop prototype of the product, performing an animal study to demonstrate modulation of disease by a therapeutic, ascertaining a critical property in a material that will demonstrate a product's superiority, or coding a software prototype with minimal feature sets. The results of these early-stage activities will often determine the future of the company: it might be that the technology just did not work and the company should think about folding or pivoting to another application or product; the results might be ambiguous and more seed funding will be needed to reach a pivotal milestone; or the results might be promising and warrant investor-grade capital. In a few cases where the technical risk is low at this stage (which is rare for most university start-ups), the seed capital is used to pay for management or consultants to further develop the business and marketing side. These steps may include business development activities; partnership development with an industrial partner; or market research activities to better define the market need, trends driving the market, and market growth. The amount of seed capital varies but is usually not more than a few hundred thousand dollars.

At the preseed and seed stages of investing, the value of the company is often difficult to determine. The company rarely has a product to sell, much less significant revenue. Valuations are often a best guess, and they are often a point of significant contention between the company, which wants a high valuation and less dilution, and the investor, who wants the opposite.

A popular way to invest at this stage is in the form of a loan or convertible note. A convertible note sets forth terms for loaning the money to the company (the capital provider holds the "note"), and the note can be converted into equity at the first institutional financing round (e.g., Series A). A typical scenario involves the note converting to equity with a discount (e.g., 25 percent) to the current stock price, reflecting the risk taken by the note holder in putting money into the company at an earlier, riskier stage. There are several advantages of a convertible note:

- DELAY IN SETTING VALUATION. By setting the valuation at a later date, more sophisticated investors (angels or VCs) are setting the stock price and the company has progressed to the point where there is measurable value.
- SPEED AND SIMPLICITY. The issuance of a convertible note, given the reduced negotiations around valuation and other terms, can be done in days, as compared to months for an equity investment. The simplicity of the transaction also results in lower legal fees.

- RETAINING CONTROL. The convertible note, as compared to equity, does not usually provide the investor a board seat or veto rights.

The level of preparation to get seed capital from an investor varies with the investor, the amount needed, and the stage of the company. An example of a convertible note can be found at researchtorevenue.com.

SBIR Grants

SBIR (and the related STTR) grants are one of the best sources of nondilutive funding for technology development, feasibility, prototype development, or proof of concept (for an overview of the SBIR grants, see Chapter 2 or go to SBIR.gov). An overview of the SBIR grant application process is shown in table 3.13.

In preparing an SBIR/STTR application, it is important to keep in mind the funding agency's review criteria. The following are the NIH's SBIR/STTR review criteria:

SIGNIFICANCE. Does the project address an important problem or a critical barrier to progress in the field? If the aims of the project are achieved, how will scientific knowledge, technical capability, and/or clinical practice be improved? How will successful completion of the aims change the concepts, methods, technologies, treatments, services, or preventative interventions that drive this field? Does the proposed project have commercial potential to lead to a marketable product, process, or service? (In the case of Phase II, Fast-Track, and Phase II, Competing Renewals, does the Commercialization Plan demonstrate a high probability of commercialization?)

Here, emphasize the critical unmet need, the commercial potential of the innovation, and/or the societal benefits. In addition to explaining how the technology will solve an important problem, if applicable, show how the solution is relevant to the funding agency.

INVESTIGATOR(S). Are the PD/PIs [principal directors/principal investigators], collaborators, and other researchers well suited to the project? If [they are] Early Stage Investigators or New Investigators, or in the early stages of independent careers, do they have appropriate experience and training? If established, have they demonstrated an ongoing record of accomplishments that have advanced their field(s)? If the project is collaborative or multi-PD/PI, do the investigators have

TABLE 3.13 Timeline for a SBIR/STTR grant submission

MONTHS BEFORE SUBMISSION	ACTIVITY
6–8	Determine eligibility
	• Do you have a principal investigator (PI) with > 51% of time devoted to the company? (SBIR)
	• Is the company owned > 51% by individuals?*
	• Are you U.S. owned?
	Identify solicitation topic and agency that fits the company's technology
	• NIH: http://grants.nih.gov/grants/funding/sbir.htm
	• NSF: http://www.nsf.gov/eng/iip/sbir/
	Contact program officer from target agency and review proposal concept
3–5	Obtain government registrations for electronic submission
	• DUNS number: required for all U.S. government grantees: http://fedgov.dnb.com/webform
	• System for Award Management (SAM) registration: www.sam.gov/portal/public/SAM/
	• SBIR company registration: http://www.sbir.gov/registration
	• eRA Commons registration (NIH): https://public.era.nih.gov/commons/
	• Fastlane registration (NSF): https://www.fastlane.nsf.gov/fastlane.jsp
	Outline application structure
	Begin writing application
	Obtain letters of support and subcontracting agreements
1–2	Get feedback
	Edit/revise
	Proofread
0	Submit 5 days before submission date in case there are any last-minute glitches with the electronic submission
Postsubmission	Track submission via eRA Commons or FastLane
	Expect scoring and feedback 6–7 months after submission

Source: Adapted from NC Fisher Research, LLC (www.ncfisherresearch.com)

*This requirement has recently changed to allow VC-backed companies to apply for SBIR grants; check the latest eligibility requirements.

complementary and integrated expertise; are their leadership approach, governance, and organizational structure appropriate for the project?

Securing principal investigators for SBIRs is one of the more difficult tasks in the application process. Many faculty founders who would be the best PIs can't leave their academic post to serve in this capacity.[40] The next-best option is a graduating Ph.D. student or a postdoc. Their lack of experience can be a deficiency but can be overcome with several consultants (including the faculty founder).

INNOVATION. Does the application challenge and seek to shift current research or clinical practice paradigms by utilizing novel theoretical concepts, approaches or methodologies, instrumentation, or interventions? Are the concepts, approaches or methodologies, instrumentation, or interventions novel to one field of research or novel in a broad sense? Is a refinement, improvement, or new application of theoretical concepts, approaches or methodologies, instrumentation, or interventions proposed?

Reviewers are looking for an innovative approach to an existing problem that can involve a completely new solution or a significant reduction in cost or increase in efficiency of a current solution. It is important to understand the difference between the innovative nature of the proposed study and the innovation of the technology. The proposed study might simply be reproducing, under much more rigorous conditions, the results demonstrated by the university laboratory. The proposed study might not appear innovative but the necessary first step in bringing the innovation to market. Make sure the reviewer sees the innovation as the backdrop to the proposed study.

APPROACH. Are the overall strategy, methodology, and analyses well-reasoned and appropriate to accomplish the specific aims of the project? Are potential problems, alternative strategies, and benchmarks for success presented? If the project is in the early stages of development, will the strategy establish feasibility and will particularly risky aspects be managed?

If the project involves human subjects and/or NIH-defined clinical research, are the plans to address 1) the protection of human subjects from research risks, and 2) the inclusion (or exclusion) of individuals on the basis of sex/gender, race, and ethnicity, as well as the inclusion

---

40. If a nonacademic PI can't be found, the STTR route is best.

or (exclusion) of children, justified in terms of the scientific goals and research strategy proposed?

Reviewers are looking for well-designed experiments for adequately testing the feasibility of the concept. This includes appropriate reagents, controls, and statistical design. It is important to acknowledge potential problem areas and propose alternative approaches.

ENVIRONMENT. Will the scientific environment in which the work will be done contribute to the probability of success? Are the institutional support, equipment, and other physical resources available to the investigators adequate for the project proposed? Will the project benefit from unique features of the scientific environment, subject populations, or collaborative arrangement?[41]

In addition to the criteria listed, one should do the following:

- WRITE TO THE REVIEWER. Most reviewers are not experts in your field, so don't assume they have intuitive knowledge of your proposal or know the acronyms and jargon of the field. Effectively communicate the importance of your work relative to the field (have a colleague outside your field read the application to assure good communication).
- BE CLEAR AND CONCISE. One of the most common comments from applicants is "the reviewer did not understand my technology." This is due to either 1) not gearing the explanation of the technology to the reviewer's knowledge level or 2) lack of clarity and conciseness. To this latter point, make every word count and throw out the ones that don't.
- HELP THE REVIEWER. The reviewer has to review many applications. The longer he/she spends trying to figure out what you are saying or what the point is, the less time he/she has to give the application careful consideration. Keep in mind, too, that the reviewer has to complete the evaluation form. Make it easy for him/her to identify the significance, innovation, and approach with key words: "The significance of this work is . . ." or "This innovative approach will . . ."
- BE PASSIONATE. The application needs to tell a compelling story about the innovation, its relevance to the agency, and its future impact on the world. Don't be shy about letting your passion about what you are doing shine through.

---

41. "Definitions of Criteria and Considerations for SBIR-STTR Critiques," Office of Extramural Research, National Institutes of Health, http://grants.nih.gov/grants/peer/critiques/sbir-sttr.htm (accessed 13 November 2013).

The major components of the application include the Abstract/Specific Aims, Research Plan, Budget and Justification, and Personnel Information.

Abstract/Specific Aims (one page)

Here you will outline the objectives of the proposed studies and activities. This is one of the most important parts of the application since it provides a concise summary of the project and sets the stage for the research plan. Consider the following when writing this section:

- Think of this section as the "executive summary" of the application. You must make a compelling case here or the entire application will appear weak. This is likely the only section of the proposal that anyone other than the primary reviewers will read.
- Set up the specific aims this way: 1) identify the problem or unmet need, 2) discuss the current solutions to that problem, 3) point to the gaps and shortcomings of the current solutions, and 4) explain how your innovative solution will solve the problem.
- Propose aims that are measureable and quantifiable. The reviewer needs to know how you will measure success. For example, don't simply claim to make an "improvement," but claim a "threefold improvement" relative to the current approach.
- Propose aims that are achievable. Less is more with specific aims. One of the most common mistakes is to put forth too many or difficult to achieve aims or to underestimate the time required to achieve the aims. It's best to propose two or three aims that can be achieved in the intended time frame that will support the subsequent proposal for a larger, Phase II application.
- SBIR/STTR funding is for non-hypothesis-driven research and development. Do not propose research whose goal is to answer a hypothesis. The research should answer very specific questions that will demonstrate the feasibility of the technology, which is the purpose of Phase I grants.

The structure of this page should be as follows:

INTRODUCTORY PARAGRAPH:

- Statement of long-term health-related goal (one sentence)
- Background/significance of the problem (one to two sentences)
- Preliminary data/state of the art (two to three sentences)
- Data gaps/controversy (one to two sentences)
- Clearly defined hypothesis/specific goal (one to two sentences)

SPECIFIC AIMS/MILESTONES:

- Two to five aims (one sentence each)
- Each focused to prove hypothesis/develop product
- Logical order with no dead ends

SUMMARY STATEMENT:

- Emphasize novel product and innovative approach and impact on field (2–3 sentences)

Research Plan (six pages)

At the core of the SBIR/STTR application is the research plan, which outlines the objectives and activities for the studies to be conducted. It should be broken down into three sections: Significance, Innovation, and Research Design/Methods. For most faculty founders, this section will be familiar since similar information is required for many federal research grants. You should describe a detailed experimental plan for each aim as well as anticipated problems and alternative approaches. Refer to the review criteria often when writing this section.

Budget and Justification

The budget spells out the financial support needed by the company to complete the proposed specific aims. In preparing a budget, your first consideration is what expenses are allowable and which are not. In general, an expense is allowable if it is reasonable (i.e., in accordance with company policy and award conditions), allocatable (i.e., is chargeable to a project), and consistent (i.e., is treated consistently according to company policy and general accounting practices). According to Federal Acquisition Regulation (FAR) 48 Part 31, unallowable expenses include advertising costs, bad debt costs, compensation for personal services, contingencies, contributions or donations, entertainment costs, fines and penalties, independent research and development costs, insurance costs, interest and other financial costs, legislative lobbying costs, organization costs, patents costs,[42] relocation costs, royalty costs, taxes, travel costs, and alcoholic beverages.

The next step is to determine whether the costs are direct or indirect. Direct costs are those that can be identified specifically with a particular project or activity (i.e., easily/readily attached to a project with a high degree of accuracy), for example, salary, equipment, supplies, animals, consultants.

---

42. Although patent costs are not specifically allowed, some companies have used the SBIR fee to pay for patent costs. Consult with SBIR consultants and the SBIR program officer to verify.

Indirect costs are those incurred for common or joint objectives that cannot be readily or specifically identified with a particular project or other company function (e.g., utilities, telephone, offices supplies, insurance, postage, legal.)[43]

When in doubt about whether a cost is direct or indirect, refer to the funding agency's guidelines. If doubt remains, provide ample justification of how the cost will impact the ability to complete the project.

Assemble the budget on a spreadsheet that lists the following budget items: salaries, benefits, consultant fees, materials and supplies, equipment, travel, subcontracts, core facilities and other services, animals, indirect costs, and the fee. Phase I award limits and project time frames vary by agency, generally ranging from $100,000 over six months to $250,000 a year for two years. Funding agencies publish these guidelines, but they are only guidelines. A well-written proposal with the right justification can sometimes be funded above the guidelines.[44] Once the budget has been developed, it needs to be transferred to the standard online budget sheets provided as part of the grant applications. Table 3.14 shows each component of the Research and Related (R&R) budget sheets to be completed.

Personnel Information

Include a biosketch for all key personnel and named consultants using the biosketch format page (four-page limit, 15 publications). The personal statements should demonstrate that these individuals have the experience and knowledge necessary to successfully complete the project.

Additional Documentation

If relevant, the application should include other supporting information.

HUMAN SUBJECTS PROTECTION/VERTEBRATE ANIMAL CARE. If animal or human subjects are going to be used as part of the project, information must be provided as part of the application. Instructions spell out the required information (e.g., Institutional Animal Care and Use Committee).

CONTRACTUAL ARRANGEMENTS. Any subcontracts the company will engage in need to be shown with either actual contracts or letters from subcontractors outlining the scope and cost of work to be done.

---

43. Thank you to Jim Peterson, Research Solutions Consulting, for providing this information.
44. If the request is for significantly more than $250,000 and one or two years, consider a FastTrack application that combines Phase I and II into one submission. Though appealing, it does require significant work to anticipate and outline a large number of specific aims as well as to develop a cogent commercialization plan.

TABLE 3.14 Budget detail for an SBIR/STTR grant

BUDGET SHEETS (DATA ENTRY SCREENS)	COMPONENT	DESCRIPTION AND NOTES
Components A and B	A: Senior/key personnel	
	B: Other personnel	
Components C, D, and E	C: Equipment	Must list any equipment over $5,000
	D: Travel	Travel to consultants domestic and foreign
	E: Participant/trainee support	
Components F–K	F: Other direct costs	Materials/supplies, publications costs, consultant services, computer services, subawards, equipment or facility rental
	G: Direct total	Sum of A through F
	H: Indirect costs	For Phase I, 40% typical
	I: Total direct + indirect	
	J: Fee	Not more than 7% of total
	K: Budget justification	Information to support the budget request—should justify A through J; upload one pdf document. A sub-award budget requires a separate budget justification.

Source: Used with permission of J. Peterson, Research Solutions Consulting.

Subcontracts can be made to the university (e.g., core lab) or another third party (e.g., contract research organization [CRO], machine shop, software developer). Only one-third of the work can be subcontracted for an SBIR, although higher limits are permissible for an STTR.

LETTERS OF SUPPORT/COLLABORATION. Include letters addressed to the PI from all key personnel and consultants that outline the resources they will provide as part of the collaboration and/or reiterate the innovation and impact of the product, making sure they are recent and include the title and grant solicitation (no blanket letters).

FACILITIES AND EQUIPMENT. This is an opportunity to highlight the facilities and equipment that will help make this project successful. If the company is going to be housed in an on-campus incubator, highlight the access and synergy that location will provide.

Finally, as you begin assembling the SBIR or STTR grant applications, keep the following in mind.

- Allocate enough time. Writing the research plan can take up to 70 hours, and the time it takes to assemble the application can approach 40 hours. Allow for enough time for external review by colleagues and coworkers (approximately two to three weeks turnaround) and time to address the feedback.
- Don't be afraid to pull the plug at the last minute if the application is not complete. If it's not ready, wait for the next submission period. It is better to submit a complete, well-thought-out application than a rushed one.[45]
- If the technology has multiple applications, consider multiple applications to different institutes (e.g., the National Institute of Allergy and Infectious Diseases [NIAID] and/or the National Cancer Institute [NCI]).
- Consider an SBIR contract, which is different than a grant. Many agencies will issue requests for small companies with innovative technologies to produce, under contract, some tangible item (e.g., nanoparticle, reagent, mouse model, polymer material, etc.). The contract can help to develop and validate the company's technology.

Resubmissions[46]
According to the NIH, these are the most common reasons SBIR/STTR applications are rejected:

- Lack of innovative ideas
- Lack of sufficient experimental data
- Lack of knowledge of published relevant work
- Lack of experience in essential methodology

45. Be aware of the timing cycling for grant submissions. For example, results of an April NIH submission might not be available until November, which would preclude a resubmission by the August deadline and perhaps the December deadline. This could mean a one-year cycle time for an application.

46. The NIH's resubmission guidelines are in the process of changing. Rather than addressing individual reviewer's comments separately, you might be able to simply submitting a new application that incorporates the reviewer's comments.

- Uncertainty concerning future directions
- Questionable reasoning in experimental approach
- Unfocused, diffuse, or superficial research plan
- Absence of acceptable scientific rationale
- Overambitious

If the application does not score well enough to be funded, wait for the comments to come back and talk to the program officer to get an idea of the discussion around the table about your application. Also review the comments ("Summary Statement") and take the comments to heart. A common reaction to the comments is that the "reviewers just did not get it," which may be true and indicates a need for clarity. From the comments and the discussion with the program manager, make an honest assessment about the likelihood of a better score upon resubmission. If the comments point to specific addressable points, then consider resubmission. If the comments point to a lack of clarity, poor overall approach, or lack of innovation, then maybe a resubmission is not advisable.

KEY STEP Finding Space

With some initial capital, from either investors or grants, space may be needed to begin company operations. The space can be office space for company personnel, meeting space, or lab space for technology-development studies and product-development activities. Start-up space requirements will depend on the company's activities and the mix of those activities to be done in company-leased space versus those outsourced to a third-party vendor. In some cases, especially early on, the most capital-efficient approach is to outsource as much as possible to others, which will reduce the need to purchase capital equipment or to rent high-cost wet-lab space. For example, in pharmaceutical development, it is possible to outsource almost every aspect of the operations, from lead discovery and optimization to animal and human testing using CROs. Outsourcing has limitations, however, especially where specialized scientific equipment or technology know-how can be found only among the founders. Outsourcing is also limited by certain grant requirements. For example, SBIR grants require that a majority of the work is done by the company in company facilities.

Many universities and regions are developing incubators and accelerators for early-stage start-ups. Although the definition of the term "incubator" varies depending on who's using it, an incubator generally offers space and equipment for a company, and it is sometimes shared among a number of companies. Accelerators are incubators with some "value-added" services such as advisers or "entrepreneurs-in-residence," seed funding, or interim management. These facilities are ideal for start-ups for a number of reasons. First, the cost for leasing the space is appealing because the rent may be subsidized and the amount of space rented is small or shared (e.g., one lab bench versus an entire lab). Second, the obligation of the company is small since lease terms are typically short (one or two years), thus reducing the risk if funding becomes tight but also allowing the company flexibility to move to a larger space as it grows (most commercial leases are for five years). Finally, working in a facility with other companies provides the opportunity for synergy and cross-talk between companies. The other companies can be good sources for investor references, legal help, or technical advice. Another option utilized by some campuses is to house the company in the founder's lab. Although conflict of interest and confidentially issues need to be managed, this can be an ideal option for a company with SBIR grant funds needing a single bench and access to specialized equipment that exists in the founder's lab. In this case, the company pays rent for the space and pays a fee for use of certain pieces of equipment. A copy of a university Facility Use Agreement can be found at researchtorevenue.com.

Leasing Commercial Space

As a company grows, it will need more space and will often move into leased commercial space. Finding commercial space involves either dealing directly with commercial real estate firms that have space for lease or engaging a real estate agent who will represent the company. In the latter case, it is customary to sign an agreement with the agent for a period time (e.g., 6–12 months) whereby the company and the agent will have an exclusive relationship. In other words, during that time, the company cannot sign a lease agreement independent of the agent, and the company will not use another agent. Agents make their money by collecting a percentage of the lease deal, and they are not going to work hard to find the best space if the exclusive arrangement is not in place. The cost of renting most commercial real estate is based on a price per square foot, usually on an annual basis. So if you are looking at a 3,000-square-foot space and the price per square foot quoted is $15, then the annual rent is $45,000 ($15 × 3,000, or $3,750 per month). It is important to know what is included in the price per square foot. It often includes the charges associated with the property ownership: real estate taxes, insurance, and common area maintenance charges (TICAM). These charges are typically split pro rata among the different tenants leasing space in a building. Leases that include these charges are referred to as net leases, NNN leases, or "triple net" leases. The real estate agent might say, "That space is $15 a foot, triple net" or "$15 a foot, all in." That means the 3,000 square-foot space will cost $3,750/month with no additional costs, other than utilities or perhaps space improvements (see below).

When it comes time for leasing space, it is important to understand the elements of a lease agreement:

- IDENTIFICATION INFORMATION. The owner (lessor), tenant (lessee), leased premise address, and square footage of the unit with accompanying drawings depicting the space are listed here.
- LEASE TERM. This includes start and end dates and details of any free-rent or reduced-rent time given.
- LEASE PAYMENTS. This defines the annual lease amount and the interval payments (e.g., monthly, every four weeks, etc.). It may show a break-down of the lease amount into the base rent and the other charges (e.g., TICAM). This clause will also spell out when the interval payments are due (e.g., first day of each month) and how to make the payment (send a check or wire transfer). For a start-up, some property owners might be open to a partial deferment of the lease payments (e.g., the total over five years split into different amounts among the years; the payments in year one will be much lower than year five) to give the company more cash up front for operations.
- IMPROVEMENTS AND ALTERATIONS. In some cases, the space may need to be altered or improved prior to the company moving in (in an extreme case, the space may be a shell). These leasehold or tenant improve-ments are usually undertaken by the owner (lessor) and a portion of the improvement may be included in the lease payments (e.g., spread over the term of the payments). The amount included in the lease payments is a point of negotiation: the more specialized the tenant improvements, the more the tenant may be asked to pay (painting the walls is generic so the owner likely will cover this cost, but special-use improvements, that don't increase the overall value of the space, such as creating a clean room may need to be paid for by the tenant). Alterations or improve-ments made after the company moves in are usually company-specific (e.g., a fume hood installed) and therefore are typically the responsibil-ity of the tenant. The owner often needs to approve the work and may

do the work (and bill the company) or approve of a contractor to do the work.

- USE OF SPACE. This defines the activities permitted in the space as well as any restrictions (e.g., research and development but not manufacturing, or restrictions on chemical or biohazards).
- REPAIR AND MAINTENANCE OBLIGATIONS. This outlines who is responsible for repair and maintenance of the facility (i.e., the tenant vs. the owner).
- COMMON AREA DEFINITION. Common areas are those areas and facilities that the owner or others in or near the space might furnish for general common use (e.g., parking lot, grassy area, reception area).
- COMMON AREA MAINTENANCE CHARGES. These are charges the lessor pays to maintain common areas (e.g., cutting the grass in front of the building). These are part of the TICAM charges.
- REAL ESTATE TAX CHARGES. Each city/county charges property tax on land and buildings. This clause outlines who is responsible for paying the tax bill. Usually part of TICAM.
- ASSIGNMENT AND SUBLEASING RIGHTS. This is a very important clause for start-ups since things rarely go as planned. The company might have funding difficulties and need to go dormant for a while or move into a smaller space before the end of the lease, or it might grow so quickly that it needs to move out before the end of the term. In either case, the company has an obligation to the owner for the term of the lease. One option is to assign or sublease the space to a third party.
- UTILITY OBLIGATIONS. Some lessors include the cost of utilities as part of the lease payment; others have the lessee pay for utilities separately.
- ENTRY AND INSPECTION NOTICES. These are the rights of the lessor to enter the facility and inspect it for proper use or damage.
- INSURANCE RESPONSIBILITIES. Insurance must exist for fire, theft, flood, and liability. This clause outlines who is responsible for paying those insurance premiums. Often part of TICAM.

An alternative to leasing space directly is to sublease space from another tenant. In an area with significant start-up activity, there likely will be start-ups on either side of the growth curve: not getting the funding/revenue necessary to maintain their space or growing too fast for their space. In these cases, a start-up might only be several years into a five-year lease and need to sublease. This can be an ideal situation for a new start-up seeking space at a possible discount for the short term.

KEY STEP **Raising Growth Capital**

Up to this point, the company has gotten at most a few hundred thousand dollars from grants or seed capital from friends or families or an angel investor. Growth capital is the cash for making the company operational: completing the management and technical teams and making significant progress in product development, sales, and marketing. The source of this capital is usually an institution (venture capital group or angel group) and comes in the form of an equity (dilutive) investment.

Selecting Funds to Target

The chances of successfully raising growth capital are related to how closely aligned the start-up's market focus and business strategy is with the investment focus of the funders. There are four main criteria by which to select VC funds to target: industry focus, stage of investing, fund size, and geographic reach. Some VC firms will focus on one specific industry segment (e.g., life science or information technology), whereas others will consider several segments. A VC firm's choice of industry focus is usually based on the fund partners' past experience in running companies in that industry or what they have learned from past investment experience. An easy way to understand a firm's industry focus is to look at the companies in which it has previously made investments.

In general, the smaller the fund, the earlier the stage at which the start-up can be to be considered for investment. The relationship between fund size and stage of company comes down to the amount the firm invests in each start-up. For a firm with a $100 million fund needing to make 10–15 investments to see an appropriate return, each investment is going to be on the order of $5 million–10 million, which is in line with funding amounts needed by an early-stage company (e.g., $2 million Series A + $6 million Series B). A firm with a much larger fund size would be investing in a later-stage company (e.g., a $10 million Series C or a $25 million series D, etc.). Another aspect of this relationship between fund size and stage of the company involves the cost to the investor of doing the deal (e.g., partner time, due diligence cost, legal fees, etc.): it costs a firm nearly as much to do a $1 million deal as it does to do a $10 million deal, so unless there is a compelling reason to do so, large firms don't typically do small deals. Of course there are exceptions to every rule. Some of the larger firms will reserve a small amount to invest in early-stage start-ups, but usually these types of deals are reserved for a management team they have backed in the past or for a CEO with a stellar track record with a game-changing technology.

Sorting firms by geographic reach can significantly limit the pool of funds to target. Angels and VCs tend to invest in their geographic region. That's great if your start-up is located in Silicon Valley but not so good if your start-up is based in Billings, Montana. Some firms invest strictly locally (e.g., in Boston) because they have enough "deal flow" in that locale, whereas others invest regionally (e.g., the Southeast) because the density of start-ups is lower. Investors tend to limit their investment geographically for several other reasons. First, their network of deal sources (e.g., entrepreneurs, universities) and talent tends to be centered around their geographic location. Second, companies are hard to manage from afar. Attending board meetings and face-to-face meetings with management is easier when the investor can drive or take a short flight to the company. In some cases, investments may come from outside the region when the local investor "syndicates," or brings other investors in on the deal. (This usually happens when the local firm needs to share risk or reach a level of funding that it can't reach by itself.) The easiest way to find these nonlocal syndicate partners is to look at press releases from local VC firms; they often list the other syndicate firms in the deal.

Introductions and Calls

Once the list of targeted investors has been made, the company needs to make contact with one of the partners of the firm or a member of the angel group. The worst way to make contact is to submit a business plan to a firm's website. Those go into a black hole and rarely result in follow-up, primarily because investors are extremely busy and they need some filtering mechanism to decide which opportunities are the highest priority. To increase your chances of getting the attention of an investor, you need a connection to the investor. This is where networking becomes invaluable. For example, the CEO might know an investor and make the contact directly. More common, a "friend of a friend" knows the investor. For example, one of your board members or key advisers might know the investor and can make an introduction, usually by e-mail, and perhaps attaching an executive summary of the business plan or the one-pager. Next is a follow up with a brief call (15 minutes, max) to introduce the company with an expanded elevator pitch and time for Q&A. The purpose of the introduction and call is not only to start building a relationship with the investor but specifically to get a face-to-face meeting to give the pitch.

Meetings and Pitches

The investor who takes the call is usually, but not always, the one who will be bringing the deal to the partners or angel group for consideration. Thus, not only does the investor need convincing about the upside of the opportunity, but he/she also needs help to make the case for the opportunity to others. The investor needs to understand the many aspects of the opportunity, its potential upside, and its potential risks. Given the limited time the investor has to concentrate on each potential investment, this information needs to be presented clearly and in bite-sized chunks he or she can assimilate easily. This convincing/educating starts with the first face-to-face meeting and the company pitch. The first meeting may be with any one or a combination of the following: A partner, an associate/junior partner, or a venture partner, the latter having specific domain expertise around your technology and product. The meeting will rarely last more than an hour and is where the company pitch is made.

The Company Pitch

Much has been written about preparing and making the company pitch. In general, two presentations are created: the "pitch deck" for the face-to-face meeting and a "reading deck," which is the pitch deck filled out with more text and details and polished so that it is clear to a person reading the deck without the presentation. In building the company pitch, it is important to understand how a university start-up pitch differs from a non-university-based company pitch. Although both pitches need to tell a story about how the world will be a better place with a product (or at least customers or patients will be happier, healthier, or more productive), both will describe a strategy for developing the product, and both will point out their product's competitive advantages, the university start-up is usually built around a key technology, innovation, or discovery derived from the academia. Thus, the pitch must address three things: 1) how the technology is going to be embodied in a product, 2) what key attributes of the technology and product will play out in terms of customer benefits and competitive advantages, and 3) what technical risks are associated with the technology/product.

There are a number of rules of thumb for putting together a pitch deck. Guy Kawasaki, best-selling author of *The Art of the Start*, has develop the 10/20/30 rule: there should be 10 slides, delivered in 20 minutes, and no slide should have a font size less than 30 points.[47] At minimum, the slides described below should be included, but if more are needed, be sure to keep the number to no more than 15.[48] Note that much of this information is derived from the business plan.

COVER/TITLE. This features the company name, logo (if any), and company tag line (if any). Also include the full contact information for the person handling the investor relationship (CEO, founder, etc.).

PROBLEM. Tell a story about how the world is today, emphasizing the inadequacies of current practices, the unmet needs, the obstacles in the way. If you can, make the problem specific using a person or a situation to illustrate your point. Make it clear how widespread the problem is (market size) but don't go into too much detail at this point.

SOLUTION. Tell a story about how the world will be a better place or patients will be healthier or customers will be more productive or businesses will be more profitable by using your solution or buying your product. Emphasize your product's benefits, but don't dive too deep into the technology yet (there will be time for that in later slides). A mocked-up image of the product makes it more real for the investor. If you have a widget that you can pass around, all the better.

TECHNOLOGY. Describe the underlying technology or "secret sauce" that will give the company a significant competitive advantage. Site a number of enabling features of the technology and how those translate into customer benefits. Note: this section can be combined with the Solution section if the technology and product are closely related.

BUSINESS MODEL. Investors in particular need to know up front how you plan to make money. For an early-stage, technology-based company, this section might not be completely formed. If there are options (e.g., licensing the product versus direct sales) choose the one that makes the most sense, but make the investor aware you have several strategies for value creation that will be more clear as the company matures.

MARKETING AND SALES. This will vary widely depending on the stage of the company and its business model. For a company that will have a product ready to launch in the next year or two, this slide provides a

---

47. "The 10/20/30 Rule of PowerPoint," *Guy Kawasaki* (blog), 30 December 2005, http://blog .guykawasaki.com/2005/12/the_102030_rule.html (accessed 11 December 2013).

48. Although Microsoft's PowerPoint is the standard tool for presenting the pitch, more impactful approaches should be considered. Prezi (prezi.com), for example, combines zooming and panning features with graphics to create stunning presentations.

high-level overview of your "go-to-market strategy," or how the product will be launched, marketed, and sold. For companies with a much longer lead time to product launch, this section may not have many details. For start-ups that will likely partner with another company (e.g., a pharmaceutical company), this slide can address business development (i.e., the development of a partnering deal).

COMPETITION. Present a simple table that the investor can easily understand (this is harder than you think!) that shows your product features and attributes relative to other products. Try and present a balanced but favorable comparison. Saying that there is no competition is rarely true or smart.

TEAM. Talk about the management team and key advisers. Put a (good looking) picture of each on the slide and talk about each in a sentence or two. Emphasize experience or domain expertise.

PROJECTIONS. You will need to sum up at the company's financial projections with a high level overview for three to five years.[49] At this level, presenting charts and graphs of the financials is sufficient. Don't make the mistake of putting up a spreadsheet with numbers and complexity that will bog down the presentation. The investor will focus on the answer to three questions: 1) Is the growth rate reasonable for this opportunity and market? 2) Are the gross margins reasonable for this industry? and 3) How much money will be lost before the company gets to revenue? The answer to the third question gives the investor an idea of the amount of investment required. Link the projections to milestones. For example, show a simple chart for the income statement and the year in which the company will reach certain milestones (e.g., prototype complete, regulatory approval, product launch). As mentioned, some companies (e.g., therapeutic companies) are going to be years away from revenue and gross margins, so the projections will be limited to expenses related to key milestones.

STATUS. Include short updates on various aspects of the company (e.g., product development, hiring the team, fund-raising, IP). An effective way to demonstrate the company's status is with a timeline showing where the company is today relative to past milestones that have been

---

49. Some argue that projections beyond three years are just guesswork, but for companies requiring significant product-development money (e.g., where regulatory approval is required), it might take several years of investment before significant revenue can be made.

achieved and the company's future activities, fund-raising, and milestones over the next 12–24 months.

THE ASK.[50] Summarize the presentation with three key points and end with the ask, indicating the amount of capital requested and providing a short list of "use of funds" and associated milestones.

There are a number of do's and don'ts when it comes to making the company pitch:

DO'S

- Tell a story, since stories are easy to remember and an easy way to engage the listener. The story should start with the Problem slide.
- Focus on the situation today (e.g., status quo, unmet needs, problems) and what the world would look like with your product (i.e., paint a picture of the future). Make the "between today and the future" as large and as believable as possible.
- Consider a tag-team presentation if it has considerable technical content, since the investors need to see that the faculty founder or CSO has a grasp of the complexities of the technology. A possible structure is first the CEO paints the picture of the vision, then the founder/CSO dives into the benefits of the technology, and then the CEO lays out the strategy for realizing the vision.
- Use short video clips (one to two minutes, max) where appropriate.
- Get your key points made early, since many presentations never get finished because of questions and tangents.
- Keep it short; 20 minutes, max.

DON'TS

- Don't put too much text on the slide; if you do, the audience will be reading while you are talking, and your presentation will lose its impact.
- Never read from your slides; if you need prompts, use images and graphics. Your slides should form a backdrop to support the key points you are making, guiding the listener through the presentation.
- Never put up a slide and then talk about something else. The audience will be reading while you are talking.
- Avoid overly technical language and acronyms that the investor may not be familiar with.

---

50. An alternative approach is to put the ask up front, on the second slide. This gets the number on the table so that the rest of the presentation is a justification of why the company needs that amount of money.

- Don't let tangents take control of the meeting; unless the discussion is productive to getting your pitch across, gently get the presentation back on track (e.g., "Your time is important so I want to make sure we cover all the points.").
- Don't spend too much time talking about the technology unless it's closely related to the product. Investors invest in products, not technology.

At end of the meeting, the investors will usually be very pleasant and might even be enthusiastic, but don't let this enthusiasm give you false hope; they see hundreds of pitches a year and are enthusiastic about many of them—but very few get funded. Don't let the meeting end with the investor saying "We'll be in touch." Ask if additional information is needed (e.g., a reading deck of the company pitch, a more complete business plan, customer references, etc.). A common response from the investor is "We really love the deal. Come back when you have a lead investor." This means either 1) they like the deal but don't have the time/expertise/energy to lead the deal, which entails conducting the due diligence and negotiations, 2) they like the deal but need some validation like other investors committing to the ideas, or 3) they don't really love the deal and this is a way to say "not interested." It's worth taking time to try to figure out what's really happening.

If the presentation goes well, the investor will bring the investment opportunity to the general partner meeting, which usually takes place weekly, where the partners discuss the company as a possible investment. The outcome of the meeting will be either a "pass" (no interest), interest but a need for more information (e.g., more company information or a phone call to a key opinion leader or consultant with expertise on the technology), or an invitation to present to a larger group of partners. If the company makes it to the next stage of consideration, the partners will agree to go ahead with due diligence and to draw up a term sheet for making the investment.[51] Although many things can derail the investment, making it to this point is a very positive sign.

In putting together the materials for the pitch, one essential perspective must be kept in mind. Investors get thousands of requests for their time and see hundreds of pitches and business plans to get to perhaps five or ten investments a year. In their screening process, they are looking for the "quick no"; that is, the red flag on the management team, the gap in the strategy,

---

51. Some investors may take an intermediate step before due diligence and a term sheet, especially for very early companies. If the company needs to do a "killer experiment"—that is, one whose outcome will either kill or validate the technology, the investor may write a check, usually under a promissory note, to fund the experiment.

the insurmountable technical hurdle, the small market size. Whatever it is, they are looking for it and can find it quickly so they can move on the next deal. This may be an unfair system for screening opportunities, but for investors who can't spend too much time or energy studying individual potential investment opportunities, it's the only approach for getting to a promising investment—even if it means missing something really revolutionary that could result in a big win. As such, it is crucial to get as many eyes as possible on these materials to look for sources of the "quick no."

Due Diligence, Term Sheet, and Deal Close

After several meetings and several pitches, the investor and the company will enter into an iterative process of information exchange and negotiation in order to close the round of investment. For the investor, the process might look something like this:

STEP 1. BEGIN DUE DILIGENCE. The investor will request information that addresses many aspects of the opportunity (e.g., business plan, ownership details, incorporation documents, financials and supporting assumptions and details, patents and patent applications, etc.). After reviewing the information, the investor might reach out to his/her network to get opinions on the opportunity (e.g., competition, market size) and/or do some additional research. At this point, the investor is getting an initial read on the risks and rewards associated with the opportunity.

STEP 2. NEGOTIATE COMPANY VALUATION. In parallel to some of the initial due diligence, the investor will negotiate the value of the company, the premoney valuation or "pre." This valuation sets the stock price and percentage of the company ownership the investor will receive.

STEP 3. DRAFT A TERM SHEET. If there are no obvious red flags (e.g., weak IP or a license agreement that will be difficult to renegotiate), and there is general agreement on the valuation, the investor will provide a draft term sheet outlining the terms of the investment. This will be the investor's first "offer" for investment and will include the investment amount, the share price (and thus the valuation of the company), and all the rights and stipulations that go along with accepting the investment. This is a draft and is open to negotiation.

STEP 4. MORE DUE DILIGENCE. If the draft term sheet or a modified version is close to being acceptable by both investor and company, additional in-depth due diligence is performed. The investor does not want to spend too much time during the initial due diligence (Step 1) if the investor's and the company's expectations of valuation differ too much. At this stage, if he/she has not already done so, the investor might bring in other investors to syndicate the deal.

STEP 5. FINAL TERM SHEET. The due diligence might have uncovered some details that affect the value of the company (rarely upward, e.g., a significant competitor or interfering patent), and the founders and management have had time to reflect on the term sheet, so the term sheet is negotiated to a final form that can be converted into the document to close the financing.

STEP 6. EVEN MORE DUE DILIGENCE. With a finalized term sheet, the investor does not want to leave any stone unturned until the final bits of due diligence work are completed.

STEP 7. CLOSE THE DEAL. The investor's attorneys prepare the final documents for the financing and small details are negotiated, but at this point the process should be close to being over. With the final documents printed, all of the parties sign to close the deal. Shortly afterward, the investor will wire the money to the company's bank account.[52]

Term Sheet Basics

One of the most critical but often the most misunderstood aspects of raising capital is the terms associated with the start-up taking an equity investment. A good attorney can help explain many of the terms, but here's a short primer.[53]

Price. The value the investor is placing on the company is determined by two terms, the amount to be invested and the number of shares (or percentage ownership) to be acquired for the investment. Thus, the stock price (price per share) sets the value of the company and can be compared to the previous rounds. As described in Chapter 2, the price also determines the amount of

---

52. It is often said that neither party is happy with a good deal because both have given up something. Whether this is the case usually depends on how far apart the parties were at the start of the negotiations. Investors often say that they learn the most about a company at the first board meeting after the investment. It's not that the company has withheld information during due diligence but that a business can be complex and the nuances of those complexities and the decisions surrounding them only emerge once an investor is fully engaged in the business.

53. Adapted from a series of blog posts by Brad Feld at *FeldThoughts* (blog), www.feld.com (accessed 2 January 2014).

dilution the current owners will receive. One aspect of this term involves the option pool, the pool of stock to motivate current and future employees. If the pool is too small, many investors will insist on increasing its size prior to the investment, which will lower the value of the company (more shares in the price-per-share equation). If the pool significantly lowers the value, the founders are motivated to negotiate for a higher premoney valuation. You may see language in the term sheet like this:

Amount of Financing: An aggregate of $_____ million, representing a _____% ownership position on a fully diluted basis, including shares reserved for any employee option pool. Prior to the Closing, the Company will reserve shares of its Common Stock so that _____% of its fully diluted capital stock following the issuance of its Series A Preferred is available for future issuances to directors, officers, employees, and consultants.

Or:

Price: $_____ per share (the Original Purchase Price). The Original Purchase Price represents a fully diluted premoney valuation of $ _____ million and a fully diluted postmoney valuation of $_____ million. For purposes of the above calculation and any other reference to fully diluted in this term sheet, fully diluted assumes the conversion of all outstanding preferred stock of the Company, the exercise of all authorized and currently existing stock options and warrants of the Company, and the increase of the Company's existing option pool by _____ shares prior to this financing.

The price an investor offers you is dependent on a number of factors: 1) how many other deals like yours the investor is looking at, 2) how many other investors are interested in your deal, 3) comparable deals made in the past, or 4) current macroeconomics. As Brad Feld put it so well:

In early rounds, your new investors will likely be looking for the lowest possible price that still leaves enough equity in the founders' and employees' hands. In later rounds, your existing investors will often argue for the highest price for new investors in order to limit the existing investors' dilution. If there are no new investors interested in investing in your company, your existing investors will often argue for an equal to (flat round) or lower than (down round) price then the previous round. Finally, new investors will always argue for the lowest price they think will enable them to get a financing done, given the appetite (or lack thereof) of the existing investors in putting more money into the company. As an entrepreneur, you are faced with all of these contradictory motivations in a financing, reinforcing the truism that it is incredibly important to pick your early investors wisely, as they can materially help or hurt this process.[54]

Premoney and postmoney. These often confusing terms simply refer to the value of the company prior to the investment (premoney or "pre") and after the investment (postmoney). As outlined in Chapter 2, the premoney valuation divided by the number of issued shares is the stock price, or the price the investor is willing to pay for the company. For term sheet negotiations, the premoney term is the one most often used since most investors have rules of thumb for premoney valuation of companies. For example, if an investor says, "We are thinking about investing $2 million on a $3 million pre," this means that the VC will own 40 percent of the company after investing $2 million (percentage ownership = investment ÷ (premoney valuation + investment).

Liquidation preference. This term defines how the company's assets will be divided in the event of a liquidity event. The event can be either a positive event (acquisition or IPO) or a negative event (bankruptcy). The term can be confusing because there are two different aspects that take into account how things are split up, the preference and the participation, both of which are often lumped under liquidation preference. The preference pertains to how money is returned to a holder of one series of stock compared to another (e.g., Series A versus common). The preference is usually a multiple of the purchase price. For example, the preference term may call for the investor, who's holding Series A stock, to get two times the Series A purchase price, ahead of the common stock holder. After payment of the preference, any remaining money will be paid to all shareholders (common and preferred) on a pro-rata basis. The preferences and participation allow the investor a certain return, even for a moderate liquidity event. But because the investor is "first in line" based on these terms, the founders and management can be left with little or nothing, a demotivating factor. As Brad Feld notes:

> Most professional, reasonable investors will not want to gouge a company with excessive liquidation preferences. The greater the liquidation preference ahead of management and employees, the lower the potential value of the management / employee equity. There's a fine balance here and each case is situation specific, but a rational investor will want

54. "Term Sheet: Price," *FeldThoughts* (blog), http://www.feld.com/wp/archives/2005/01/term-sheet-price.html (accessed 2 January 2014).

a combination of "the best price" while insuring "maximum motivation" of management and employees. Obviously what happens in the end is a negotiation and depends on the stage of the company, bargaining strength, and existing capital structure, but in general most companies and their investors will reach a reasonable compromise regarding these provisions. Note that investors get either the liquidation preference and participation amounts (if any) or what they would get on a fully converted common holding, at their election; they do not get both.[55]

Board seat. The term sheet will usually include a term calling for a board seat for the investor (or lead investor in the case of a syndicate). The rationale is based on the need for the investor to be a party to business discussions at the board level, as well as to have a say in key decisions. Depending on the size of the board and the negotiations, the board seat might be a full seat with voting rights or an "observer" seat, where the investor can be present at the meetings but has no voting rights.

A full term sheet for a life science deal can be found at researchtorevenue .com.

KEY STEP Developing the Product

With money in the bank, the company has the resources to begin developing the product in earnest. As described Chapter 2, product development takes different paths depending on the product and its associated risks and hurdles. In broad terms, product development falls into two categories: Development requiring federal approval (e.g., FDA) for commercial sale and those not requiring approval.

Development of Regulated Products

The Food and Drug Administration is responsible for approving drugs, devices, and diagnostics sold in the United States, with analogous agencies approving these products in the rest of the world. Product development of regulated products involves more prescribed steps with approvals along the way. The approval requirements are proportional to the potential harm the

---

55. "Term Sheet: Liquidation Preference," *FeldThought* (blog), http://www.feld.com/wp/ archives/2005/01/term-sheet-liquidation-preference.html (accessed 2 January 2014).

product can do to the customer (patient). A new kind of examination glove or surgical gown has very low regulatory hurdles compared to an invasive surgical device or a cancer therapy. For potentially harmful products, a company must first test the product with a nonanimal assay (i.e., in-vitro testing), then test it with animals (i.e., in-vivo, preclinical testing), then, finally, test it with humans (clinical testing or clinical trials). It must submit the results of each step of testing to a regulatory body before moving to the next. Reaching the different milestones indicates the mitigation of a certain level of risk, setting the stage for additional investments. In addition, because of the cost and complexity of developing government-regulated products, partnering may come into play at this stage. Partnering with a company to develop the product can provide not only capital but also expertise to help surmount regulatory hurdles.

The Customer Discovery Process

For products without significant technical or regulatory hurdles, product development focuses much more on the market and the customer. (This doesn't mean that developing regulated products is void of customer input but means that the technical and regulatory risk can be significant compared to market risk, as addressed here.) Steve Blank's approach to customer development, as opposed to product development, involves a process of customer discovery.[56] A company with a cutting-edge technology can be easily fooled into thinking that the technology will create customer demand (technology push thinking). It's only after testing a number of hypotheses with customers that a company can be confident of the proper path for developing the product. The customer discovery process is an iterative process, beginning with stating the hypotheses about the business (product, customer need, etc.). From there the product hypothesis is tested and verified, and, if necessary, adjustments are made to the original stated hypotheses.

Phase 1: State the Hypotheses

Each hypothesis below should be explained in a brief, which outlines the facts and assumptions about the hypothesis:

---

56. Stephen G. Blank, *The Four Steps to Epiphany: Successful Strategies for Products That Win* (cafe press.com, 2006).

PRODUCT HYPOTHESIS. The product hypothesis is a product brief consisting of product features, benefits, intellectual property, and the product delivery schedule. In addition, it should include an assessment of things outside of the company's control that have to happen for the product to be effective (e.g., issuance of a government regulation) as well as consideration of all of the costs the customer must bear in purchasing the product (e.g., hardware to run the software).

CUSTOMER AND PROBLEM HYPOTHESIS. Analogous to stating hypotheses about the product, one needs to state assumptions about the customer (e.g., who are they?) and the problems they have to create a customer brief. This brief will not only outline the types of customers (end users, economic buyers, influencers, etc.) and their problems but can include a comprehensive view of customers ("a day in the life") and how they see the value of the product (their return on investment).

DISTRIBUTION AND PRICING HYPOTHESIS. This hypothesis covers first assumptions about how the product will be distributed ("sales channel") to the customer (direct sales, online, retail, third-party resellers, telemarketing, etc.) and how much the customer will pay. Pricing assumptions are best derived from similar products delivering similar features, much the way the customer looks at pricing.

DEMAND CREATION HYPOTHESIS. This addresses the strategy for driving demand for the product, namely what methods will be employed to influence the customer to purchase the product. These hypotheses will depend on the type of product being sold, the customer type, and the sales channel.

MARKET TYPE HYPOTHESIS. The company needs a working hypothesis for the market type, but actual commitment to a specific market can come later in the customer-development process. Most companies sell into one of three market types: an existing market; a resegmented market, where a product is being positioned in a unique niche within an existing market; or a new market, wherein customers' needs are not currently being met by products on the market.

COMPETITIVE HYPOTHESIS. In existing and resegmented markets, customers buy on product attributes. This brief outlines the features and benefits of competitive products and makes a first pass at how the new product will stack up.

Phase 2: Test and Qualify the Hypotheses

Once the hypotheses have been stated and briefs developed for each, the hypotheses need to be tested. This is an iterative, learning process during which potential customers are contacted and presented information about the product and the problem it solves. Blank breaks the process down as follows:

FIRST CUSTOMER CONTACTS. The purpose of this step is to identify and contact potential customers to learn about their needs. This is one of the hardest steps because a) it's difficult to get strangers to give you the time and b) sometimes finding the right people to call on is a challenge because of a limited network from which to draw. It helps to use your fledgling network (friends, family, advisers, attorney, colleagues, etc.) to identify potential customers (and getting a referral from them helps even more). The goal is to get 5–10 scheduled visits for testing your hypotheses.

PRESENTING THE PROBLEM. This may seem counterintuitive, but this is a presentation to the customer about the perceived problem, not just a presentation about the proposed product or solution. The goal is to learn from the customer, not just to make a presentation. This presentation involves three steps: 1) listing problems, 2) listing current solutions, and 3) demonstrating the start-up's solution. It is important to move through each step thoroughly to make sure the customer agrees with the current problems and the current solutions. The temptation is to move quickly through the first two and enthusiastically show how the start-up is going to solve the problem better than anyone else. By not listening to customers, it is easy to miss their needs, which can translate into a product with less market appeal.

UNDERSTANDING THE CUSTOMER. During these conversations with customers, it is important to broaden the knowledge about them and their work and to understand the problem in the context of their workflow. Will solving this problem simply create a bottleneck somewhere else? Do others in the organization have similar problems? Other information can be gathered at this point as well: How much would you pay for a product like this? What other features could you use? Finally, some of these contacts might be important in future steps in the testing process. They might also refer the product to others or act as advisers.

UNDERSTANDING THE MARKET. A further broadening of market understanding places the customer in the context of a broader market. Talking to industry leaders, analysts, and people in adjacent markets will
help with this. One of the most valuable and efficient ways to gather
market information is to attend trade shows. The presentations will
highlight trends in the industry, and the exhibition hall will be full of
customers, thought leaders, and competitors.[57]

Phase 3: Test and Qualify the Product Concept

Having learned from potential customers about their problems, their perception of current solutions, and their initial reaction to your solution, it is
time to begin testing in earnest the assumptions about the product. As Blank
outlines it, this is an iterative process involving a number of reality checks.
The first reality check involves taking the customer feedback and adjusting
the product specifications to be more aligned with what was learned earlier
about the problem, the customer, and the market. This can be challenging
since many of the assumptions going in may have been significantly different
from what was heard from customers. At this point, only one of two options
is viable; you can a) identify a different set of customers with problems more
aligned with the currently conceived product, or b) change the currently
conceived product to be more aligned with the customer feedback. From
here, a product presentation is developed with the goal of reconfirming that
you have identified a significant customer problem and validating the product
features and benefits (avoid trying to convince customers or sell the product).
The presentation is given to as many of the original contacts as possible as well
as new contacts, perhaps derived from the original contacts. As in earlier steps,
use this time with the customers to explore topics related to how they buy
products: for example, purchasing decision-makers, buying process (approvals, timelines), pricing sensitivity, budgeting for new products, channels they
buy from. After these presentations and interviews, a second reality check
ensues where the customer feedback is discussed relative to the conceived
product and adjustments to the product concept are made. According to
Blank, customers react to the product in one of four ways:

1 They love the product and no changes are needed.
2 They like the product but would like more features.

---

57. Ibid., 58.

3   They understand the product after a long explanation, but they don't show much excitement.

4   They don't see a need for the product.

If customers react the first way, then you can move onto the next phase. The second kind of reaction, cautions Blank, can lead to expansion of the product specifications, especially if no features are dropped, which can delay the first shipment. It is better to get a minimum viable product into the hands of paying customers right away than to delay launch to develop a more full-featured product. The last two reactions are common for technology-based products where technology push (creating a new value proposition) plays a larger role than market pull (displacing an existing one). It is tempting to presume customers who react the latter two ways simply don't know they have a problem but that if they would just try the product out they would see how cool and useful it is. Some products have been successfully developed this way (the personal computer with graphical user interface being a famous example), but this is rare. There are several ways to address unengaged or flatly negative customer reactions. One approach, outlined by Blank, is to repackage the technology so the consumer better understands it. This may involve breaking the product down (e.g., software) into more easily understandable features or introducing a basic version that has very few features and thus is easier to use. Another approach is to build a customer education component into the plan. Though this is not ideal, some customers may need to be educated or convinced that the product solves a problem. For research-based products, publications in peer-reviewed journals can help educate customers (e.g., doctors) of the product's ability to solve a problem.[58]

Phase 4: Verify

At this point, a significant amount of the customer discovery process has been completed. Now several aspects of the customer problem and product solution need to be verified. The verification process involves taking stock of what has been learned from customers and deciding if more information is needed. If so, repeat some of the steps taken in Phase 3. Beyond verifying the hypotheses about the customer and product, it is important to verify the business model, or how the company will make money selling the product. Blank suggests that you use information gathered through this customer

58. Ibid., 65.

discovery process to revise the product-development plan and the financial plan, by first answering the following questions:

- How does the projected selling price differ from the initial business plan assumptions?
- How many units will the customer buy over the next three years?
- How will the product be sold to the customer?
- What is the cost of distribution through channels?
- What is the current best estimate of the sales cycle and how will it affect cash flow?
- How much will it cost to acquire each customer (e.g., sales and marketing expenses)?
- Is the market still large enough to meet the revenue projections?
- Based on revised product specifications, have the product-development costs changed?
- How much will the product cost to produce? How does it compare to the original plan?
- Based on the current understanding of the product, the costs for developing, the costs of the product, and the market size, is this still a profitable model?[59]

The answer to the last question is the most important since it will determine whether you want to move ahead with the start-up as currently conceived, iterate again to better understand the market, or fold the venture.

Product Prototype and Testing

The customer discovery process provides valuable information about customer needs and how the product can meet those needs. Product specifications are derived from that process, and the initial product is built using the specifications. Most products go through a prototyping phase during which an initial product is assembled to demonstrate the product's features and usability. In some industries, such as software or web-based applications, this is called the "minimum viable product." For hardware and instruments, this is called the alpha or beta test unit. These prototypes allow for testing of certain aspects of the product (performance, reliability, etc.) but are also used for customer testing. Needless to say, the product at this point is in a fragile state; many things can fail or not perform to specification. The failures provide

---

59. Ibid., 73.

feedback to the development team as to what needs attention. Customer testing is vital at this point because it can provide "real-world" testing of the product with the customer's application. However, given the nascent state of the product, "beta testing" must be done with care. The customer that the company chooses to test the prototype must understand the application well and tolerate failure. The company must closely communicate with the customer, setting expectations about performance, features, reliability, and so forth, for the customer and getting valuable feedback from the customer. In these cases, the customer rarely pays for the product but might get a discount on a future purchase in compensation for his/her time. Some customers are so excited to be involved in the cutting edge of product development that being part of the process is compensation enough. The risk at this stage is overselling the features and benefits of the product only to have the product fail miserably in the hands of the customer. Since customers talk and reference each other, word can get out that the product is a failure, affecting future demand. Thus choose beta customers with care.

KEY STEP Establishing Manufacturing

The logical extension of product development is manufacturing. Generally speaking, this involves the processes and procedures necessary to turn raw materials into a high-quality, reliable product. One way to think of the spectrum of manufacturing is the extent to which value is added during product development versus manufacturing. Three cases can illustrate the breadth of this value add. First, cloud-based software has most of the value added in the product-development phase. Manufacturing, if you can call it that, is simply providing the user access to the software server. Second, a pharmaceutical has value added in product development (e.g., clinical trials) and during the manufacturing process, especially if the pharmaceutical is complex (e.g., a protein therapeutic). Finally, scientific instruments or medical devices have a significant amount of value added during manufacturing where high-precision and complex steps transform raw materials into a sophisticated product. No matter where the value is added in producing a product, the company must have established, reproducible processes and procedures (e.g., "standard operating procedures," or SOPs) so that each and every product produced is the same and of the highest quality.

Although a start-up may be years away from manufacturing a product, it must consider manufacturing as part of its overall business strategy as it will affect management hires and capital requirements. In establishing a manufacturing plan, the first order of business is determining the cost of making the product. For the moment, assume the product will be manufactured by the start-up (we'll consider outsourcing below). The costs, referred to as cost of goods sold, or COGS (sometimes called the cost of sales or cost of revenue; see table 3.9), involve the labor and material for manufacturing, testing, and shipping the product. Material costs can include the cost of raw materials, of items purchased for resale, or of parts used to build the product. Other costs, referred to as direct costs, include production labor, supplies, shipping, and any overhead costs directly associated with manufacturing (e.g., rent and utilities). Occasionally indirect costs, such as distribution and sales force costs, are also included in COGS. In producing a product, such as a pill or hardware, the COGS are fairly easy to calculate, given that material and labor go into the manufacturing process. For a software company, where the product may be a CD, a downloaded file or app, or a hosted application on the cloud, the traditional contribution to the COGS is small or nonexistent. One might include in this calculation the cost of supporting the product (hosting, storage, customer support) and developing the product (beyond feasibility). Sales and marketing expenses are not typically included in COGS.

At this point in the company's development, many of these manufacturing costs may be difficult to assess accurately. However, a rough calculation will go a long way in helping the management and investor understand the risks associated with bringing the product to market. A common mistake academic founders make is to simply add up the costs to build the unit for the lab and call that number COGS without considering the many hours of labor required to put a unit together, the indirect costs, or any special equipment needed to produce the product. The good news is that smart manufacturing people can dramatically drive the cost of a product down through purchasing in bulk, outsourcing, partnerships, and so forth.

The second thing to consider about the manufacturing plan is who will make the product. There are a variety of ways a company can get a product manufactured. At one end of the spectrum, the company can opt to receive the raw materials and manufacture the final product itself, and at the other, the company can opt to develop the detailed product specification and a have third party manufacture it. In between those two ends of the spectrum are a variety of options. The company could contract a third party to manufacture key components or intermediates and then assemble those components into the final product, or the company might create the key component for a third party to assemble into the product. The decision about where the company should reside on this continuum comes down to cost and expertise.

Establishing a manufacturing operation is expensive. The capital costs of the building and assembly and test equipment can be enormous. In addition, there is the cost of purchasing the raw materials and components in large quantities prior to revenue coming back to the company. For some products, expertise may reside within the company (e.g., the product-development engineers), an argument for keeping some portion of manufacturing in-house, whereas external expertise (e.g., access to clean-room facilities) may argue for outsourcing.

KEY STEP **Engaging the Customer: Marketing, Sales, and Business Development**

In a sense, all the previous steps come down to this step of engaging the customer to purchase the product, the primary purpose of a company. This step can be broken down into two parts: creating appeal for the product (marketing) and the transaction between the company and the customer (sales and business development).

Marketing Activities

The purpose of marketing is to create a demand for the product. Products don't sell themselves; people need to be made aware of the product and its features and benefits. Today, this is accomplished through the Internet and social media, advertising, and trade shows. The marketing effort should reflect the many audiences being targeted. First and foremost are the customers, but in the early stages of the company, the marketing activities should also be relevant to investors and future employees.

Website

The company website will be the primary source of information about the company and its products. It is usually where investors or customers will get their first impressions about the start-up. Since there are few second chances for first impressions, don't launch a website until the funds and expertise are available to launch a credible site. The site needs to be informative, intuitive, easy to navigate, and aesthetically pleasing. There are many do-it-yourself options for site design, but there are many parts of web design that require an experienced professional. A professional can help you answer questions like, What images invoke the culture of the company? What opening text best positions the product and the company? What navigational structure is the most intuitive but also allows for site growth? A website designer will cost money, but as is the case with a good attorney, it is usually money well spent. A common way for start-ups with limited funds to proceed is to have designers develop the site layout, navigation tools, and graphics in a format such as WordPress. The company can then add content. This is especially important since a young company is dynamic in the early days: management and board members change, products and technology develops, and business strategies shift.

E-Marketing

Having a website is useful for convincing investors that the company is legitimate, but customers are the real target for a website. Beyond the company's site being on the first page of Google search results, customers need to have an additional incentive to visit it. Internet marketing provides that incentive by building brand and increasing traffic to the destination website. It can take many forms, including the following:

NEWSLETTERS. An effective marketing strategy, especially for companies who have relevant information to share, is the newsletter. A monthly or quarterly newsletter can provide updates on products, company news, industry trends, application notes, customer testimonials, etc. The most effective newsletters are easy to read (headlines and a few sentences with a link to the full article) and provide useful content. The website should have an easy way for visitors to sign up for the newsletter.

BLOGS AND SOCIAL MEDIA. Blogs are an alternative to a newsletter, but the blog structure can make it difficult for readers to quickly find relevant information. Facebook, Twitter, LinkedIn, and other forms of social media are an excellent way to reach customers.

Whatever marketing methods are used, the goal is to transmit your message on the same frequency the customer is receiving it. For example, doctors interested in a medical device are more likely to learn about the results of pivotal trials published in a leading journal than from a company's Twitter feed. By contrast, a health specialist's blog post about a weight-loss app is going to have a bigger audience than a mention of the app in a trade publication.

Trade Shows and Conferences

The trade show can be an effective and efficient marketing tool for an early-stage company.[60] Trade shows bring together a group of people interested in the same topic (cancer therapeutics, cloud computing, environmental safety, etc.). They might be organized in conjunction with a scientific meeting (where there are many presentations and posters and a small exhibition area) or they might be large enough that they feature a large exhibition space. So how does a start-up navigate the world of trade shows and conferences? Here are a few options, in order of expense:

JUST ATTEND. Many faculty founders go to scientific meetings wearing their academic hat. Much insight can be gained by attending the meeting and looking through the lens of technology commercialization and start-ups. Walk the exhibition floor looking for both competitive companies and potential partners, as well as seeing how companies position and promote their products on the floor (through, e.g., well-designed booths, giveaways, workshops, etc.). It can also be instructive to attend scientific talks by representatives of other start-ups in the field that may be competitive or to attend softer science talks (e.g., workshops and technical application talks) sponsored by industry leaders.

PRIVATE SHOWING. The cost of a booth may be prohibitive during the early days of a start-up. An alternative would be to have private showings of the product in a hotel suite. Here the company can demonstrate the product to both investors and customers in an intimate setting, perhaps made more comfortable with a beverage of choice, where attendees can give candid feedback. Private showings work best when you invite individuals ahead of time, although "pulling viewers from the crowd" works too.

SHARE-A-BOOTH. There might be companies that are potential partners or that would like to work with the start-up in the future. If that is the case, they might be open to letting you set up a product display in their booth, giving them a chance to see not only the product but also potential customers' response to the product.

---

60. Trade shows and conferences can also be valuable for very early-stage companies as sources for market research. They bring together target customers as well as key opinion leaders, many of whom may be giving presentations on related technologies. The trade show floor is a great way to survey the competition and look for potential partners.

COMPANY BOOTH. Having a company booth gives the company the opportunity to interact with customers who are looking for your company (through an invitation or having marketed to them), as well as those at the show who may be interested in the product. Like a website, the booth provides the first impression of the product and company and thus needs to look professional. A full pop-up booth may be cost-prohibitive, but several pull-up banners with a large computer display can suffice. Sitting behind a draped table with a couple of brochures and the exhibition-provided company sign is not the way to go. In terms of booth design and etiquette, here are a few suggestions:

- Make the booth inviting. There is nothing more unfriendly than talking to someone from behind a table, so move the tables aside.
- Always be there. Trade shows can be long, but an empty booth speaks volumes about how important the show is for your company. Have two people at the show so you can split booth duty.
- Don't eat in the booth.
- Stay off the phone and the computer when in the booth. There may be some low traffic times when this is OK, but a company representative always needs to be ready when someone interested in the product comes by.
- Get out. Spend time wandering the show to look at the competition and to look for potential customers. Some of the best customers may be in a booth one aisle over.
- Get information. Without being overly aggressive, gather as much information from the booth visitor as possible. Many shows have barcode scanners for an extra fee allowing you to scan an attendee's badge to collect his/her contact information. They are worth it.
- If you have literature, save it for the most interested customers. You can give away a lot of expensive literature to uninterested customers. Some companies won't bring any literature and will follow up with an e-mail and an electronic brochure.
- Bring plenty of business cards.

Publications

For technology-based university start-ups, peer-reviewed publications can be the lifeblood of early marketing efforts. They are powerful because they provide a level of validity that a company brochure cannot. A scientific publication (e.g., a validation study for a biomarker) can showcase the attributes of the technology or innovation that will give rise to the product. An article published by a collaborator using the technology might demonstrate its utility in solving a problem. Finally, a publication on the findings of a study might mention that the start-up's product was used as part of the study's experimental methods (e.g., software for analysis or measurement instrument) and materials (e.g., a reagent). In any of these cases, the company should purchase a reprint of the publication (digital and/or paper) and post it to its website or send it to potential investors/customers as promotional material.

Other kinds of publications developed for marketing can be equally effective. Trade journals often publish articles showcasing a product or technology. Some of the articles are start-up-paid placements, but they make nice marketing pieces. Some trade journal articles are original pieces about a cutting-edge technology (e.g., stem cells) that mention a number of companies. Having periodic conversations with the editor will help get a mention when an article is being written.

Business Development and Sales

At the core of any business is the exchange of something of perceived value, the company's product, for some type of tangible currency, usually cash. This transaction can occur on may levels, depending on the complexity of the transaction, the level of engagement by the company to consummate the transaction, and the amount of the transaction. We'll consider the broad spectrum of transactions, from the most complex (business development) to the simplest (Internet sales).

Business Development

For many university start-ups, getting a product to market will require a partner who will assist in product development, manufacturing, or sales and marketing. The start-up must think about the value of its product from two vantage points: the partner's and, if the partner is taking the product to market, the end-user's. For example, a university start-up may be developing a novel semiconductor material for a new generation of optical switches. Given the capital-intensive nature of developing, manufacturing, and distributing an optical switch, the start-up should consider partnering with an Intel, Siemens, or Cisco. In this case, the partner company is the customer and must be convinced of the value of the potential product for it *and* its customers. This is an important distinction when positioning the business: the market for electronics components is different from but also related to the market for a product enabled by that component.

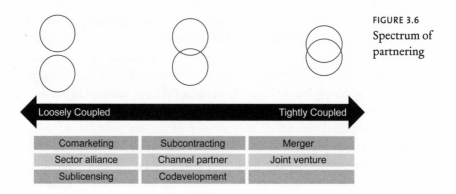

FIGURE 3.6
Spectrum of
partnering

Partnerships can vary by the degree of coupling between the start-up and partner (fig. 3.6). In a loosely coupled partnering, the start-up and the partner might copromote (or comarket) a product or the start-up might sublicense IP to a partner for the partner to develop.[61] In a tightly coupled partnering there is more collaboration between start-up and partner. For example, the start-up's scientists and engineers might work closely with their counterparts in the partner company in product development. The most coupled type of partnering involves the companies either forming a joint venture, typically a separate company owned by the partnering companies, or merging the two companies together.[62]

The decision to partner and the type of partnering arrangement a start-up chooses are driven by a number of factors. One must weigh the cost-benefit of partnering—that is, the cost (financially and in terms of control) versus the benefit (access to capabilities, time to market). Put another way, what is the cost of developing the capability in-house versus partnering. One of the biggest barriers to establishing these partnerships is underestimating the knowledge capital that can be made available by the partner. When weighing the decision, it is important to understand what each party brings to the table and what each gets in return.

61. Sublicensing can span the spectrum of partnering, depending on the terms of the sublicense. The most loosely coupled situation provides the sublicensee with the right to develop the product with little or no input from the licensor. If the sublicense involves more collaboration (e.g., codevelopment), then the partnership is more tightly coupled. Some codevelopment agreements even go so far as to allow the partner, at some point, to acquire the start-up (merger).

62. A separate field of business development is mergers and acquisitions (M&A). Although the terms are not strictly defined, mergers tend to be the joining of two companies of comparable size (e.g. Glaxo + Wellcome = Glaxo-Wellcome). Acquisitions usually refer to a larger entity acquiring a smaller entity (e.g., Google acquiring Waze).

For a start-up, partnering with an established company can provide the following:

CAPITAL. A partner can invest in the start-up or it can provide access to capital equipment and infrastructure valuable to the start-up (e.g., research labs, pilot plants).

CAPABILITIES. The knowledge capital and capabilities of the partner can be critical to the start-up. Experience obtaining regulatory approval, knowledge of the competition and markets, or capabilities in scale-up manufacturing can be invaluable.

VISIBILITY AND VALIDATION. Partnering with an established company, especially one well known in the industry provides a level of visibility and validation for the start-up. The partner's willingness to take a risk on the start-up demonstrates that the start-up has passed muster with a major player. The start-up can leverage this validation to raise money or to establish other noncompetitive partnerships.

For the partner, a partnership with a start-up provides the following:

ACCESS TO NEW MARKETS. Many established companies are looking for a rapid means to gain access to new markets with innovative products. Like the start-up, they are weighing the cost-benefit of developing a product internally versus accessing the market with a product from a start-up.

ACCESS TO INNOVATIVE EMPLOYEES. For the most part, employees of start-ups tend to desire working in a creative and innovative environment, have domain expertise in certain technical areas, and tolerate risk and uncertainty. Partnering with a start-up can provide an established company access to an innovative talent pool.

FIRST RIGHTS. Many partnerships, especially those involving product development, give the established company "first rights." By investing in the partnership with time, money, or people, the established company has certain rights, ahead of anyone else, to the start-up's technology or product or to the start-up itself. For example, a big pharmaceutical company may partner with a biotech start-up to develop a drug. The partnering agreement may stipulate that after a development milestone is reached (e.g., completion of a phase II clinical trial), the pharmaceutical company has the right to license the drug for further development.

Sales

When the transaction between the customer and the company is less complex, with few or no legal documents, and involves simply paying for the product of service, as opposed to an ongoing relationship between the customer and company, then the transaction moves from a business development deal to a sales transaction. The process of selling a product varies according to the type of product, the price of the product, and the customer buying the product. The mode of selling is referred to as the sales channels and involves a distinct set of activities surrounding the transaction and for getting a product to the customer. The choice of sales channel will be influenced by the company's business model and usually revolves around this central question: What is the most capital-efficient way to reach the most customers and sell the most product in the least amount of time? The following are typical sales channels:

DIRECT SALES. With direct sales, the company hires its own employees as sales people and deploys them to call on customers. Traditionally, there was a distinction between inside sales and outsides sales (sales reps), the former residing at the company office, generating leads and closing sales over the phone or by e-mail, and the latter traveling most of the week to visit customers, demonstrate the product, and close the deal. With the Internet and customers having less time for sales calls, the line between inside and outside sales has blurred. The advantage of direct sales is being able to train a sales force on all aspects of the product and the sales process as well as deploy them in specific regions targeting certain customers. Direct sales also provide a direct link to the customer, the customer's applications, and its feedback on the product. (Using a third party for sales such as a distributor does not provide that direct link.) In the early stages of selling the product, support of and feedback on the product will be invaluable, and having that link can be essential. The downside to direct sales is the cost of hiring the sales force and the time to train the sales reps before they start generating revenue.

INTERNET SALES. The Internet provides an efficient means for selling product. In this case, the cost of selling is low since the sales process is "self-serve": customers peruse the product offerings, make a selection, and place the order on their own. There are three options for Internet sales: 1) direct Internet sales from the company's website, 2) sales by another entity specializing in that type of product (like a distributor), or 3) sales through a "mega-aggregator" like Amazon. Which option you choose will depend on how much traffic the site receives, how the product will be displayed on the site, the fee for carrying the product on a third-party's site, how the order will be fulfilled (who ships the product), and how the product will be supported. Internet sales can be appealing, but for products that are creating a new product category or have sophisticated features and benefits, a more proactive sales effort (e.g., sales reps) may be needed, with the Internet providing important product information (online brochure).

DISTRIBUTORS. Distributors are third-party organizations that provide sales and support for a product. They can cover certain regions or specialize in certain product types or industries. They can provide a range of services, from marketing, sales, and product support to just sales reps for hire. One advantage to using a distributor is that it has a sales force already on the ground actively calling on customers, which reduces the time to market and revenue. A medical device distributor of endoscopic probes, for example, is already calling on the target doctors. Such a relationship can be especially important in entering new geographic regions (e.g., Europe), where the distributor can help navigate certain culture issues or import regulations. The disadvantages are the fees the distributor charges for those services and the indirect link between the start-up and the customer, where customer feedback might get lost in translation through the distributor.

Keep in mind that one can always use more than one sales strategy and it can always change. For example, a direct sales force can be used in one region (e.g., North America) and distributors in another region (e.g., Europe). Or distributors can be used for a certain period of time until the company has the capital to hire a direct sales force.

The Sales Cycle and Product Adoption

One of the biggest areas of risk for a start-up, and the one most difficult to assess, is the length of the sales cycle. The sales cycle is the time from the customer first being introduced to or showing interest in the product (a lead) to the closing of the sale.[63] The sales cycle is important for a start-up

---

63. The closing of the sale can be defined in different ways and has implications on how the company reports revenue. The closing of sales can be defined as 1) receiving a purchase order from the customer, 2) shipping the product to the customer, 3) invoicing the customer, or 4) receiving payment from the customer. Although a sales person may recognize 1 as a sale, the CFO or accountant may only recognize 4.

because the company needs to spend capital on sales and marketing before revenue comes in the door. The longer the sales cycle, the more capital that is required. A common mistake start-ups make is underestimating the time it take to close a deal. In the academic market of university researchers, few researchers have discretionary funds over $5,000, so if they want to purchase something that costs more than that amount, they need to apply for a grant from an extramural funding source. The grant cycle is often longer than nine months and is not guaranteed. Product adoption also affects the sales cycle. For example, a truly revolutionary product may take time to be adopted by customers because of issues related to the "chasm" (see the "Barriers to Adoption," section on page 147). In his book *Crossing the Chasm*, Geoffrey Moore describes a scenario that many technology-based companies will be familiar with:

> In the first year of selling a product—most of it alpha and beta release— the emerging high-tech company expands its customer list to include some technology enthusiasts, innovators, and one or two visionary early adopters. Everyone is pleased, and at the first annual Christmas party, held on the company premises, plastic glasses and potluck canapés are held high. In the second year—the first year of true product—the company wins over several more visionary early adopters [and makes] a handful of truly major deals. Revenue meets plan, and everyone is convinced it is time to ramp up—especially the venture capitalists who note that next year's plan calls for a 300 percent increase in revenue. (What could justify such a number? The technology adoption profile, of course! For are we not just at that point in the profile where the slope is increasing at its fastest point? We don't want to lose market share at this critical juncture to some competitor. Strike while the iron is hot!) This year the company Christmas party is held at a fine hotel, the glasses are crystal, the wine vintage, and the theme, à la Dickens, is "Great Expectations."
>
> At the beginning of the third year, a major sales force expansion is undertaken, impressive sales collateral and advertising are under-written, district offices are opened, and customer support is strength-ened. Halfway through the year, however, sales revenues are disap-pointing. A few more companies have come on board, but only after a prolonged sales struggle and significant compromise on price. The num-bers of sales overall is far fewer than expected, and growth in expenses is vastly outdistancing growth in income. In the meantime, R&D is badly

bogged down with several special projects committed to in the early contracts with the original customers.

Meetings are held. The salespeople complain that there are great holes in the product line and that what is available today is overpriced, full of bugs, and not what the customer wants. The engineers claim they have met spec and schedule for every major release, at which point the customer support staff merely groan. Executive managers lament that the sales force doesn't call high enough in the prospect organization, lacks the ability to communicate the vision, and simply isn't aggressive enough. Nothing is resolved, and, off line, political enclaves begin to form.

Third quarter revenues results are in—and they are absolutely dismal. It is time to whip the slaves. The board and the venture capitalist start in on the founders and the president, who in turn put the screws to the vice president of sales, who passes it on to the troops in the trenches. Turnover follows. The vice president of marketing is fired. It's time to bring in "real management." More financing is required, with horrendous dilution for the initial cadre of investors—especially the founders and the key technical staff. One or more founders object but are shunted aside. Six months pass. Real management doesn't do any better. Key defections occur. Time to bring in consultants. More turnover. What we really need now, investors decide, is a turnaround artist. Layoffs are followed by more turnover. And so it goes. When the screen fades to the credits, yet another venture rides off to join the twilight companies of Silicon Valley—enterprises on life support, not truly alive and yet, due in part to the vagaries of venture capital accounting, unable to choose death with dignity.[64]

Customer Service and Product Support

Another important aspect of sales, which is often overlooked, is the support of the product. Product support can span a large portion of the sales process. For a highly technical product, the sales team may need to rely on product engineers or technical support scientists for "pre-sales" support, which entails demonstrating how to use the product or helping to explain the product's technical capabilities to fit the customer's needs. The latter support function is particularly important with platform technologies that have multiple applications. At the other end of the spectrum, "post-sales" support will need

64. Moore, *Crossing the Chasm*, 23–25.

to be provided as the customer uses the product. The product may not work as intended or malfunction or need to be repaired. Someone will need to interact with the customer, either remotely or on-site, to take care of the issue. A related aspect is product maintenance and upgrades. Complex hardware should be on a periodic maintenance schedule, and software has continuous bug fixes and upgrades. Both of these activities can be a significant source of revenue.

Reimbursement

In most of the economy, the transaction of selling a product is relatively straightforward. The customer purchases the product, and the company ships the product to the customer. Minor layers of complication can involve outsourced manufacturing, a fulfillment group (picking and shipping), or a distributor. In the healthcare space, however, the transaction is complicated by the fact that many medical procedures and treatments are not paid for directly by the consumer. In most cases, an insurer (private or Medicaid) pays the medical bill, with the consumer paying a portion directly (e.g., copay, deductible) and a portion indirectly (insurance premiums). Complicating the transaction further is the involvement of a "benefits" manager and/or rebates to various intermediaries.

KEY STEP The Exit

Most university start-ups are built around an innovation that requires capital to bring that innovation to market. The source of capital, as discussed, is typically an investor who expects some return on that investment. The return expectations are usually commensurate with the risk the investor assumes when making the investment. A seed-stage investor is expecting much more return than is a Series C investor, and a Series C investor is expecting more return than is a banker making a loan to the company. In addition to the return on investment, the investor is also expecting a return on that investment in a certain period of time. A VC needs to see a return within a period of five to seven years in order to bolster fund-raising efforts for the next fund. "Non-financial" investors are seeking a return as well. Founders and management have invested time and effort into launching and growing the company. Many members of the management team may have gone years with a salary well below their market value and have worked many more hours than a typical big-company job would require. For this, they are hoping for some financial upside at the end of the day.

For all of these shareholders, the "exit" occurs when the company shares are exchanged for cash or a cash equivalent, which makes the shares "liquid." The two most common exits, or "liquidity events," are an acquisition or an initial public offering.

Acquisition

The acquisition of a company by another company involves the acquirer purchasing all of the shares of the company, along with any assets (e.g., IP, buildings, cash) and any liabilities (e.g., debt). The acquisition, like an investment or a licensing deal, involves a term sheet that the acquirer offers to the target company outlining the terms of the acquisition. Term sheet negotiations, along with due diligence, proceed until both parties sign a deal. The following are the major terms of an acquisition deal:

ACQUISITION PRICE. The price the acquiring company is paying for the target company, like the value of the target company during a round of investing, is open to plenty of negotiation. However, at this stage, more data about the progress of the company in developing and selling the product is available, and there are comparables in the industry to guide the valuation discussion, since many of these acquisitions are done by publicly traded companies who have to disclose these transactions.

FORM OF PAYMENT. How much the acquirer is willing to pay for the target company is only part of the equation. The acquirer has to pay for the acquisition some way, and the form of payment is usually either cash or equity (acquirer stock) or a combination of the two. The choice of payment form will depend on two factors: 1) the financial implications of paying cash versus equity for the acquirer (e.g., does it result in debt?) and 2) the attractiveness of the payment to the target company (other things being equal, an all-cash deal is better than a deal involving all publicly traded stock, and a deal involving all publicly traded stock is better than one involving all privately held stock).

TIMING AND TERMS OF PAYMENT. The final financial term relates to how the payments will be made. A number of options exist, and the one chosen will depend on the deal structure. For example, the payment could be all publicly traded stock given at the closing of the deal. However, shareholders of the target company, with their newly acquired public stock, may be restricted from selling it immediately. For example, the terms may stipulate a "lock-up" period (typically 6–12 months) during which the stock may not be sold or only a certain percentage may be sold each month. This prevents a flood of stock being placed on the market and depressing the stock price and wards off the perception that the new shareholders don't have confidence in the acquiring company. Another common approach is to have an "earnout," where the target company, after being acquired but running independently, must achieve certain milestones over time. With the earnout, payments are made to the target company employees. For example, there may be significant disagreement over the value of the company in the future. The target company may defer part of the purchase price until after certain milestones are achieved (e.g., $100 million in revenue in three years).

OPERATIONS AND EMPLOYEES. From an operational perspective, an acquisition can have many different outcomes, both short term and long term. On one extreme, the target company can continue to operate independently postacquisition but with access to capital and infrastructure support from the acquirer (e.g., human resources). This scenario is common when the acquisition depends on earnout milestones. In this scenario, most employees are incentivized to stay and earn what may amount to half of the purchase price. At the other extreme, the target company's operations are fully merged with the acquiring company's. In this scenario, since there are likely redundancy and economies of scale, some people are let go. There also might be incentives for higher-level managers (e.g., CEO, VPs) to stay for a period of time (e.g., six months) to ensure a smooth integration of operations.

Initial Public Offering

The second common form of exit is the IPO (an exchange of privately held stock for publicly traded stock). In this case, the company hires an investment bank to assist in the public offering process (documentation, pricing, initial sale of shares). Senior management works with the bank to create a prospectus that describes in detail the investment opportunity. The bank sets the price for the stock offering (a price per share) and gets commitments from both institutional and retail buyers. Depending on the demand for the stock, private investors (venture, private equity) might commit to purchasing a certain number of shares. When the stock goes public (in the United States typically via the New York Stock Exchange [NSYE] or the NASDAQ), the commitments are turned into buy orders. The shares of the start-up shareholders are exchanged for shares of the now publicly traded stock. To prevent the flood of stock into the public market, owners are usually subject to a three- to six-month lock-up period.

Mergers and Acquisitions versus Initial Public Offering

Some start-ups that have grown to the point of contemplating an exit have a choice between going public or being acquired. The option likely won't be at the same moment in time but rather, for example, whether to enter into a partnership that will likely lead to an acquisition or go it alone in hopes of going public. In thinking about these two options, it is important to consider the following:

THE INVESTOR'S PERSPECTIVE. In thinking about an acquisition versus an IPO, an investor will always look at the risk-return equation. For an acquisition, the liquidity is short term, with the exception of when future milestones are part of the deal. Many investors see an IPO as a mark of success; that is, an IPO offers a greater long-term return. The risks, however, are higher due to both internal factors (product development, execution) and external factors (macroeconomic conditions, wars, natural disasters). Liquidity through an IPO can also take time, perhaps as long as two years, since investors, who are insiders, have restrictions on their ability to sell stock.

THE MANAGEMENT'S PERSPECTIVE. Company employees may have a different view of the differences between an M&A and IPO. If their company opts for an acquisition, they may be looking beyond the financial return. Is there a good fit between the companies in terms of culture, product strategy, or corporate mission? What is the risk of being laid off, and is that risk mitigated by the companies' synergy and the acquiring company's resources? With an IPO, there is the rapid access to capital with more freedom on how to use the capital. On the downside, an IPO comes with public scrutiny, additional regulations and filings, and additional dilution, up to 40 percent in some cases.

The Bumps in the Road

The key steps to a start-up described above outline the typical path a start-up takes in bringing a university innovation to the market. Not every start-up goes through all the steps in the defined order. Some skip steps, some proceed through the steps in a different order, and some have to repeat steps when things don't go as planned. On this point, one of the truths about start-ups is that planning is important, but things rarely go as planned. In other words, be prepared for the unexpected. These bumps in the road can, at best, cause a change in direction of the company and at worst slow the company's progress or even worse, result in the company going out of business. Below are some of the typical bumps in the road to be prepared for:

Lack of seed capital to launch the company. In this scenario, a company is formed, management and advisers are recruited, technology is licensed, and the business plan is written. After a number of pitches to investors, however, all pass. The investors give various reasons for passing, but most center around "too early." This is one of the first and biggest hurdles most university start-ups face. These are some of the reasons why:

- The company is looking for money in the wrong places. For example, an angel deal might be appropriate for the company, but the company has only talked to venture capitalists (or vice versa). Or the investors you have selected don't invest in your type of company (wrong stage, wrong industry).
- The technology is too early and either grants to the faculty member's lab or SBIR grants might be required to de-risk the technology.
- The company is asking for too much money. The "bite-size" might be too big for the investor (e.g., an angel investor), or the investor might feel there is too much risk for the amount of money being requested. To raise the initial seed round, the company might need to show several "tranches," or rounds of investment, to get to the product launch, a partnership deal signed, a break even, etc. So rather than asking for $5 million to get the product launched, the company should ask for $500,000 to build several production prototypes, complete beta tests, and acquire customer feedback.

Disagreements with the university. Anytime two parties engage in a business transaction, there is always the possibility for disagreement. The following are some typical areas of disagreement between a start-up licensing a technology from a university and the university:

- Most universities require initial payments as part of the license, either up front or over time, in most cases to cover the costs of the patent. For some start-ups, the fund-raising may not go according to plan, so they are unable to make the payments. In these cases, TTOs exercise varying degrees of flexibility in terms of collecting payments. In general,

TTOs will be more flexible if there is demonstrated movement toward raising capital (e.g., term sheet negotiations or a pending SBIR grant). In this case, the remedy may be an amendment of the license to restructure or delay the payments. In some cases, out of a matter of procedure, the TTO will issue a breach indicating that the company has violated a term of the license and that it has a certain number of days to rectify the breach. One positive aspect of a breach letter is that it often speeds up the negotiations with an investor.

- Related to payments, most licenses stipulate that certain performance or diligence milestones must occur at a certain time to ensure that the company is making reasonable progress in commercializing the technology; for example, a prototype has to be completed by a certain date or the first commercial sale has to occur within a certain number of years from license. Since things usually take longer than expected, these timelines can slip. Again, most universities understand this and can be flexible, if there is good reason for the delays and the company is making demonstrable progress. In both cases (payments and diligence), flexibility is likely to come at a cost. In lieu of current payments, the university may change other aspects of the license. For example, it may increase the equity stake it has in the company or increase the royalty percentage.

- For start-ups commercializing technology, the faculty member will inevitably make improvements to the technology. When the improvements occur in the university lab, the question arises as to where the improvement stands in terms of the license. Is it a) part of the licensed technology and therefore covered under the current license, b) not part of the license technology and subject to a separate license agreement, or c) not an improvement at all but a new discovery, which means not only would it be subject to a separate license agreement, but the license might be to a third party? To avert potential disagreements the original license should account for improvements and make provisions for their license.

- An improvement or discovery might be made by the company and there are disagreements on ownership of the IP. Ownership usually resides with the inventor. If the inventor is an employee of the company, then the company usually has rights to the invention, per the employment agreement. The stickier area is an invention that is conceived by the faculty member consulting for the company, where the terms of the consulting arrangement are not made clear. Some universities will not allow traditional consulting arrangements (e.g., any discovery or invention made by the faculty member during consulting is the property of the consulted company). Again, a well-conceived and transparent relationship between the faculty founder and the start-up can prevent potential discord.

- Patent infringement can also be an area of friction between start-up and university. The license usually does not give the start-up the right to pursue infringers of the university IP. Rather, that right rests with the university. However, universities don't often have the resources to pursue infringers, especially if they are established companies with deep pockets. Some TTOs, however, can be flexible in this area, provided that a) the start-up has the resources to pursue the infringer, and b) the start-up and the university's interests are aligned in the pursuit.

Change in direction. There is no definitive data, but many university start-ups change directions one or more times before bringing a product to market. These changes, or "pivots," might involve the product being developed (e.g., different application, different product) or how the product is going to be delivered to the market (e.g., different business model, type of partner). In some cases, the reason for a pivot is clear (e.g., FDA rejection letter, lawsuit by competitor), and the decision to change direction is rapid and unanimous. In other cases, the reason behind the change is not so clear, at least not to all parties, and thus leads to disagreements within the company. For example, a start-up might decide to de-emphasize a key aspect of the university technology based on market research or customer interviews. For faculty founders, this change not only can reduce their technology's impact in the market but also can reduce the importance of the faculty founder to the company, since his or her insights and expertise won't be as essential going forward.

Changes in direction can also create friction with investors. They have invested in a certain company developing a defined product for an identified market need. Any change to that plan needs to be rational and well justified. At the end of the day, however, the decision to change direction is often based on limited input and past experiences. Since investors make a living in the world of best guesses with limited input, their approach to the decision may be different than company management's. Furthermore, the objectives of the investors and the company management can differ. Although both parties are aligned in terms of the desire to increase shareholder value, they may disagree about the means to do so. For example, a VC might see an acquisition as an immediate way to get return on his/her investment, whereas management might see the acquisition as selling short before the long-term value of the company can be created.

Personality clashes and job fit. In a start-up, since there are very few people involved initially, the relationships, or "people chemistry," is important. When the chemistry is not there, then personality clashes can occur. This is why it is important to make each addition to the start-up carefully and to work with people for some period of time before bringing them on. Related to personality clashes is job fit: Is this person a good fit for the job? In some cases, the answer is no, but often the founders or management team spend time and energy forcing a fit that may not exist. Although it is tough to do, it's in the best interest of everyone to let that person go. Remember, there are no bad people, just bad fits.

Product failures and slow adoption. Sometimes the product fails in development (e.g., clinical trial) or in the market (poor revenues). For some products, these failures are harder to overcome. For example, a drug failing a clinical trial is hard to overcome without starting over with another compound. Other failures during development might be solved by spending more time and money to redesign, modify, or tweak the product. Market failures occur when the customer is not buying the product, or at least not at the rate expected. Most product adoption problems arise from a lack of fit between the product's value (perceived or otherwise) and the customer's needs. This can be remedied by either changing the product to deliver more or different value or changing the perception of value through intense marketing. Both of these solutions, unfortunately, require more time and money, both of which are in short supply in a start-up. A common trap, outlined above in the discussion of Moore's *Crossing the Chasm*, is to think product adoption is going well when in realty the demand is only by early adopters.

4

Case Studies

In Chapter 3, we walked through the key steps in forming a start-up based on a university scientific or technical innovation. To both illustrate the key steps and show the diversity of options and approaches available at each step, we present the following case studies. The companies are fictitious, but the specifics of each company are based on our own experiences. The case studies represent the breadth of start-up technologies—a cancer therapeutic, a solid-state sensor for environmental monitoring, and software for optimizing web servers—and demonstrate how those technologies influence the approach to building a company.

Oncotica

The Oncotica case study describes the development of a cancer therapeutic and the eventual acquisition of the company by a pharmaceutical partner. Figure 4.1 provides an overview of the significant events for the company.

Dr. Davis, from the University Cancer Center, discovered a novel protein kinase that is activated in cancer resulting in tumor cell growth (vascular formation). His lab, working with several collaborators, cloned the gene, expressed the protein, developed antibodies to the kinase, isolated the natural ligand, did an initial screen of small molecule compounds, and identified several hits (compounds that inhibit the activity of the novel kinase). From those hits, several compounds were optimized via medicinal chemistry and tested in animal models of cancer. One of the compounds showed a significant reduction in tumor growth in a preliminary study involving a xenograft tumor mouse model.

Recognizing the opportunity. Dr. Davis recognized the novelty of the kinase as a therapeutic target as well as the broader medical need for more selective therapeutics in oncology. He went beyond the target to identify several

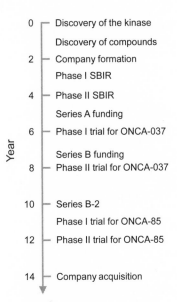

Year	
0	Discovery of the kinase
	Discovery of compounds
2	Company formation
	Phase I SBIR
4	Phase II SBIR
	Series A funding
6	Phase I trial for ONCA-037
	Series B funding
8	Phase II trial for ONCA-037
10	Series B-2
	Phase I trial for ONCA-85
12	Phase II trial for ONCA-85
14	Company acquisition

FIGURE 4.1 Timeline for Oncotica

chemical compounds that appear to modulate tumor growth. In thinking about the unique capabilities of the technology, he emphasized both the target (kinase) and the chemical compounds (inhibitors). The kinase is a novel target, previously not described in the literature, and acts as a "master switch" in tumor growth. The inhibitors were novel chemical compounds that were patent protectable, but Dr. Davis realized that limited testing had been done on their efficacy and toxicity. One of the challenges was identifying the specific type of cancer on which to focus further efforts. That focus would be driven in part by the unmet need and in part by the demonstrated efficacy.

Disclosure to the university. Dr. Davis was preparing a presentation to be made at the American Association of Cancer Research, and he wanted to discuss the novel kinase target and the compounds that showed inhibition. Thus, he made an invention disclosure to the university's technology transfer office. A licensing officer with the TTO interviewed Dr. Davis. During the interview, the following additional facts were identified and discussed:

- A graduate student had been instrumental in discovering, cloning, expressing, and characterizing the kinase target.
- A second graduate student had developed the antibody to the kinase and had isolated the natural ligand for the kinase.

- Dr. Davis had collaborated with Dr. Switzer, a medicinal chemist with experience in kinase inhibition, to design the series of compounds to be tested in the xenograft model.
- The compounds had been synthesized by a contract synthesis lab in India.
- All of the work had been funded by the National Cancer Institute at NIH.

With the situation of potentially multiple inventors on the discovery of the novel target and compounds, the licensing officer contacted patent counsel at an experienced external IP/patent law firm to sort through the inventorship question.

Filing for IP protection. In considering the value of the intellectual property and what patents to file, the TTO considered the kinase target of limited value and the compounds of high value. Patenting the use of the target for diagnosing cancer patients was considered briefly but abandoned given that the TTO had limited financial resources and that no data had been generated on validating the target as a diagnostic biomarker. For the compounds, a high level of inhibition (nanomolar activity) showed, at least on one level, the potency of the compounds. This was going to be a key selling point in outlicensing/partnering the compounds. The inventorship question came down to Dr. Davis and Dr. Switzer (since the kinase was not going to be patented, their contribution to it was moot). Outside counsel interviewed each, and, although their contributions were not equal, both had contributed to the discovery and were considered co-inventors. The last wrinkle involved the contract synthesis lab. Dr. Davis had asked for the academic rate from the contract lab. In consideration for the lower rate, the lab retained the right to commercialize any compounds it synthesized. However, the right the contract lab retained was exclusively for India. Although this could be problematic in the future (it would exclude another company from selling the product in India), for the moment it was not enough of a concern for the TTO. In addition, the patent counsel determined that the contract lab was not an inventor on the intellectual property, since it was just synthesizing compounds as directed by Dr. Switzer. Thus, the TTO decided to file a provisional patent on the compounds, with both Dr. David and Dr. Switzer as inventors, even though the data was preliminary.

Recruiting advisers and mentors. Drs. Davis and Switzer discussed the possibility of starting a company around these kinase inhibitors. They both agreed it would be a great opportunity and that the patient need was significant. They also saw little interest from the pharma companies contacted by the TTO because of the early stage of the molecules. Potential pharma companies all said the data was too preliminary and to come back when there was more animal data on the toxicity of the compounds. Also at this time, Dr. Switzer decided that since he was coming up for tenure in a few years, he did not want to be distracted by the start-up. He was open to consulting from time to time but could not take an active role in the company. Dr. Davis, on the other hand, already had tenure, wanted to learn more about entrepreneurship, and so was going to take the lead in forming the company.

Before forming the company, both Davis and Switzer felt that more input was important from business people with experience in cancer and drug development. They decided to gather a group of potential advisers. Working with the TTO and several faculty who had launched start-ups in the past, they identified several local people. One adviser worked in big pharma for a number of years, left to start a biotech start-up as chief medical officer, and helped bring a compound to Phase IIb. Another was a medical oncologist from the University Cancer Center and a local business-development consultant who was working on several projects with pharma and biotech. Drs. Davis and Switzer met with the group and presented the data. The group was enthusiastic, but the technical, regulatory, and funding risks involved in bringing the product to market tempered their enthusiasm. They also recognized the need to identify the type of cancer to be targeted with the compounds.

Developing the business case. The advisers suggest that before the doctors took the traditional steps of writing a full business plan and incorporating the company, they should develop a business case, which would outline the opportunity and help build (or detract) from the rationale of starting a company. Mr. Andrews, the adviser with pharma and start-up experience, agreed to help develop the business case.

The first task for Davis and Andrews was narrowing the therapeutic scope of the product since the compounds were unlikely to address a wide range of cancers. Dr. Davis noted that since the kinase was highly expressed in cancers of the GI (colon, bladder) and since the initial testing was done in a colon cancer model, those cancer types were to be considered initially. Incidence rates of GI cancers were obtained, and it was determined that they supported a significant market size. Davis and Andrews's next task was to ascertain the current standard of care for GI cancers. Through a series of interviews with GI oncologists (i.e., primary market research), they gained a clearer picture of the treatment options, effectiveness, and success rates of current approaches. Next, they addressed the highest barriers to success: technical and regulatory hurdles. They began by laying out the preclinical development plan, determining which parts could be completed using Dr. Davis's research funding and which would need to be completed using other means (grants, investment).

With this information in hand, they gathered their original advisers, plus a few additional people (a GI oncologist and a preclinical CRO person), and laid out the business case. There was general enthusiasm for the approach, but several concerns were raised. The obvious ones (e.g., Will the compound work better than current treatments? Will it be safe?) could not be answered without future experiments and funding for those experiments. The less obvious question was whether investors would consider this a "one-trick pony"—that is, would the drug work against only one type of cancer. Given the ubiquity of this kinase in other cancers, though expressed in lower amounts, the team felt that this concern could be addressed if the first drug was partnered and if the company identified additional compounds to develop for other cancers.

Forming the company. With the generally positive response from their ad-hoc advisory group, Davis took the lead on founding the company. He had hoped Mr. Andrews would be a cofounder as well, but he found another job and didn't have the resources to work for equity alone for the next 6–12 months. Davis initially want to name the company Kinase Research Labs, but one of the advisers thought it sounded too much like a research institute. He considered Oncolera, but that sounded like "cholera," so he eventually settled on Oncotica after some web searches for the availability of the name. Working with a local attorney, he incorporated the company as a C-corporation in Delaware, knowing that the company was likely going to need venture capital in the future. Dr. Davis wanted to reward with equity the people who had contributed over the years. When he presented the list of 23 people (former grad students, postdocs, and collaborators) to his attorney, the attorney advised against that, since, with a few exceptions, most had made only minor contributions, and giving them all equity would complicate the incorporation and might be a stumbling block to investment from venture capital firms in the future (just keeping up with this number of founders to inform them or get their consent would have been a huge undertaking). Dr. Davis narrowed down the list to two former students and then tackled the issue of equity for Switzer.

At first, the division of equity between Drs. Davis and Switzer was contentious, with Dr. Switzer feeling he had contributed as much or more to the discovery and development of the compound. A tense meeting with the attorney ended amicably when Dr. Switzer realized his equity represented his past contributions and Dr. Davis's equity represented past and future contributions, namely building the company, organizing and leading the SAB, contributing to grant writing, and providing the biological insight for drug development. As a compromise, Dr. Switzer received slightly less equity. For the moment, Davis and Andrews (Andrews agreed to continue to advise the company) would be the sole board members, with the attorney acting as the corporate secretary. Equity was distributed as follows:

SHAREHOLDER	SHARES	PERCENTAGE OWNERSHIP	VESTING
Dr. Davis	4,500,000	45	25 percent vests now, 75 percent over three years
Dr. Switzer	4,000,000	40	25 percent vests now, 75 percent over three years
Student 1	400,000	4	100 percent vesting
Student 2	400,000	4	100 percent vesting
Advisers/SAB	500,000	5	25 percent vests now, 75 percent over three years
Attorney	200,000	2	100 percent vesting
Total	10,000,000	100	

The vesting schedule was different for different founders, based on the following reasoning. Davis and Switzer needed to be engaged at some level going forward. For Switzer, he needed to at least contribute by being on the SAB and the board; if he did not participate, he would lose any of his unvested shares. The same applied for the advisers. SAB members needed to be involved over the long term to receive the full number of shares. The students contributed in the past, so there was no point in vesting for them. The attorney waived some legal fees in return for equity, so those shares were considered compensation. Based on advice from his corporate attorney, Davis did not set any equity aside for the future management team, and he decided that the equity owned by the individuals listed above would be diluted pro rata since equity was distributed to the future management team.

Building the management team. With Oncotica launched, the founders began to recruit a CEO. With no funding, they experienced the common problem of start-ups: How do you get a seasoned biotech executive to take a huge risk with only equity as compensation? As an alternative, they found Ms. Jan

McCallister, a person recently laid off from big pharma with business development experience. They decided to bring her on board as VP of business development for equity plus a percentage of the value of any deal she closed in the next 12 months. She was young, but they liked her aggressiveness and her deep list of pharma contacts. By putting in place a VP of business development, they could begin to test the waters for partnering, and if there is interest, they could potentially recruit a CEO and/or begin raising VC money. In addition, Dr. Davis organized Oncotica's first scientific advisory board meeting, which was very productive both in terms of scientific directions and in terms of contacts in the industry.

Licensing the IP. For licensing the technology from the university's TTO, Dr. Davis turned the negotiations over to the company's corporate attorney and the external board member. Since the company was still very early, they agreed to take an exclusive option to the technology, giving them the right to take a license at a later time. The option agreement was for 12 months, and the cost was $10,000, which could not be applied to the license agreement. Davis and Switzer each agreed to contribute funds to secure the option agreement but wanted the terms to be prenegotiated as part of the option agreement. The university would not do that, arguing that the value of the company in 12 months could not be predicted. As a compromise, they agreed to the following terms, with ranges acting as placeholders to be negotiated at a future date (e.g., when the option expired):

Exclusivity, territory, field	Exclusive, worldwide, all diseases
Up-front licensing fee	$0–25,000
Equity	5–15 percent with no dilution until $1 million raised
Royalty on sale of product	1–3 percent
Sublicensing income	10–20 percent
Patent costs	Incurred costs paid back over 180 days, plus ongoing costs

Gathering market information. Additional studies in the lab confirmed the compound's activity in a colon cancer model, so the company focused its market research on this indication. Through personal and professional connections (SAB, advisers), oncologists specializing in colon cancer were identified and interviewed. The interviews probed the challenges of treating colon cancer, as well as the first-line and second-line therapies, the weakness of each, and pricing and reimbursement. Dr. Davis and Ms. McCallister also met with a key executive at a large health insurance company to understand reimbursements for cancer therapies. Ms. McCallister developed a matrix of potential partner companies with products targeting colon cancer. She identified products that were in clinical trials (at www.clinicaltrials.gov) and products currently on the market and when they were scheduled to go generic (patent expiration). This information provided a landscape of products and companies, helping to identify which partners to approach.

Through interviews with doctors and several retired FDA officials, the company determined that the major market drivers for colon cancer therapeutics were safety and effectiveness. The interviews also revealed that, given the lifesaving nature of cancer therapy and the levels of toxicity seen with current treatments, to a certain extent, effectiveness trumped safety. In an effort to determine how much more effective its treatment needed to be to get FDA approval, the company focused on current and future therapies in development. This information, combined with information on companies' product pipelines and what products would come off patent in the future, provided a realistic view of what the market would look like in 7–10 years, at which time Oncotica's product would likely be launched.

Defining and refining the business model. As with most therapeutic companies, Oncotica was likely to partner at some point during the clinical development cycle. The point at which it partnered would depend on the level of interest by a partner (big pharma or a biotech company) in this drug, which would be driven by the partner's strategy and its current products in the pipeline. Typically, pharmaceutical companies become most interested when proof of concept has been demonstrated in humans (i.e., after Phase II clinical trials). They may show interest at the preclinical or earlier clinical stage, when there is a compelling unmet medical need for the drug, or when the strategic fit is exceptionally high. The biggest challenge for this type of start-up is finding the capital to fund the preclinical and early clinical (Phase I) development, which could easily amount to five to ten million dollars. The most likely source for this large funding is venture capital firms that invest in biotech.

When Oncotica did find a partner, the relationship would depend on Oncotica's capital needs and the expertise of the partner company. If Oncotica had raised sufficient capital to reach meaningful milestones, then the pharma partner might provide only advice and support until larger clinical trials were required. On the other hand, the partner might conduct the vast majority of the studies, with the Oncotica team working with the partner to design and execute partner-funded studies.

Marketing the company. Using an online logo-development site (logotourna ment.com), the founders settled on a logo. It wasn't easy since everyone had an opinion on the 10 different options. The founders reserved the domain oncotica.com for their website and, using a WordPress template, created a simple site that had an "about" page, a "founders and management" page, a "technology" page, and a "contact" page. They also provided links to the most relevant publications. The purpose of the site was to serve as a convenient access point for recruiting advisers and management. It would also serve as the nucleus for the full site to be developed as the company began raising capital.

Writing the business plan. The initial Oncotica business plan was written as a PowerPoint deck with 20 slides, including a number of appendix slides to support the main set of slides (e.g., data graphs and spreadsheets). The plan focused on several key areas. First was differentiating Oncotica's drug from other oncology drugs. The mechanism was discussed in enough detail to convince the nonexpert and the scientist alike. In addition, other therapies in the colon cancer area were discussed and contrasted with Oncotica's. Care was taken to differentiate only where differences could be supported by data (e.g., the fact that it was a novel mechanism), and not where there was lack of validation (efficacy and safety). The second area of focus was on product development. Here, the team did its homework on the preclinical development that the FDA required for submission of an IND: animal models, toxicity testing, pharmacodynamic/pharmacokinetic studies, chemistry manufacturing, and controls. Included in the appendix slides were detailed quotes from several CROs to verify the company's capital needs. Next, the plan addressed the intellectual property, with particular emphasis on patent searches that had been completed, which showed the patent landscape for the company's compounds. A list of filings and office actions was included in the appendix slides. The plan then outlined the partnering strategy, including the names of potential key partners, and the rationale behind their being chosen (e.g., compounds coming off patent, oncology compounds but few in colon cancer, etc.). The plan ended with management bios and high-level financials accompanied by a spreadsheet in the appendix with more detail. The emphasis was on the cost to get the compound over three hurdles: the submission of the IND, the first-in-human trial (Phase I), and the first efficacy and safety trial (Phase II). If the Phase II data looked good, the plan was to license the compound to a large pharmaceutical company for continued development in return for a significant up-front payment, milestones, and royalties to Oncotica.

Raising initial capital. The company took two routes to raise capital: it applied for SBIR grants and sought seed-round funds from venture capital. As expected, the VC fund-raising went very slowly. Out of the 20 firms the team approached, 8 took initial calls and 3 invited the team in for a presentation. Although the team generated much excitement and many questions at the meetings, every firm felt that the company was "too early" and that it should come back when it had more data.

Fortunately, the company was able to get a Phase I SBIR grant from NIH/NCI to achieve two milestones: It was able to synthesize a series of 10 compounds derived from its first hit and to set up a medium-throughput assay to test those compounds using the labs at the university's incubator. The result after nine months was a lead compound with low nanomolar potency and a backup compound with high nanomolar potency. The company got a Phase II SBIR grant for a period of 12 months to begin the initial toxicity and pharmacodynamics and pharmacokinetic studies. Although the funding was helping generate good data, the company still had financial needs not served by the grants—namely, paying for regulatory consultants to help prepare for a pre-IND meeting with the FDA, as well as the mounting IP costs for covering previous and new patent filings.

With the data in hand, the team went back to the eight initial VC firms and got meetings with two. The company was asking for $2.5 million to get the studies to complete an IND, to initiate the first-in-human trial (Phase I), and to provide additional working capital for the company. One of the VC firms, Peak Ventures, liked the company but wanted to see the results from the Phase II SBIR studies first. The firm agreed to invest $250,000 as a convertible note (seed round) to help cover some of the patent costs and to enable the company to get a regulatory consultant to help map out the regulatory path, and especially to determine the cost of the IND-enabling studies.[1]

Finding space. The company was already working out of the university incubator, but with the seed round, it signed a two-year sublease from a company that had gone bankrupt three years into its five-year lease. The space was only office space and a conference room, but it provided not only a place to have meetings and review data, but also a "sense of corporation" for the company.

---

1. The convertible note had standard terms. It was interest bearing at standard rates, and it converted to preferred stock at Series A with a 25 percent discount on the share price.

Raising growth capital. After 12 months, the Phase II SBIR data for Oncotica's lead compound, ONCA-037, looked promising. The toxicology results were somewhat ambiguous, but they were potentially addressable with the back-up compound. With the data in hand, the company was able to get a term sheet for the Series A preferred investment from Peak Ventures. Through due diligence and discussions with the regulatory consultant, Oncotica estimated that it needed a total of $3 million: $1.5 million to complete the IND-enabling studies, $750,000 for the Phase I trial, and $750,000 in working capital (for salaries, IP costs, rent, consultants, etc.). The term sheet had the following major terms:

- Investment: A $3 million investment would be tranched, with the first tranche of $2 million to enable the company to submit the IND. The remaining capital would be released after the IND submission.
- Valuation: The premoney valuation of the company was pegged at $5 million. With an investment of $3 million, Peak would own approximately one-third of the company.
- Stock options: In order to provide incentives for the future management team, a stock option pool of 1 million shares was issued (approximately 6 percent of the company).
- Board seat and management. Since Oncotica did not have a CEO, Dan Rivers, one of Peak's managing partners, become the interim CEO and chairman of the board. The plan was for the company to recruit a full-time CEO as the company approached the IND filing. Having positive results would enhance the ability to attract a top-shelf CEO.

The founders raised concerns about giving away a third of the company, but the difficulty in raising capital and the experience Dan brings to the table made the deal acceptable. This coupled with the comparable data on other VC investments in the biotech industry convinced the founders to accept the funding. Dan had founded a biotech start-up a number of years ago and took it public. Eventually, the company signed the term sheet.

Developing the product. With the investment, the company worked to complete the IND-enabling studies. Given the growth in the CRO industry, the company was able to outsource most of the studies. It also hired a VP of R&D as well as a project manager to plan and oversee the studies. The studies had some hiccups along the way, but the data was solid, so the company submitted an IND to the FDA, paving the way for a first-in-human trial as well as releasing the additional capital from the VC.

After the IND was filed, the company hired a chief medical officer (CMO) who would oversee the clinical development of the drug. The CMO had taken several products through the clinic previously and understood the regulatory hurdles of each phase of the process. However, he came from big pharma and was not accustomed to working on such a tight budget. This, along with his large ego, resulted in a number of heated discussions with the VP of R&D and the CEO. In addition to the CMO, the company planned to hire several clinical and regulatory affairs people, but there was not enough funding to bring them on.

Engaging the customer. Jan McCallister, the VP of business development and one of the first company employees, had been wearing many hats over the previous several years. She was instrumental in putting together the business plan, determining the market need, developing the regulatory plan, and helping to make pitches to the VCs. With the funding and the arrival of a CEO and VP of R&D, she turned her attention to developing relationships with potential pharmaceutical partners. She was considering a range of partners, from small pharma start-ups whose products would complement Oncotica's product, to large pharma and biotechs whose products were coming off patent or who needed to fill a gap in their oncology franchise. She was also open to any type of partnership—from joint development to acquisition of the company. She understood that few companies would partner with a start-up whose drug was in the preclinical stage, but she also understood that it takes time to build these relationships so it was a good time to introduce the company and the product to these partners. Although her efforts were admirable, even good results from the Phase I trial were not sufficient to engage a partner in any serious discussions.

More product development and more fund-raising. With the company running out of money, it turned again to Peak Ventures to raise an $8 million Series B. Peak was interested in the deal but had to get some other firms to come in as part of a syndicate. Putting together a syndicate took some time, and the company desperately needed cash. To buy some time and to avoid laying off key employees, the company agreed to a bridge loan from Peak to keep the company afloat.[2] Two other venture firms were willing to come into the deal, but with the capital markets going through a significant downturn, the premoney valuation was, from the founders' and management's perspective,

2. A bridge loan is similar to a convertible note in that it is a loan to the company to carry it between financings. Terms of the note vary, but a common term is for the amount of the loan to convert at the price of the next round of funding, sometimes with a discount to the share price.

a disappointingly low $8 million, a flat round compared to the postmoney of $8 million from the Series A. Despite the dilution, the company went ahead with the Series B so it could proceed with the Phase II clinical trial.

The Phase II results for ONCA-037 were ambiguous. The trial failed to meet its primary endpoint but did meet the secondary endpoint. After consulting with the FDA and key advisers, Oncotica decided to drop this compound in favor of a backup, ONCA-085, that had been in preclinical testing with very promising results. The safety profile was about the same as 037's, but the efficacy (survival rate) appeared about 40 percent higher. However, the synthesis of this compound was complex, and there were concerns about the company's being able to scale up enough compound for clinical trials. With the company once again running out of money and facing a risky scale-up followed by expensive Phase I and II clinical trials, the investors carefully weighed their options. They issued a bridge loan to allow the company time to get external experts to examine the preclinical data and time to determine, based on the failed Phase II trial, how to design a better clinical program that would have a better chance for success. On the positive side, an experienced team was in place and the diligence from the advisers on 085 was encouraging. On the negative side, the clinical trial would have to be enlarged with several more sites, the risk of scale-up was significant, and the investors were getting tired (Peak had been in this deal for over five years). With that, Peak decided an investment of $12 million (Series B-2) would get them to attract a partner. Although this was good news for the company, it was a bitter pill for the founders because the investors pegged the premoney at a very disappointing $8 million, a significant down round.[3] There was much gnashing of teeth, but in the end, there were no other options and the founders had long since lost control of the company, given the dilution of the earlier rounds of investment. Still, the capital would give the company the funds to get a more promising product into the clinic and perhaps to patients.

The Phase I and II clinical trials of 085 were extremely encouraging. With that data, the management team approached several of the pharma companies McAllister had teed up previously. From discussions with those companies as well as several others (a total of 40 visits and presentations and countless phone calls and e-mails), four companies were interested enough to sign a nondisclosure agreement and begin initial due diligence. Over the next six months, those four were reduced to two, Borland Biotech, a small biotech, and Force Pharmaceuticals, a medium-sized, publicly traded specialty pharma company. Borland had a recent Phase III failure in colon cancer and

---

3. In the colloquialism of venture capital, this is called a "haircut."

was scrambling to come up with a backup plan. It was fortunate in raising a significant amount of capital and could raise another round if a partnership was consummated. The initial conversations had been around licensing the colon cancer compound for development. Force had a colon cancer therapeutic coming off patent in five years and needed a new product. The initial conversation with Force seemed to lean toward acquisition of the company. The team was skillful in keeping both conversations going and subtly letting each party know another party was at the negotiating table. The conversations further developed into term sheets from both companies, but not without some finessing (Oncotica had to stall Force for six months to get both deals on the table). Borland wanted to license the compound from Oncotica and if the compound reached clinical and regulatory events, would pay the company up-front money and certain milestone payments, plus royalty on sales. Force wanted to acquire Oncotica. Below were the key terms for each deal:

Borland (licensing of compound)

Up-front payment:	$50 million
Milestone payments:	Completion of Phase III: $15 million
	Approval of NDA: $20 million
Royalty on sales:	20 percent

Force (company acquisition)

Acquisition price:	$150 million (1/2 cash, 1/2 Force stock)
Milestone payments:	50 percent up front
	25 percent at completion of Phase III
	25 percent at approval of NDA
Management:	One-year consulting contract for senior management
Lock-up:	12 months

Clearly both deals were appealing. The Borland deal had a total "bio-buck" value of $85 million in up-front and milestone payments and somewhere in the range of $160–200 million in royalties per year (assuming $800 million–1 billion per year for eight years, based on the patent life of the compound). By contrast, the Force deal was worth $150 million in cash and stock. The investors preferred the Force deal, although the lock-up and insider trading restrictions were going to delay their liquidity. The Borland deal was potentially worth more, but the time to realize the return was too long for their liking. The management and founders favored the Borland deal because some earlier work had yielded a novel compound for bladder cancer, and they felt more long-term value could be created by developing a series of compounds.

TABLE 4.1 Oncotica capitalization table

SHAREHOLDER	SHARES	%
Dr. Davis	5,500,000	9.2
Dr. Switzer	3,000,000	5.0
Student 1	400,000	0.7
Student 2	400,000	0.7
Advisers	500,000	0.8
Attorney	200,000	0.3
University	1,000,000	1.7
McAllister	250,000	0.4
CMO	250,000	0.4
Peak	48,500,000	80.8
Total	60,000,000	100.0

Heated discussions among the board of directors ensued over which deal to take. Ultimately, the investors, having a majority position in the company (see table 4.1), prevailed and the company was acquired by Force Pharmaceuticals.

So where did things end up after Force acquired Oncotica? The lead compound failed in the Phase III clinical trial because of a series of significant adverse reactions. From the VCs' perspective, the investment was not a home run, but it was not a strikeout either. They invested $20 million and got a return of $65 million, even with the failed compound. It was not the five or ten times the return they had hoped for (but they may have gotten it if the drug had been approved). The founders ended up with money in their pockets, which they were happy with. In addition, the founders negotiated with Force Pharmaceuticals and licensed/acquired the novel compounds for bladder cancer and started a new company to develop these bladder cancer compounds.

Things would not have ended up so well if the company had not been able to strike the deal outlined above. If the company had had even more problems in the clinic, or there had been an economic downturn, or the number of buyers was more limited, they might have had to sell the company at a "fire sale" price, meaning the VCs would want to get something out of the deal, and Oncotica's founders and management would have suffered.

On the other hand, if the founders sold the company for $50 million ($25 million up front), with the same Phase III failure, they would have ended up with much less money, as shown in table 4.2: The founders owned more than

TABLE 4.2 Oncotica capitalization and payout for a $50 million acquisition

SHAREHOLDER	SHARES	%	UP-FRONT
Dr. Davis	5,500,000	9.1	$181,818
Dr. Switzer	3,000,000	5.0	99,174
Student 1	400,000	0.7	13,223
Student 2	400,000	0.7	13,223
Advisers	500,000	0.8	16,529
Attorney	200,000	0.3	6,612
University	1,000,000	1.7	33,058
McAllister	250,000	0.4	8,264
CMO	250,000	0.4	8,264
Other Employees	500,000	0.8	16,529
Peak	48,500,000	80.2	24,603,306
Total	60,500,000	100.0	25,000,000

14 percent of the company but only got around $300,000. This is a great illustration of "preferred stock." When investors purchase stock as part of their investment, they are issued preferred stock, a different class of stock from common stock, which is issued to the founders and management in return for their time and nonfinancial investment in the company. Preferred stockholders are at the front of the line in terms of getting paid at liquidation (acquisition or IPO). After they get paid back their investment, then they get a share of the remaining proceeds on a pro-rata basis, as do common shareholders. In this case, the investors invested $20 million, which they got back as part of the up-front payment, leaving only $5 million to be split among common shareholders, with Peak being an 81 percent shareholder.

SensorLogix

The SensorLogix case study involves a polymer-coated solid-state sensor for detecting airborne chemicals. The company struck a number of partnering deals and was eventually acquired by one of its partners. Figure 4.2 provides a timeline for the major company events.

Dr. Xian Fang (solid-state material scientist, Department of Electrical Engineering) working with Dr. Angela Herron (polymer chemist, Department of Environment Science and Engineering) developed a solid-state sensor coated

FIGURE 4.2 Timeline for SensorLogix

with a thin polymer film that produces a signal in response to a specific gas. The gas diffuses into the film, reacts with the polymer, and produces a current that is detected by the solid-state device. The chemical composition of the film can be changed to respond to different gases.

Recognizing the opportunity. Working together, Drs. Fang and Herron collaborated to develop the initial sensor. Fang developed the solid-state sensor, the supporting electronics, and the communication system for monitoring the sensor remotely. Herron worked on the polymers, each optimized for a different atmospheric gas. The initial application involved environmental studies, where the sensor was used for monitoring CO_2 levels (e.g., in rainforest canopies). With its compact size, remote monitoring, and a potential low cost, the sensor could be deployed over large regions. Although that application drew considerable attention in the literature and resulted in significant grant funding, Dr. Herron recognized the broad utility of the technology, with applications across many problems and many markets. The initial commercial applications she considered were oxygen-sensing in aircraft, pollution monitoring in urban areas, and chemical warfare monitoring. When talking about these applications, she emphasized the key features of the technology: fast response time, gas selectivity (based on the type of film), multiplex capabilities (multiple sensors/films in one package), and small size.

Disclosure to the university and filing for IP protection. A graduate student presented a poster on the sensor at an environmental sciences meeting. The attention and buzz from the show convinced Herron of the commercial potential with this sensor. She disclosed the invention to the TTO, who let her know that the poster was considered a public disclosure and that this might jeopardize patent protection. Herron was shocked, thinking that a publication, not a poster, was public disclosure. An IP lawyer working for the TTO reviewed the poster and concluded that some, but not all, protection outside the United States had been forfeited. The poster only disclosed the sensor film used for CO_2 detection, which was chemically distinct from other films being developed for other gases. The solid-state sensor, without the polymer, had previously been disclosed and filed as a provisional patent. Thus, the TTO decided to file a provisional patent for several of the polymers sensitive to gases other than CO_2.

Recruiting advisers and mentors. Fang and Herron had challenges in finding the right advisers. Because the gas sensor technology can be applied across many applications, it was hard to know whether to recruit a person who understood the target areas and their needs (military, pollution, aerospace) or someone with experience in sensors (e.g., accelerometers, smoke detectors). Through a contact, Herron met Jim Wiggins, who was a product-development engineer for a company that built sensors for screening luggage in airports. Though Wiggins was not in a senior level position, the application was a reasonably close fit with the possible military application, and he had experience working with the government. Through another contact, Fang was approached by Bob Rolf, a semiretired executive who had worked for several large semiconductor companies at the senior executive level and had more recently been involved in a number of material science start-ups.

Developing the business case. With Wiggins and Rolf as advisers, Fang and Herron began monthly meetings to begin developing the business case for the company. The purpose of these meetings was to begin mapping out the product opportunities for the sensor technology. The team began by better defining the applications for the technology. Although the initial application was CO_2 monitoring for global warming, which might not have represented much of an opportunity because of the IP, the team explored many other

TABLE 4.3 Importance of features to customers for SensorLogix applications

	FEATURES				
APPLICATIONS	FAST RESPONSE TIME	MULTIPLEX CAPABILITIES	SMALL SIZE	LOW PRICE	REMOTE SENSING
CO_2 monitoring of rainforests	+	+	++	+++	+++
Oxygen monitoring in airplanes	++	+	+++	++	+
Industrial air pollution monitoring	+	+++	+	++	+++
Home/office air quality monitoring	+	+	++	+++	++
Confined space oxygen monitoring (firefighting)	+++	++	++	++	+++
Chemical warfare	++	++	+++	+	+++

applications. With the assistance of several industry contacts, it developed a matrix that mapped out the fit between the application and the technology (table 4.3).

For each cell in the matrix, it was determined, through general industry knowledge, as well as some market research provided by an MBA student intern, how important each attribute was for the specific application (the more pluses, the more important). For example, small size was not considered important for air pollution monitoring since the device would be mounted in a fixed location. Multiplexed analysis (multiple gases) was important for pollution monitoring since a wide range of chemical pollutants are found in the environment. By contrast, a sensor for chemical warfare would need to be small since soldiers would be wearing the device. Likewise, it was determined that detecting a wide range of chemical agents was not as important as it was for air pollution since fewer agents are used in chemical warfare. Based on this cursory analysis, the team decided to initially focus on a product for the military that rapidly detects chemical warfare agents. The team understood this market was small (only government customers), but it identified significant grant funding and believed that successful demonstration of the product in this area would lay the groundwork for additional applications and products.

Forming the company. Fang and Herron, working with their advisers, decided on the name SensorLogix. They incorporated the company as an S-corporation to avoid double taxation and because they wanted to fund the company through government grants (DOD SBIR) and perhaps a small amount of angel investment. Fang and Herron each contributed $25,000 to the company as a convertible note to help pay for upcoming university patent expenses. The equity was distributed as follows:

SHAREHOLDER	PERCENTAGE OWNERSHIP	VESTING
Herron	45	50 percent vests immediately, 50 percent over the next three years
Fang	25	75 percent vests immediately, 25 percent over the next three years
Wiggins	4	vesting over four years
Rolf	4	vesting over four years
Corporate attorney	2	fully vested
Future management	20	(reserved for CEO, etc.)

The equity split between Herron and Fang was contentious. Herron, who developed the novel polymers, felt her contribution was at least equal to or even greater than Fang's contribution of the solid-state device. In addition, Fang was not that interested in being part of the start-up. Fang felt the solid-state device was essential to making the sensor work, had suggested the initial collaboration with Herron, and the IP protection for the material was very broad. Eventually they reached a compromise where Fang would have less equity but more of it vested sooner, signifying his lack of engagement in building the business. Herron planned to take a one-year sabbatical to be the CSO of the company when the company had acquired a small lab to conduct studies for product development. The lab she occupied was small and funding thus far had been difficult. She decided that she would leave her academic position if the sabbatical was successful and if the company could raise more money. She liked the idea of working in a start-up rather than the university. Fang planned to be an adviser and consultant to the company but to stay at the university (she would come up for tenure in two years).

Building the management team. The SensorLogix board was composed of Fang, Herron, and Rolf. Wiggins, who was going to help with product development and market research, was excited about the technology but could not leave his day job. He agreed to work nights and weekends to explore product opportunities by doing market research to identify the applications of the technology and to drill down into specific applications to get more customer feedback. He was also willing to help out with writing government grants to develop a chemical warfare product. Building the rest of the management team would have to be put off until more funding was acquired.

Licensing the IP. This university had a template license that contained a number of nonnegotiable, predefined terms specific to start-ups and was generally favorable to a start-up. Because equity per se was not part of the license, the negotiations proceeded fairly quickly. The company signed the template license with the following terms:

Exclusivity, territory, field	Exclusive, worldwide, all fields
Up-front licensing fee	$0
Equity	1 percent liquidity fee[4]
Royalty on sale of product	1 percent
Sublicensing income	15 percent
Patent costs	Incurred costs paid back at $500/month for one year; after one year, the balance of incurred plus ongoing costs paid back

Gathering market information. Although the initial market focus was the military, which would use the sensor to detect chemical warfare agents, the company realized that the market was small and the customers were few. They viewed entry into this market important because there were government grants that could pay for initial product-development costs. Even though the product would be geared toward the military, many aspects of the military product could be leveraged for nonmilitary products. Furthermore, selling into the military market would help validate the technology for both investors and customers in other markets.

Wiggins was able to speak with a program officer running a new technology-development group for the U.S. Army. Those conversations helped identify 1) a significant need by the army for a product like this, 2) the process of getting funding for developing and testing the product, and 3) the procurement process for selling to the government. In addition, with his ties to the aviation industry, Wiggins began talking to a number of engineers about

4. This fee was 1 percent of the value of the first liquidity event—either an acquisition or a public offering. The university derived this number from the average university equity holdings at the time of liquidity for a number of previous start-ups.

the use of the sensor for oxygen detection in airplanes. It turned out that the oxygen-sensing unit in planes today is large, expensive, and heavy. Federal regulators had been pressuring the airline manufacturers to install more sensors (only two installed today: one fore, one aft). The anticipated price and size of the SensorLogix sensor made it easy for the company to justify up to five per plane.

To better determine the potential applications, the team gathered information about competitive products on the market. With this information, they developed several market maps showing competitive sensors. The first map compared size versus cost for sensors detecting chemical warfare agents, of which there were only a few. Using the product specification of those sensors, the team created a second map of cost versus sensitivity. That map showed that the SensorLogix sensor was about half the (estimated) price of the competitors' sensors but much less sensitive. The company needed to revisit the sensitivity aspect of the sensor to determine how important it was to the customer. The team created another map to look at size versus cost for oxygen sensors used for airplanes. Well over a dozen competitors were found in this space, but one obscure product appeared to be very close to the SensorLogix sensor in terms of size and cost. The company needed to dig further to understand why this sensor did not have better market penetration.

Defining and refining the business model. The business model for SensorLogix could take several forms, depending on the final product configuration, the establishment of partnerships, and the distribution strategy. One option was for the company to make the sensor module: the semiconductor would be produced offshore, and the company would produce the polymer (that was unlikely to be outsourced because of Herron's expertise in synthesizing the polymer), apply it to the semiconductor (a potential trade secret since it was not disclosed in the patent or otherwise published), and package it into a module. From there, the company could sell the module to a third party for incorporation into a product, or the company could make the product itself and sell it directly to the customer or sell it through a distributor.

Given the lack of capital and infrastructure at this point and the need to show some market traction, partnering with a third party was attractive. For example, if the company developed a wearable, battery-powered sensor for the military that issued an alarm when it sensed one of the target gases, then partnering with a manufacturer that could incorporate the SensorLogix sensor into the final product, had experience building to military spec, and had the relationships with government procurement officers would allow rapid entry into the military market. The downside of this approach was having to share some of the revenue potential with the partner. From there, the company planned to enter the nonmilitary market with an oxygen sensor for the aerospace industry. For this, the company planned either to raise money or to use profits from the military product to develop a product for selling directly to airline manufacturers. For this, they needed to hire a business development person who had ties to that industry, since the number of manufacturers was small and having the relationships with key industry leaders would be important. Finally, if the company moves into a consumer product (e.g., for home/office air quality monitoring), then a different model might evolve to include a third-party manufacturer who could produce the sensor on a large scale to drive down costs. In addition, the sales and distribution channel might include online sales as well as distribution through home improvement and office supply chains.

Marketing the company. The team members brainstormed about how to position the company, the technology, and the future products. With SensorLogix as the company name, and the web address secured, they turned their attention to the platform technology. A name for the technology would give them the opportunity to talk broadly to potential investors, partners, and employees about the capabilities of the company without having to go into product details, which they were thin on. They considered a number of names, including PolySense, SensorMatix, MagicSense, 7thSense, and so on. Although not everyone approved, they eventually settled on QuantiPlex and hoped to use it when talking about their products (e.g., "Powered by the QuantiPlex technology"). The name captured the quantitative and multiplex capability of the technology. Given that the team members were uncertain about where the company was heading with the technology, they struggled to come up with product names, but they did decided to at least choose one for the military application. Eventually they arrived at the QIP 1000 for the product name. It was not the most memorable name, but for military purposes, it was perfectly adequate.

Writing the business plan. In preparing the business plan, the team wanted to focus on several key points:

1 The unique and key enabling features of the QuantiPlex technology to quantify a wide range of gasses simultaneously.
2 The competitive advantage the company had with both its intellectual property and trade secrets.

3   The wide range of product opportunities the QuantiPlex technology
    provided, given the range of polymers that could be synthesized and
    used for different applications.
4   The stepwise strategy the company was pursuing to focus on near-
    term product opportunities (military), which would lay a foundation
    for medium-term (aerospace) and long-term (consumer product)
    opportunities.
5   The team, by members' own admission was adequate but incomplete
    to execute the strategy.

Putting together the business plan provided the structure and discipline
the team needed to dig into each of the opportunities. Team members built
on their previous market research to flesh out the competitive landscape
in terms of product specifications and pricing. In putting together the
competitive landscape, they were cognizant of the fact that many of their
competitors could be partners for some of the product opportunities. In the
long term the competitors could be possible acquirers. The "ask" was a seed
round of $400,000, which would allow them to bring on Wiggins as director
of product development to lead the effort to develop the military sensor.
Team members anticipated that they would need another $600,000 to get
the product to a state where they could partner with a player in the military
equipment space to manufacture the product. The result was a well-written
business plan configured in several forms for communication to investors: a
written document (25 pages), a slide deck for reading (20 slides), a two-page
overview, and a presentation for pitching the company live to investors. In
addition, they put some of this material on the website, knowing that people
who receive the two-page executive summary (e.g., forwarded by a colleague)
might want more information.

Raising initial capital. The team targeted several local angels and three regional
angel groups. They made a dozen presentations (some preliminary pitches,
others in more depth). Although the reception was good and the feedback
from the investors was helpful, the investors all viewed this opportunity as
too early. The team was dejected at the response, but more than that, they
had spent almost a year chasing investors. During this process, though, they
began to sense the technology was not developed enough to attract investors.
For example, the only demonstration of the technology had been with CO_2.
It was clear that they had to demonstrate the technology with other gasses,
which would require the company to develop additional polymers. They also
realized that they would need to be able to apply multiple polymers to the

sensor for simultaneous detection of multiple gasses. Anticipating that more product development would be required, Wiggins and Rolf, working with the faculty founders, put together several grant applications for developing the technology further.

With most of the technology development focused initially on the polymer, Herron considered applying for academic research grants. However, her area of research was environmental chemistry, so grants to develop polymers to detect chemical warfare agents (e.g., nerve gas) were going to be difficult to win. The university offered a TTO-sponsored technology-development grant for $200,000, divided into a $50,000 Phase I and a $150,000 Phase II. Herron applied with Fang as a collaborator to develop two polymers, each specific to two nerve agents for Phase I. Phase II would be application of the two polymers to the semiconductor substrate to demonstrate sensitivity, selectivity, reproducibility, and simultaneous detection. At the same time, the company applied for an SBIR grant through the U.S. Department of Defense for developing polymers for nerve agents not outlined in the university grant. For the SBIR grant, Wiggins was the PI, with Fang and Herron as consultants. Wiggins was willing to leave his current job and join the company if the grant was awarded.

The Phase I university grant was awarded, but the SBIR grant did not score well enough to be funded. The comments back from the SBIR grant were encouraging enough that the company reapplied at the next opportunity. Meanwhile, the university grant allowed Herron to develop the novel polymers in her lab to the point where she could demonstrate the detection of the different gasses.[5] However, given the close chemical structure of the two nerve gasses, the selectivity was very low between the two polymers. Herron realized she should have chosen agents that were more chemically distinct. Given the low selectivity, the TTO decided to not award the Phase II grant. Meanwhile, the Phase I SBIR grant was awarded ($225,000), allowing Wiggins to leave his job and join SensorLogix.

---

5. The work being done in the lab using the university grant caused a minor controversy. The only person who had the skills to synthesize the polymer was a graduate student, so the COI committee insisted the student be able to publish the work. Wiggins and Rolf, who represented the company, objected since publication would require that a provisional patent be filed. Filing a provisional patent not only would cost the company money but would start the clock ticking on the patent life. The company wanted to keep the polymer a secret until it could demonstrate more utility. As a compromise, the adviser found another polymer that could be published, the COI committee let the student work on the weekend for the company, and the IP would be retained by the university and licensed under the existing terms of the license agreement.

Finding space. With an SBIR grant in hand, the company contemplated rent-ing flex space in a local industrial park. Although there was money for rent, the landlord required a five-year lease, which would put the company in a financial bind if the Phase II SBIR grant did not get awarded. Further, if SensorLogix did raise a substantial seed round, the space would not be large enough for the anticipated personnel and activities. Finally, the space did not have a fume hood for the chemical synthesis work. Through several rounds of negotiations with the landlord, the parties agreed to 1) the landlord paying for the installation of a fume hood, 2) an increase in the rent to cover the cost of the hood, 3) a five-year lease with provisions for the company to sublease the space only with the approval of the landlord.

Raising growth capital. Getting the SBIR grant gave the company's technology some level of validation, and the work from the SBIR grant and the univer-sity technology-development grant allowed the company to demonstrate feasibility of a military sensor product. Thus the company decided to make another pass at raising money. Before investing more time and effort in the fund-raising, they spent time trying to recruit a CEO to fill a major void in the management team. Wiggins, who at this point was working for the company, began discussions with Peter Turner, a VP of business development with Sig-maTec, Wiggins's former company. Turner, who had a BS in chemistry and an MBA in finance from a top-twenty business school, had been with SigmaTec for seven years. During his tenure, he had closed several deals around the company's flagship product, a sensor for detecting explosives. He liked his job but he was young and aggressive and wanted the opportunity to lead a company. Although the fit was good, Turner wanted 20 percent equity in the company along with deferred salary of $180,000. The board met to discuss Turner and his offer. He had the business background and industry experience the company needed to do deals with partners. However, he had never raised money or worked for a start-up, so there was potential for a steep and perhaps bumpy learning curve. On the other hand, he understood the importance of building relationships and had demonstrated that by taking each of the SensorLogix owners to lunch for detailed discussions, which allowed him to do his own due diligence on the company.

The discussions around Turner were contentious. The faculty founders foresaw Turner taking the entire allocation of equity for future management, meaning future employees would dilute the current owners. They were opti-mistic that the Phase II SBIR grant would come in and that, with a potential $1 million, they might not need to raise capital for a while and the business development would involve only the military, so they wondered whether they would still need Turner. Rolf and Wiggins argued that even with the SBIR grant, the company would still need to raise money for the nonmilitary applications and to look for partners in those applications. In fact, they added, Turner's current employer would be an excellent partner for developing a product. In the end, there was general agreement that Turner should come on board but that the terms of his employment needed to be negotiated.

Over a two-month period, Turner and the company agreed to bring him on board as the CEO on the following terms:

- 20 percent equity vesting as follows:
  - 10 percent vesting over four years with a one-year cliff
  - 10 percent vesting on the following milestones:
    — 5 percent for the first $500,000 of equity investment with an additional 1 percent for each $100,000 above $500,000

    or

    — 5 percent for an exclusive partnering deal or procurement contract and an additional 5 percent for the first $1 million in revenue associated with the deal or contract
- $120,000 deferred salary for up to 24 months
- A seat on the board of directors

With a shiny new CEO on board, the team revamped the business plan to include the data from the studies funded by the grants and more specifics on the products and product development. During this process, the Phase II SBIR was awarded ($750,000), which was a huge boost for both validation of the technology and essential product development. With the funds in place, the business plan focused on the near-term development and deployment of the military product using a military vendor to manufacture the product around the SensorLogix module.

The company sought from investors $1 million to develop a product in the airport security space (a new class of explosives for which there was not good sensing technology), leveraging Wiggin's and Turner's experience, as well as an oxygen sensor for the aerospace industry. The $1 million put the company outside most angel investors' reach, although perhaps not outside that of a large angel group, of which there is one in the region, or a small venture capital firm. Turner and the team aggressively pursued the angel group and the two local venture firms. There was enough interest from the angel group and one of the VC firms that a co-investment was a possibility, provided the VC led the deal. The discussions went well until they got to premoney valuation. The current owners considered the investor's preliminary valuation of $1 million as a deal breaker, so both parties agreed to table the valuation until more due diligence was done.

Preliminary due diligence was done by the VC firm, with some help from a few of the angels with experience in this space. The pace, in Turner's mind, was glacial, especially as the summer months ensued and August passed with almost radio silence from the investors. Given the slow pace of the negotiations, Turner approached the CEO of SigmaTec, his former company, about working together. With new explosives coming into the market and the lack of sensing technologies for airports to detect them, the CEO was intrigued. Turner knew this market was relatively small but felt that another application demonstration would help the company raise money to attack larger markets in the future. Turner and Wiggins met with the CEO and the SigmaTec product-development team. Luckily, Turner was well liked at his former company and had left under good terms, so the meeting went extremely well. The product engineers were concerned about the risk of being able to synthesize novel polymers to detect this new class of explosives. After the meeting, Turner proposed a joint agreement between the two companies where, together, they would develop a novel sensor product for this class of explosives. They spent several months negotiating a deal with the following terms:

- Up-front payment: $250,000
- R&D payments: $400,000 a year for two years to pay salaries and supplies
- R&D milestones: prototype sensor unit capable of distinguishing between four different explosives representative of this new class of explosives
- License: Exclusive option to the technology for three years with the terms of the license, if taken, being:
  ▸ Exclusive for airport security applications; worldwide
  ▸ $1 million milestone payment upon introduction of the product
  ▸ 3 percent royalties on product sales

With this deal in place and the SBIR Phase II grant awarded, the discussions with the investors continued, but the urgency lessened.

Developing the product. At this stage, the company had two products in development: a sensor for chemical warfare agents for military use and a sensor for a new class of explosives for airport security applications. For the military sensor, the company was able to use the SBIR funding to get the sensing module built and tested and ready for incorporation into a final product, a wearable sensor. Company representatives met with military personnel to better understand the requirements of the sensor (speed, sensitivity, types of gasses, etc.) and to map out how the sensor would be incorporated into a final product. Even though SensorLogix would not be producing the final product, certain specifications of the product would drive the development of the sensor module. For example, the product needed to weigh less than one pound and hold a charge for at least three days. These requirements set limits on battery weight and capacity and thus power consumption by the sensor module. One of the thorniest product-development issues was sensor contamination. The polymer film was gel-like and could be easily fouled by dust and particulates. The team considered several designs to create a barrier to keep particulates from the sensor but allow the gasses to reach the polymer film.

Even though SensorLogix was not ready to manufacture the product, given the impact of the product specifications on the sensor module design, the company identified a product-development and manufacturing partner. The partner, Greenfield Technologies, made an accelerometer-based product for the military and had the experience and the capability to deliver a SensorLogix-based type product. The two parties struck a deal with the following terms:

- Field of use and scope: military, worldwide
- Exclusivity: Exclusive to Greenfield (SensorLogix is prohibited from providing the sensor module to another manufacturer for a military application).
- R&D payments: $1.5 million to be paid for packaging of the sensor and producing 50 production prototypes for testing. These payments will cover the development of the packaging to exclude dust and particulate matter. Payment made only after the prototype sensor meets the agreed-upon specifications (power consumption, sensitivity).
- Greenfield personnel: A part-time project manager and a full-time product engineer will be dedicated to the effort.
- Manufacturing: SensorLogix will produce the first 50 production prototypes and then transfer the production know-how to Greenfield for production of the modules. Greenfield will incorporate the production prototypes into the final product for testing and then be responsible for producing the modules for production.
- Royalty: 1 percent on product sales

Turner tried to negotiate a higher royalty rate but Greenfield was firm on this point, arguing that the sensor module was only a small part of the cost of the final product. In the end, Turner saw the long-term advantage of this relationship in not only developing the technology for nonmilitary uses but also validating the technology by getting a product on the market.

With the agreement signed, the two companies met with military procurement officers and others to identify the specifications of the product, namely weight, battery life, sensitivity, selectivity, and the range of agents needed to be detected. SensorLogix used the SBIR grant, along with R&D payments from the manufacturing deal, to deliver a working prototype to Greenfield.

Meanwhile, the company was working with SigmaTec to develop the explosives detector. The specifications were less stringent (no battery, no fouling) so the product development proceeded smoothly. As the company approached a working prototype, Turner amended the agreement with SigmaTec to include more specifics about manufacturing, which were left open in the original agreement. Using the Greenfield agreement as a template, the two companies came to terms for an amended agreement.

Engaging the customer. At this point, the customer had been engaged indirectly by the two partners, SigmaTec and Greenfield. The partners were selling directly to the customers (government and airports) using the SensorLogix module as the key enabling feature of the products. Although the royalty streams might be nice in the future and the R&D payments and the SBIR grants were keeping the company afloat, Turner wanted to capture more value for SensorLogix, as opposed to handing the value over to a partner. He was able to raise a seed round of $1 million from the angel group, this time with a favorable valuation. The money was tranched in two parts: $500,000 initially to develop the product specifications and a working prototype and the second $500,000 to build the first production units. The money allowed Turner to pursue SensorLogix's first "real" product, an oxygen sensor for firefighters. Although the oxygen sensor for airliners looked initially appealing, a competing product appeared to be very similar to the SensorLogix product and was going to be on the market a year in advance of a SensorLogix launch.

Through some preliminary market research, Turner identified an opportunity for selling a product into the firefighter market for sensing oxygen levels in a confined space. Ancillary markets might include oil rigs, mines, or other confined spaces (e.g., underground utilities). With the funding from the angel group, Turner hired John Holladay, an experienced business-development and marketing executive. Holladay's duties included: 1) meeting with a number of customers to understand the requirements of the product and how current products were not meeting the needs of the firefighter, 2) understanding the purchasing process of products like the one proposed (e.g., do municipalities buy direct or from a distributor) as well the key decision makers involved, and 3) identifying several groups willing and able to test prototypes of the sensor.

Holladay leveraged the work being done for the military to get important meetings with thought leaders in the field. These meetings revealed several important deficiencies with current products. Although two wearable sensors for oxygen levels were available, neither was specifically designed for firefighter use; rather, both were repackaged from other applications. One product had a very slow response time (minutes), which limited its utility for a firefighter quickly moving from room to room. The other product had failed several times due to soot and ash contamination. Holladay and Turner were excited to learn about these weaknesses because their sensor had a fast response time (seconds), and they hoped the lessons learned from the military application could be leveraged to prevent contamination. The discussions also uncovered the need for multiple gas detection (e.g., oxygen, carbon monoxide), which was an opportunity to take advantage of the multiplex capabilities of the technology for future products.

Armed with information on the initial product specification, Turner and Holladay brought on a product engineer to lead the development of the "Oxy-Logix" product. With the polymer production capability developed through the other two products and several approaches to reducing contamination underway, they quickly developed a working prototype. They identified a fire safety trade organization that put them in touch with several groups capable of testing the sensors under simulated situations. They delivered the first prototype for testing, and it passed all the initial tests but failed when exposed to high heat. Although this appeared to be a setback, after talking to a number of customers, it turned out that the heat exposure was outside the range most firefighters would be exposed to. With this testing done, Turner and Holladay approached several large municipalities about testing the prototype alongside sensors currently used by firefighters. The objective of the tests were to 1) determine the time response, 2) test contamination during real situations, and 3) measure long-term drift and the need for calibration. The result of the tests was so positive that the beta customer was ready to commit to ordering enough units to outfit its 200-plus firefighters.

Given the positive results from the beta customer and its commitment to buy the product and the meeting of milestones in developing the sensors for explosives and chemical warfare agents with partners, Turner returned to the angel group for a Series A round of financing. There had been several delays and cost overruns in product development, so more capital was needed to begin production. He was able to raise an additional $1 million from the angel group, who syndicated with another angel group outside the state. With this new infusion of capital, the company was able to establish manufacturing operations for the OxyLogix product.

Establishing manufacturing. With the Series A money, the company established not only polymer production capabilities that would allow large-scale synthesis of the sensing polymers but also an assembly and test facility for the automated application of the polymer to the semiconductor substrate. Because of the sophisticated nature of making and packaging the semiconductor, it continued to be outsourced to a third party. Once the polymer was applied and cured, the sensor module was packaged into the unit and tested.

Scaling up of the polymer synthesis was not trivial. What was doable on a bench-scale proved to be problematic on a production scale. A chemical engineer spent six months getting the batch-to-batch reproducibility acceptable. The chemical engineer also worked with a production engineer to set up an automated dispensing unit for applying the polymer to 48 sensor substrates with the requisite thickness and uniformity. In addition, the two engineers developed a station for curing the polymer after application. Given the trials and tribulations in setting up the production facility and the delays in developing the other products (Greenfield was acquired, causing delays due to layoffs and reorganization; SigmaTec fumbled a product introduction, which set its revenue projections behind and impeded R&D efforts), Turner and Holladay approached the partners about having SensorLogix take over the manufacturing of the product. Greenfield declined to renegotiate the agreement, even though it was paying diligence payments with no revenue because it was not convinced that SensorLogix could meet the stringent military specifications required. SigmaTec, on the other hand, was willing to renegotiate the agreement.

Building sales and marketing. Sales and marketing activities were split three ways: supporting the two partners' efforts (Greenfield and SigmaTec) and efforts to market the company's own product, OxyLogix. To support these diverse marketing efforts, Turner hired Joan Preston, an experience sales and marketing executive. She had run a 150-person global sales force and oversaw marketing for a major aerospace industry leader. She had grown tired of corporate life and wanted to be involved in building something from the ground up. In doing so, however, she realized she would be managing less and taking a more hands-on approach to the marketing (writing ads, attending trade shows, traveling with sales reps) at least until sales ramped up and she could bring more people on board.

SigmaTec was less engaged on the marketing front given that its only customers would be governments and they bought based on specifications and less on technology and branding. Greenfield heavily relied on Preston to help position the explosives sensor for direct selling to airports and the security groups that manage airport security. Greenfield had developed the new product as the SED-5000 (Sensitive Explosive Detector) to add to its other SED products but needed a little more sizzle to compete against another product introduced several months before. They liked the QuantiPlex Technology branding developed by Preston and used "Powered by QuantiPlex" as the tag line for the SED-5000.

For the OxyLogix product, Preston hired two sales reps, giving them huge initial territories (East/West Coast of the United States). Armed with the positive results from beta customers, they were charged with focusing on large municipalities. In deploying the sales reps, Preston learned a number of important things: 1) the sales cycle was dependent on the budget cycle of a municipality (if the rep made the first sales call too far into the budget cycle, there would be less discretionary money for the purchase; the product needed to get into the budget for the following year), 2) for many municipalities, the fire chief's decision to purchase was driven by endorsement of the fire and safety trade organization, and 3) some buyers only went through distributors with whom they had prenegotiated contracts. Overall, however, the reception of the product was extremely positive, even if the number of orders did not reflect it.

To further build the marketing and sales effort, the company got a booth at each of the two major fire and safety trade shows. In a full-court press, the sales reps, as well as Preston, Turner, and Holladay, attended the shows in order to accomplish the following: 1) generate more sales leads for the reps, 2) canvas the exhibition looking at competitive products, 3) learn the process for getting trade organization endorsement (one of the shows is run by the trade organization, and the venue will provide easy access, and 4) identify potential distributors in case they chose to go that route. Each day the team met at the bar of the hotel convention center to compare notes from the day. By the end of the second show, Preston had what she needed to rev up the sales and marketing machine and deliver on the revenue numbers she had promised Turner.

The exit. Although the initial marketing efforts for OxyLogics yielded sales, the customer adoption was slow. Some of that was attributable to the slow sales cycle, but the company soon learned that only the larger municipalities had money or interest in a sophisticated sensor, which limited its market size.

Compounding the company's troubles was the Greenfield acquisition. The acquiring company did not see the strategic alignment of the SensorLogix-Greenfield partnership. After delays due to integration, the acquirer canceled the agreement. Although there was a cancellation payment, the termination eliminated a source of revenue the company had counted on (and had hired people in anticipation of the product launch into the military).

With a launched product and a healthy royalty stream, the SigmaTec partnership was going well. But even with that, Turner had to lay off employees with the latest turn of events. Given the current situation, Turner had several options: 1) he could raise more capital to find a new partner for the military product and pursue new products (e.g., an oxygen sensor for airlines or a home carbon monoxide detector) or 2) he could consider selling the company. A number of contentious board meetings ensued. On one side, Turner was convinced that the oxygen sensor for airlines and the consumer product home sensor would be blockbuster products, but getting these off the ground would require another $2 million in investment and several years of development and marketing. On the other side, the investors had been in this company for five years and needed a liquidity event for their limited partners. The seven-person board (Turner, Heron, Fang, Rolf, two investors, and an independent board member) agreed to explore the acquisition option for six months to see what the appetite was for the company. Reluctantly, Turner and Holladay hit the road to pitch the company to a few potential acquirers. One of the obvious stops was SigmaTec, although Turner was not excited about the idea of working again for his old company. SigmaTec had recently gone public and was on the hunt for small companies with cutting-edge products and technologies. It was familiar with SensorLogix through the partnership. In addition to not wanting to work for his former employer, Turner knew its strategic focus and thought it unlikely it would be interested in developing the consumer product. It was also unlikely that SigmaTec would be interested in keeping him around after the acquisition. He pursued several other possible acquirers, but given the company's dwindling cash reserves, the investors' impatience, and the company's strategic fit with SigmaTec's focus on defense and aerospace applications, he pursued a SigmaTec acquisition. The initial offer was $5 million, based on current sales of $1 million. The board was appalled and considered this a low-ball offer. Turner went back to SigmaTec and argued that, given the broad IP protection and the military product that had been dropped by Greenfield, there was much more value in the company. He was able to renegotiate an up-front payment of $7 million, with an additional $3 million possible over the next two years if the company reached certain revenue milestones. In the end, the company signed the deal

TABLE 4.4 SensorLogix capitalization and payout after acquisition

SHAREHOLDER	SHARES	%	UP-FRONT	EARNOUT	TOTAL
Herron	2,250,000	18	$1,265,625	$542,411	$1,808,036
Fang	1,250,000	10	$703,125	$301,339	$1,004,464
Rolf	200,000	2	$112,500	$48,214	$160,714
Wiggins	200,000	2	$112,500	$48,214	$160,714
Attorney	100,000	1	$56,250	$24,107	$80,357
Turner	1,000,000	8	$562,500	$241,071	$803,571
Holladay	400,000	3	$225,000	$96,429	$321,429
Preston	250,000	2	$140,625	$60,268	$200,893
Other employees	350,000	3	$196,875	$84,375	$281,250
Angel investors	6,444,444	52	$3,625,000	$1,553,571	$5,178,571
Total	12,444,444	100	$7,000,000	$3,000,000	$10,000,000

to be acquired by SigmaTec. The division of the proceeds from the acquisition is shown in table 4.4.[6]

Assuming that the milestones were achieved, the investors made approximately 2.5 times their investment—not a home run but a reasonable return nonetheless. The management team members made money, but not all of them viewed this in a positive light. Some had taken a significant pay cut to join SensorLogix, and the return did not make up for the lost wages. Others saw the value in the non-economic return of "the ride," that is, the opportunity to build a company from the ground up and experience the lows and highs of bringing a product to market. The founders both made money and got an invaluable education, especially Herron, who had left the university to join the company full time.

Cylent

The Cylent case study explores a university innovation that was bootstrapped initially, followed by a novel investment deal. The timeline for Cylent is shown in figure 4.3.

Dr. Vladamir Volkov, from the Department of Computer Science and Electrical Engineering, along with his graduate student, Shuu Kato, developed software algorithms to manage the data load on servers. The software could

6. Not included in the cap table is the payout to the university of $100,000 for the liquidity payment under the terms of the license.

FIGURE 4.3 Timeline for Cylent

predict server load, based on historical data and current trending, and allocate traffic to underutilized servers. In so doing, server speed could remain at optimal levels during peak usage.

Recognizing the opportunity. Dr. Volkov was a recognized expert in server software and had consulted for both government and industry. Through these consulting engagements, he recognized the problem of server traffic dramatically slowing the performance of server software. Volkov was also an endurance athlete who competed in marathons and long-distance triathlons. He had personally been perplexed and frustrated with a number of event registration sites that would slow to a crawl or crash as registration opened for a popular event. With this problem in mind, he developed novel algorithms to optimize resource allocation among servers.

Disclosure to the university. The idea for the software came to Volkov from discussions he had with a leading Internet company during a series of consulting engagements as well as his own personal experience. After disclosing the software to the university TTO, the tech transfer officer examined the consulting agreement, which included terms that assigned any inventions developed during the consulting engagement to the Internet company. Given that the idea came through Volkov's interactions with the company, and the company was not in the server or server-optimization business and that the software was developed ("reduced to practice") using National Science Foundation funding, the TTO determined that the intellectual property belonged to the university, by way of Bayh-Dole, and could be licensed to Volkov's start-up.

Filing for IP protection. Given the uncertainty in patenting software[7] and enforcing software patents, the TTO decided to file a copyright for the server-optimization software.

Recruiting advisers and mentors. At first Volkov did not think he needed an adviser, given his extensive consulting experience, but a fellow faculty member who had spun out a company told him he needed advisers to better research and position the opportunity in terms of market need. He also pointed out that Volkov eventually would need a management team that could be drawn from the advisers or identified through the advisers' contacts. Volkov identified several people through his consulting contacts who agreed to serve as advisers. Steve Humphries was head of product development for a cloud-based computing company, and Sue Clemmons was the former CEO of a small Internet service provider (ISP). She had recently left the company when it was acquired. Clemmons thought she was going to retire after her exit but realized she liked the rough-and-tumble nature of start-ups. After a number of meetings with Volkov, she became very interested in the opportunity. On her own initiative, she took an active role in conducting preliminary market research and put together thoughts on the business strategy. Together Volkov, Humphries, and Clemmons began to sketch out a preliminary list of features and benefits of the software.

Developing the business case. Volkov worked with his advisers and several industry leaders to define an initial set of product features. Although Dr. Volkov saw the market need through his consulting work, he explored the extent of the need in a broader market context through a series of interviews with cloud-based computing and ISP companies. From these conversations, Volkov concluded that the problem of server performance degradation was seen by only a handful of the top ISPs or ISPs that supported large e-commerce operations. Although there was not as broad a need as Volkov and his advisers had first hoped, they would need to do further research to verify the need or consider their situation more of a technology push than a market pull. During the interviews, they also discovered no apparent competition in this space, which was both good and bad.[8] The discovery pointed to the main risk

7. Patenting software has been controversial for years, with several cases being decided by the U.S. Supreme Court. The current state of software patents is evolving, with more software patents being issued by the U.S. Patent and Trademark Office each year. Over the last thirty years, the number of software patents (Class 717) has risen from 34 in 1992, to 341 in 2002, to 1,515 in 2012.

8. No apparent competition is a double-edged sword. On one hand, it provides a great opportunity to capture the market, but on the other, it could signal a lack of a significant market need to attract other products.

of building a business around this software: market risk. The most important question was, Will customers buy the product?

Because of the ease of creating software products and the low amount of working capital required, Volkov decided to create a minimal viable product to explore the customer needs further and to better develop the business case. He was able to initially create a working prototype that showed the minimum functionality of the product. With this, he visited several potential customers for feedback. Based on the feedback, he was able to modify a number of aspects of the product and better articulate the customer needs.

The team also began discussions about funding. Volkov estimated that a majority of the software could be developed by contracting with overseas companies. He had contacts in Hungary, but India was another consideration. Given the amount work to be done, the low costs associated with developing a software product, and the short time to market, the team planned to raise a small amount of capital (from the founders, friends and family, perhaps an angel investor), but essentially they were going to try to bootstrap the company. This would require the company to generate sufficient revenue to be able to bring on additional personnel and grow the company.

Forming the company. The team of three agreed there was enough demand for the software and decided to form a company. They named the company Cylent (pronounced "silent") and incorporated as an LLC. Volkov realized the essential role Clemmons was playing now and asked her to join as CEO of the company. The equity distribution was a follows:

SHAREHOLDER	PERCENTAGE OWNERSHIP	VESTING
Volkov, founder	70 percent	50 percent vests now, 50 percent over four years
Clemmons, founder and CEO	20 percent	four-year vest with one-year cliff
Humphries, founder and adviser	5 percent	vests over two years
Shuu Kato, graduate student	5 percent	all vests now

Giving the graduate student equity triggered a conflict of interest discussion with the department's COI committee. The committee was most concerned that the student's work was part of developing software for the company. Volkov and the committee agreed to focus the student's work on the fundamental algorithms related to server optimization, which could be published. The committee was also uncomfortable with the student holding equity, but it did not see any major conflict so they permitted it.

In addition, Clemmons negotiated a salary of $120,000, which she would defer until the company had the revenue to pay her. At her option, she would be permitted to convert the deferred salary to equity at an agreed-upon stock price. Volkov proposed a similar scheme under a consulting agreement to the company to account for the nights and weekends he was going to spend on the company. His proposal was not well received by the other founders, given the fact he had a salary from the university and he owned 70 percent of the company.

Building the management team. Since the founders would be bootstrapping the company, and most of the technical know-how resided in Volkov, the management team consisted of Clemmons as CEO and would remain lean until the company began to generate revenue.

Licensing the IP. Because copyrights have a shorter life span and offer less protection than do patents, the university offered a license for the software with the following terms:

Exclusivity, territory, field	Exclusive, worldwide, all fields
Up-front licensing fee	$10,000
Equity	1 percent
Royalty on sale of product	0.5 percent
Sublicensing income	15 percent
Patent costs	N/A

The founders needed to come up with the $10,000 for the license, in addition to initial capital for product development.

Gathering market information. Clemmons, having previously headed up a small ISP, understood the dynamics of the marketplace. She and Volkov talked to a number of small and medium-size ISPs that hosted a significant amount of e-commerce traffic. Through their discussions, Clemmons and Volkov learned that very few of the ISPs saw a problem with server performance. There had been a few complaints from clients about the delays their customer experienced placing orders, but they were not significant.

Several ISPs agreed to give Clemmons a list of clients to explore the need further. She contacted five e-commerce sites and discovered much more discontent than the ISPs had indicated. Three of the five sites had been completely shut down because of heavy traffic. Digging a little deeper, Clemmons discovered that these sites were hosting ticket sales for bands, theatrical performances, and sporting events and that the site delays and crashes only occurred during a one- or two-hour period when tickets for very popular events went on sale. She contacted a number of online ticket sites to explore this problem, and, as expected, the large players (e.g., Ticketmaster) had solved the problem by working closely with their ISP to develop a custom solution (and purchase more server capacity for peak times). The medium and smaller ticket sites could not afford a custom solution or more server capacity, especially since they needed the additional capacity only a few hours a month. Going back to the ISPs, Clemmons was able to get them excited about the software that could differentiate their ISP offering (more reliability, less frustrated customers) and target a unique client, namely ticket sites.

The market map for the Cylent product was complicated because at the time companies did not use software specifically designed to optimize performance. Most ISPs used in-house methods for optimization, with mixed results. Thus the initial assessment of the market, which yielded no competition, was not entirely correct. The internal solutions needed to be accounted for. For customers who did not have server optimization (e.g., the smaller ISPs), there seemed to be an opportunity. The open question was the extent to which the companies with in-house solutions currently would switch to Cylent's turnkey solution.

Defining and refining the business model. Cylent had several options in terms of a business model. It could sell the software to the customer (ISP), who could install and maintain the software. The customer would pay for one license per server. The license would be renewed each year, and the renewal would come with upgrades. The alternative was Cylent would host the software on its servers and offer software as a service. With this model, the customer would be paying a monthly fee. Both models were appealing, but Volkov determined that the SaaS model would be technically challenging and require Cylent to lease server space and hire additional personnel, costs that would require raising a significant amount of capital and result in dilution. In the end, they chose to sell directly to the ISPs, a sales effort Clemmons would lead. Marketing would be minimal since most of the customers would be accessing Cylent's website for product specifications.

Marketing the company. Since the founders had minimal marketing to do, they turned their attention instead to product names. They considered Optimizer, ServerMax, and PeakMaster, but in the end settled on FloodGate as the product name. The choice was not unanimous, but the more they used it, the more they liked it.

Writing the business plan. With the bootstrap strategy, the business plan was more of an operational document than a fund-raising one. It provided some information about the market, but Clemmons understood that they could do only so much market analysis and projections. The company would not get initial customer feedback until it had a product to show. And, of course, the real feedback would come from customers buying and using the product. Related to this, the founders realized that they were going to need to hire at least one customer-facing person to manage the e-commerce site, provide technical assistance, and release upgrades. They might need to raise money for that person, given that they would need that capability at product launch and Volkov would not have the time to do this.

Based on the initial customer surveys, a significant portion of the plan had to include the product specifications. Since contractors would be hired to develop the software, the specifications were written in fine detail.

The financial projections comprised the final, and most important, section of the business plan. With a bootstrap strategy, the company was trying to be as capital efficient as possible (e.g., contracting programmers versus hiring full-time employees). The founders' biggest challenge was projecting revenues. There would be a critical period after they launched the product where they would need to meet certain revenue projections. If they missed the numbers, they would have to either scramble to raise money (investors can smell a company in trouble a mile away; the result is usually a very low valuation) or lay off employees. If they met their projections, they could develop additional products as well as pay employees.

Raising initial capital. The financial calculations showed the company reaching cash-flow positive in 12 months. However, the break-even analysis showed that the company would need at least $250,000 to reach break even. Figure 4.4 shows both the monthly cash flow and the cumulative cash-flow projections for the first two years of company operations. (The lowest point on the cumulative curve represents the amount of initial capital the company would need to break even.) The founders agreed to contribute funds based on their percentage ownership. Volkov took out a second mortgage on his house, and together they committed to $100,000. For the remainder they approached an angel investor, Jim Cochran, who Clemmons knew. The founders agreed to raise $250,000 from Cochran, which would give them some room for error. Cochran, a creative investor, saw that the company was unlikely to be acquired and or to go public, so he crafted a clause to allow him to convert his equity to a royalty on revenue to ensure he would see return on his investment. For each

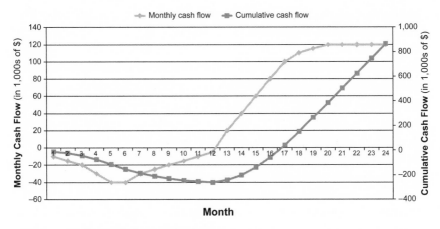

FIGURE 4.4 Cylent cash-flow projections

dollar of product sold, he would receive a small percentage of the revenue as a royalty. He proposed that the percentage royalty be sliding (i.e., it would decrease with increasing revenue). The total royalty to be paid would be capped at three times his investment. Although Volkov did not like this term, he understood that this business was unlikely to grow enough to be acquired.

Finding space. The company's space requirements were minimal. The biggest factor was high-speed Internet access. They were able to rent two offices in a local business incubator that gave them access to a conference room and video conferencing capabilities.

Developing the product. Based on the MVP developed earlier, Volkov hired programmers in India to write the code. The programmers were efficient, but Volkov could not keep up with revisions and keep his academic research group going. The grants he had to write, combined with his consulting commitments, were slowing the development. He missed a key development milestone, so the founders met to solve the problem. By this time, the graduate student, Shuu Kato, was graduating and looking for a job. The university offered an entrepreneurship fellowship for graduate students—in essence, a postdoc stint in a start-up. Given the close relationship between Volkov and Cylent, the fellowship would give Kato a chance to explore his entrepreneurial interests and experience a start-up. Just as important, given his experience in the lab, he would be able to take over some of the testing and directing the contract programmers. Furthermore, he had a good sense of design, so he would be able to craft a company website, including the e-commerce capability for selling the product online.

Engaging the customer. Clemmons was frustrated with the slow pace of the software development. She had lined up several beta customers who would likely buy if the software met their specifications. When the beta version was finally ready and shown to three beta customers, the initial demo failed miserably because of a server compatibility issue. Luckily, one of the three customers saw the value of the software and recognized Volkov's technical prowess. The customer agreed to test the next version once the compatibility issue was fixed. The team worked through a weekend to get the next revision ready and the result was a huge success. The customer not only liked the software but also thought the approach to server optimization could be game-changing for the industry. Volkov and the customer agreed to write a white paper together about the approach, which was great marketing piece for the company.

With white paper in hand, Clemmons returned to the other two beta customers. The demo went well, but they said they would like to see a number of features before they bought. An internal meeting with the technical team was intense. Volkov believed that the features were necessary and that they could be implemented in less than a month. Clemmons agreed about some of the features but argued that the entire list of features would take at least six months (optimistically) to implement. She also was not sure those features would be of value to the broader customer base. They agreed to implement two of the ten requests while Clemmons reached out to other potential customers to gauge product interest as well to get clarity on the other features. Her goal was to differentiate between "need-to-have" and "want-to-have" features and to explore price sensitivity for the product with and without the features.

The meetings with customers provided invaluable feedback on the product-development process. Clemmons, often accompanied by Volkov, met with 15 different customers to discuss the product. Through this market research, they saw a clear segmentation of features requested and identified competitive products, features, and pricing. They concluded that "super users" (people with sophisticated needs) required a certain feature set and more pedestrian users required another. They decided to launch the Flood-Gate product based on the feedback from the super users and to offer it at $59.99 per month per site, which included customer support and free upgrades for a year.

With the launch under way, Clemmons began to crank up the marketing engine. The website with e-commerce functionality was launched to both feature the products and permit sales transactions. The white paper, along with a number of early customer testimonials, helped establish a significant marketing package. Although it was expensive and time consuming, Clemmons traveled to meet potential customers with large numbers of servers. These key clients were big enough to generate significant revenue, but they also had the technical teams to understand what she considered to be a groundbreaking approach to server optimization. This three-month travel blitz paid off with significant sales. The company was excited about the market traction, but the volume of sales began to strain customer support (Kato and, when he was available, Volkov). The company's profits, along with the angel investment, allowed it to hire two people, an inside sales person and a tech support person. The inside sales person followed up on leads that came in through the website, as well as those Clemmons generated through her activities. Approaching their first year in business, they were on track to reach cash-flow positive—a rare accomplishment for many start-ups.

Raising growth capital. Over the following six months, however, sales steadily declined. Volkov and Clemmons met multiple times to discuss the problem, and much finger-pointing ensued. Volkov insisted that Clemmons do more travel, but the costs, both financially and on her family, were too great. Clemmons countered that the product was not getting the rave reviews the early customers gave it because of continued bugs and a lack of key features. She also pointed out that there seemed to be less traction with smaller customers. Volkov retorted that these customers simply lacked the "sophistication and technical depth" to understand the revolutionary nature of the product. They met with their cofounder, Humphries, who had somewhat of an objective perspective. His assessment was that the company had hit the classic chasm between early adopters and the majority of the market (see page 148). The early adopters were buying based on the technical underpinnings of the software and were willing to live with fewer features and a few bugs in exchange for access to cutting-edge software. The majority of the market, however, was less interested in groundbreaking software than in solving problems with the right feature set and needed rock-solid reliability. This assessment was consistent with the segmentation of customers they saw with earlier market research. They also acknowledged that perhaps they had designed the first product for a much higher end user, in a much more limited market than they had anticipated.

Clemmons returned to some of the customers who had shown interest but did not purchase to understand the features and reliability they needed. The market research was invaluable but it pointed to a product different from FloodGate. There was a clear opportunity here, probably bigger than FloodGate. The problem, however, was the time and money required to develop this second product. Given the current burn rate, they would be out of money before they could launch the new product. They could lay off the two employees they just hired to reduce expenses but they would need to rehire that same capability with the launch of the new product.

Clemmons and Volkov did not want further dilution from another round of financing, and they were not looking forward to dealing with Cochran, their angel investor, who had been a tough negotiator during the first round. After much deliberation, they agreed to approach Cochran for $200,000. Cochran proposed a slight up round (the good news) but changed the terms of his royalty option to both accelerate the royalty payments and raise the cap from three times to ten times his investment (the bad news). Volkov, who was known for his short temper, went ballistic, talking about lawsuits and other measures. Humphries and Clemmons calmed him down, and they agreed to counter the proposal to soften the terms. In the end, they reduced the royalty rate acceleration slightly and reduced the cap to five times the investment.

The exit. With more capital, the team members worked to develop RoboGate, their follow-on product that was much less sophisticated but easier to use and more robust. They believed that the market was much larger, so they offered the product at a lower price point. To reach this market, however, they had to reach a larger number of customers. Rather than travel to individual clients, Clemmons attended the major trade shows, bringing Volkov or Kato along to talk technical details. The team also developed a newsletter for bringing content to current and prospective customers. In addition, e-mail blasts drove significant traffic to the website, where many products were purchased with very little follow up.

For the next two years, the Cylent had good, steady growth, but, as predicted, not the kind of explosive growth that would attract an acquirer. The revenue stream (approximately $5 million/year) was enough to employ a dozen employees and pay the royalty to Cochran. It also allowed Volkov to leave his academic position and join the company full time as CTO. Meanwhile, though Clemmons had enjoyed the ride, she left the company to spend more time with her family.

Summary

The three case studies presented here show the diversity of university start-ups as well as the realistic trajectories and outcomes for a company.[9] For some companies, like Oncotica, the risk of the opportunity is huge (failing in the clinic, no FDA approval, high manufacturing costs) but the upside could be huge as well. To take on this type of risk requires significant investment by venture capital. Significant investment translates to significant dilution of the founders. Founders must be prepared for that, so understanding risk capital is essential to reach the market place (long-term) or to find a partner (short-term) willing to assume that risk (and return) in the later stages of product development. Partnering takes center stage for SensorLogix. To reach certain markets (e.g., military) they needed the expertise, experience, and relationships of their partners. Like Oncotica, the SensorLogix partners provided capital, assumed risk, and leverage their distribution channels for getting the product to market. Cylent, by contrast needed the least capital, as is typical for a tech start-up, and was able to take the product directly to the customer without a partner.[10]

These case studies also illustrate a few additional points. First, expect the unexpected. All companies, no matter the technology, backing, or management, take unexpected twists and terms. There will be bumps in the road, so be prepared by being flexible. Second, do not underestimate the importance of the right team. The tussles between founder and others illustrated here are minor compared to some that we have experienced in the real world. Disagreements are part of the game, but working with bad actors, incompetent managers, or greedy investors can turn an entrepreneurial adventure into a midnight horror show. Third, market research and customer feedback are essential, especially the closer you get to launching a product. For Oncotica, finding the right therapeutic fit for the market was important, but the technical hurdles were significant and needed to be sorted out before the company talked to customers. On the other hand, it was essential for Cylent to find its customers before developing the product, although its owners ignored some important feedback early on.

9. All three cases were successful, which is not typical for university start-ups. Many more fail than succeed. The reasons for failure are many, and determining what they are would require numerous more case studies. But heeding the lessons learned from failure can be important for moving to the next venture.

10. An equally likely outcome for Cylent would have been partnering with another software seller or "value-added reseller" to distribute the software and perhaps reach a larger market.

Finally, the return expectations of the investors are related to the size of the investment, which is related to the investor's risk tolerance. For Oncotica, only VCs and deep-pocketed pharmaceutical companies had the capital and risk tolerance to invest tens of millions of dollars to bring its drug to market. Their return expectations were very high, with the VCs expecting 10 times their investment. SensorLogix had moderate risk (some technical, some market) and needed an amount of capital that either a small VC or an angel group could invest to get the product to market. With the reduced risk, the investors knew they would be looking at a much smaller return than Oncotica's investors expected. In Cylent's case, the angel investor invested a relatively small amount, was accepting of a relatively low risk (mostly market and execution), and had the patience for very long-term return (maybe 10 years).

5

Stakeholders' Perspectives

Up to this point, we have described the entrepreneurial ecosystem in which a university start-up exists, outlined the steps that a start-up must take to bring a product to market, and provided examples of how specific types of companies take those steps. This chapter considers the perspective of the various stakeholders involved in the process of spinning companies out of universities in hopes of bringing innovative products to market. Stakeholders include the research faculty member, whose research is the subject of the start-up company and who is typically involved as a founder but can take on on other roles, 2) the entrepreneur or business leader who brings business expertise and leadership while engaging with the faculty and university to help launch and grow the business, and 3) the university research administrator (e.g., VC of research or director of the tech transfer office) who oversees certain aspects of the spinout process (e.g., licensing) but also would be interested in building a more robust entrepreneurial support program.

The Faculty

The faculty are some of the key stakeholders in companies spinning out of universities. At minimum, they are the inventors of the intellectual property, which serves as the core of the start-up. They might be the start-up founders, they might play an early role in managing the company, they might assist in fund-raising, and/or they might help to make key business decisions. As such, faculty need to determine not only their role in the company but also their motivations for starting the company. They also need to understand who owns the ideas around which the start-up is being built, what ownership of the start-up means in terms of control, and what kinds of conflicts of interest or commitment might arise.

Motivations and Expectations

If you ask faculty members why they are starting a company, there is rarely a single answer, and their motivations vary widely. Many want their research to have a practical impact in the "real world." Others see the opportunity for a significant financial return, though few will ever state that in public. Some see the start-up as a significant source of funding back to the lab. Finally, since, by nature, they are curious people, many are interested in learning about the business side of science and the exciting world of entrepreneurship.

Of course, along with these motivations come expectations about the start-up, so it is important for faculty to set realistic expectations about how this process will unfold. Here we debunk several myths about start-ups that faculty fall victim to:

MY START-UP WILL PROVIDE SIGNIFICANT FUNDING TO MY LAB. Rarely does this happen, and if it does happen, rarely is the funded research publishable, because the results are usually proprietary. The exception is in engineering fields where the lab has specific expertise or specialized equipment and the funding for development goes hand-in-hand with the work in the lab (e.g., optimization studies).

I WANT TO ALWAYS OWN AT LEAST HALF OF THE COMPANY SO I HAVE CONTROL. Rarely do faculty founders own a majority of their company at the stage that the company is fully functional or sustainable. Since most technology-based companies need significant capital to develop a product, most faculty founders have their ownership percentage reduced through dilution. The exception is where the product-development costs are low and a company can generate significant revenue early on (e.g., web-based or service-based companies).

I WANT TO FUND MY RETIREMENT THROUGH A SUCCESSFUL COMPANY. The world of start-ups is very high risk, to the point that maybe one in a thousand start-ups beginning at this early stage are successful. Even if a start-up is successful, dilution of ownership might not result in a multimillion-dollar return (but it could be enough to put a kid through college).

I BELIEVE SO STRONGLY IN MY TECHNOLOGY THAT I'M GOING TO PUT ALL OF MY RETIREMENT SAVINGS INTO THE COMPANY. See the previous point. With that said, however, showing some skin in the game signals to others you have confidence in the technology and are willing to take a risk. And putting several thousand dollars toward incorporation or patent costs is quite different from liquidating your 401k.

I WANT TO BE CEO AND RUN THE COMPANY. Rarely do research faculty members have enough breadth of experience to take on the CEO role. Furthermore, unless they are leaving their academic post, they usually lack the time to devote to the effort.

I'M NOT MOTIVATED BY THE MONEY, I JUST WANT TO HAVE IMPACT. This may be true, but the function of a start-up is to create value, and value is created by selling a product for profit. The impact will come when that product is in the hands of customers, but that only happens through the making and selling of the product.

I WANT TO SEE A PRODUCT COME OUT OF MY RESEARCH. Although extensive research on this point is lacking, there are plenty of examples of start-ups whose eventual product is only tangentially related to the founding science or technology. This happens because, as the product is developed or the business strategy is formulated, you might encounter roadblocks (e.g., technical failures, IP issues) or other opportunities might arise (e.g., alternative applications of the technology with a much larger market).

Finally, whatever the motivation or combination of motivations, it is important to 1) honestly understand your motivations, 2) understand how those motivations will play out during the course of company formation, launch, and growth, and 3) assess the likelihood that your expectations will be met.

Faculty Roles in the Start-Up

As mentioned in Chapter 2, the faculty can take on many roles in the start-up, depending on their expertise, career stage (tenure?), interest level, and other personal commitments (spouse, children). At one end of the spectrum is the start-up founded by several entrepreneurs around a university technology where the faculty member may be an occasional consultant to the company and may have a few stock options. In this case, the control and direction of the company lies with the external founders.[1] At the other extreme is the faculty

1. For these types of start-ups, the technology is either advanced to the point of being commercially ready or codified, in which case the start-up would require less input from the researcher, or the external founders are developing a product that may be derivative of the core technology, or the core technology is only a portion of the final product.

member who recognizes a commercial opportunity in his or her research, seeks out an attorney to incorporate the company, gathers a team of advisers to develop the business strategy, brings on the CEO to run the company, and helps with fund-raising. Table 5.1 shows the many possible roles a faculty member might play in a start-up.

The roles are divided according to the employment status of the faculty, since the university sets the expectation for how the employees spend their time. The time commitment of certain roles can be high, so for a university employee, that means taking personal time to carry out these roles (see conflict of commitment section below) above and beyond his or her academic role. A hybrid role might exist where the faculty member is a visiting scientist in the company, taking a sabbatical or leave of absence from the university. This temporary position results in the faculty member either returning to the university or leaving his or her academic position for the start-up.

The employment status of faculty members also raises the issue about titles. Some founders feel compelled to have someone to carry the title of CSO or CEO of the company and will take the title during the early stages of the company. This can be confusing to people outside the university (e.g., potential CEOs or investors). Unless the faculty founder is leaving the university, the title of "founder" is sufficient; it signals there is not a management team in place but the founder is actively seeking one.

The role of the faculty member with the start-up is never static since the company will grow/shrink and/or might change direction over time. Thus, the faculty member's involvement in the start-up might increase to the point that he or she decides to leave the university and work at the start-up. On the other hand, the faculty member's involvement may wane over time. The faculty founder's shift to a less active role with the company comes about for different, and at times unpleasant, reasons. Some faculty members lose interest in the company when university commitments combine with the company's less acute needs for their services (technical or strategic input). Unpleasantness can arise when either a) the company needs technical input but the faculty founder does not have the time to provide it (e.g., go on investor pitches, write grant applications) or b) the faculty founder wants to play a more active role in the company, but the company has moved beyond his or her expertise or the company has changed direction, no longer focusing on the founding technology. In the former case, the lack of technical input and guidance can strangle a company. Others can be brought in, but rarely do they fill the void. In the latter case, the faculty founder might be voted off the board or his or her consulting agreement might not be renewed. Needless to

TABLE 5.1 Faculty roles in a start-up (+ = least amount; +++++ = greatest amount)

EMPLOYMENT STATUS	FACULTY ROLE	ENGAGEMENT AND TIME COMMITMENT	COMMENTS
University employee	Consultant	+/+++	The role can vary depending on time available and the needs of the start-up. The consulting role can be informal or formal, the latter being covered by a consulting agreement that must address IP developed during consultation.
	Member/ chair of SAB	++	Usually involves monthly or quarterly meetings to advise the company on technical/scientific matters.
	Board member	+++	Weekly or monthly meetings and e-mail interactions with investors and management team.
	Visiting scientist	++++	Not typical, but some faculty founders can take a sabbatical to work for the company for 6–18 months.
University/ company employee	CSO CTO	++++	Not common. Involves working part time for company and university.
Company employee	CEO	+++++	Very rare that a faculty founder has the interest and skills to take this leadership role.
	CSO CTO	+++++	Not as rare as CEO but requires faculty founder to leave the university position.

say, this results in bitterness on the part of the founder, especially when there is lack of agreement with the direction of the company.

One important aspect of a faculty member's involvement in the company is understanding the importance of partnering with others in building out the management team. Many faculty founders underestimate the time required or expertise needed to manage and build the business. Their primary role is creating the technical underpinning for developing the product and providing technical guidance as the product is being developed. One common mistake faculty founders make is not appreciating the value of an entrepreneur or business leader in getting a company off the ground. The value of the relationships the entrepreneurs bring (e.g., service providers, investors, customers) can be significant. By the same token, many business leaders, especially those lacking a technical background, underestimate the technical hurdles (FDA approval, scale-up, etc.) a company faces in bringing a technology-based product to market. This can be an area of tension or conflict for both parties. An ideal partnership between a faculty founder and an entrepreneur is one where each has an appreciation of both the market and the technical risks the company will face and respects the skills the other brings to address these risks.

Ownership of Ideas, Discoveries, and Inventions

One of the more difficult aspects of starting a company for faculty members is determining when an invention or idea is owned by the faculty and when it is owned by the university. To put things in perspective, consider a company in private industry: it lays claim to all of your ideas as they relate to the company's business. As a condition of employment, employees often must sign an agreement that stipulates that they must disclose any ideas, discoveries, or inventions to the company in a timely manner and assign those disclosures to the company. Most universities have similar policies, but the enforcement of those policies can vary across universities. Some faculty are not even aware of these types of agreements, since often they are signed as part of the flurry of paperwork they complete when they are hired. The determination of ownership of an invention rests with the specific policy of the university. Another layer of complexity arises when considering the source of funding that led to the invention (e.g., federal funding vs. industry funding)

At this point, let's clarify some of the legal terms related to patents and ownership. The *inventor* is the person(s) involved in conceiving the idea. Collaborators who have conceived of an idea together are often considered joint inventors, though each collaborator might not have conceived of the entire invention. The inventors are listed on the patents. The patent often is assigned to a third party, or an *assignee*, based on agreements between the inventors and the third party. These agreements, as discussed, are usually blanket agreements signed by employees upon employment. The assignee owns the patent, or has all rights to "make, use, and sell" a product based on the invention. The assignee can license the patent to a *licensee,* who then has certain rights to the patent, as outlined in the license agreement.

The following are some misconceptions faculty have around university ownership of inventions:

I CONCEIVED OF THE INVENTION AT HOME, THEREFORE I OWN IT. Ownership depends on the subject of the invention. If the subject is related to the faculty member's research area, then the ownership typically resides with the university, depending on what agreements have been signed. Ownership also depends on whether university facilities or resources were used. The subject might have been outside the research area but if the invention was conceived using university computer systems (e.g., library materials, databases), even if accessed from home, ownership may reside with the university.

I CONCEIVED OF THE INVENTION AT THE UNIVERSITY, BUT MY START-UP PRODUCED IT. Invention is usually defined as a two-step process: 1) conception of the idea and 2) reduction to practice (i.e., making a working example of the idea). Inventorship relates only to the first step, though filing a patent requires both steps. Thus, conception of the idea at the university means the university likely owns the idea.

I CONCEIVED OF THE IDEA WHILE CONSULTING FOR MY START-UP. Here the lines can get a little more blurry. Take the case of a faculty member consulting for a large corporation. In this case, most universities would require the faculty member to disclose the consulting arrangements (or "external activities for pay"). The company usually has the faculty sign an agreement assigning to the company all inventions conceived of during the consulting to the company.[2] For a start-up, the lines are less clear. The start-up is typically working on a technology invented by faculty

---

2. This type of assignment was at the heart of the *Stanford v. Roche* case, which was decided by the Supreme Court in 2011. The case boiled down to the assignment language in two different agreements. The Stanford faculty member worked at Cetus, which was later bought by Roche, to learn polymerase chain reaction. Roche required that he sign an agreement stating, "I hereby do assign" all inventions to Roche. Previously, as part of his employment with Stanford, his agreement stated, "I agree to assign." That difference in verb tense appeared to have been the deciding factor. Universities are reviewing their invention disclosure and assignment policies as a result of the case.

and licensed to the start-up. Consulting with the start-up might lead to a new invention that the university may claim ownership to, since it's derivative of the licensed subject matter and was conceived as part of the faculty's university duties.

I NEVER SIGNED ANY AGREEMENT WITH THE UNIVERSITY, SO I OWN MY INVENTIONS. Several court cases have demonstrated that, with only a few exceptions, if you invent something while you are in a university's employ, the university owns the invention. Signing an agreement is not usually sufficient to argue ownership.

MY UNDERGRAD CONCEIVED OF THE IDEA, SO THE UNIVERSITY DOES NOT OWN IT. If the undergrad conceived of the idea and went to a corporation or another university to reduce it to practice, then the ownership might reside with the undergrad (but assigned to where the idea was reduced to practice). If the idea was reduced to practice by the undergrad in the faculty member's lab, then the university might have rights to the invention, depending on its patent policy, which could invoke ownership based on significant use of university resources.

So where does this leave the faculty member? Given the typical default position that the university owns most of the inventions conceived of as part of the normal course of research activities, faculty should disclose early and often to the TTO. As mentioned previously, in some cases, the TTO might choose not to patent the invention and then release it back to the inventor. The release complicates matters because the faculty member may continue to work on the invention in the lab with federal funds, perhaps making improvements to the invention (Who owns the improvements?). The release terms may vary with universities; some give full release (no obligations back to the university), while others stipulate obligations (e.g., royalty on sales) or require fulfillment of obligations to others (e.g., the federal government under Bayh-Dole).

University ownership can be viewed in a positive way. It is willing to take the risk of patenting the technology (e.g., paying costs up front, taking the time to file), will likely be open to licensing the patent to a faculty-founded start-up under reasonable terms, and will share in licensing income with the inventors. Further, when a university takes on patent costs for the invention, it provides a modicum of validation that the technology has commercial potential.

Corporate Ownership, Control, and Dilution

When a company is founded, the founders own 100 percent of the company. The faculty founders of a university spinout can own a significant portion of the company at founding. As such, they will need to decide how much of the company to share with others in order to grow the business and how much to retain for both control of the company and eventual financial return (an example of ownership and dilution is shown on page 67). Let's consider a number of issues around sharing company ownership. First, a start-up has little to offer someone but future potential, and the only way to get others' help in realizing that future potential is to give them a portion of it, namely, ownership in the company. For example, entrepreneurs who help build the business will be trading time they could have worked on other opportunities and perhaps a salary for this future potential. Likewise, investors are funding the development of the product in return for some future potential. In giving ownership (i.e., future potential) to others, the founders' ownership is diluted (the large pie slices have to be cut smaller because there is only one pie). Before founders share ownership with others, they should answer the following questions:

1   Are the new owners aligned with us in creating value so that at the end of the day the slices are smaller but worth much more?
2   How important is control to us, especially if all the owners have the same long-term interests?
3   At what point in the development of our company are we willing to be minority owners?
4   What does control look like in a start-up?

The answer to this last question is that control can be exerted in many ways. The traditional way is ownership percentage. If the founder owns a majority of the company, then it is assumed he or she has complete control because the founder(s) can out-vote the other shareholders. In reality, few decisions come to a vote of the shareholders, and if they do, they are either big decisions (e.g., the purchase of the company) or the decision has become so contentious that the team cannot reach an agreement (not a good position for the company of only a few people to be in). *Control should be thought of not in terms of voting or shares but in terms of influence and impact.* The best way for a founder to exert influence and have impact is by engaging in the operational activities of the company: creating the product-development strategy, writing grants, doing market research, contributing to the business plan, finding and hiring employees, or seeking investors. Of course, being engaged requires time and energy, which can be a scarcity among faculty members.

Investment-induced dilution is a reality for university start-ups. When the company is successful, it seems worth it. When the company is not successful, the dilution can be a source of frustration and anger. A real-life example of the realities of dilution and the angst it can cause founders comes from a case study on the pharmaceutical start-up Syntonix Pharmaceuticals:

> In 1997, when the company started, the four founders held 90 percent of the ownership: Rick and Laur about 64 percent, the two other founding researchers 26 percent, and an academic institution the remaining 10 percent. After the first round of financing, the founders owned 25 percent of the company (Rick and Laur about 18 percent), venture capitalists 29 percent (with one VC group owning 14 percent), management and employees 30 percent, and others (consultants, academic institutions, and angels) 16 percent. After round B the VC ownership went to 70 percent (with one VC group owning 20 percent), the four founders owning 7.4 percent (Rick and Laur a little over 5 percent), management and employees held 9 percent, and others owned 13 percent. As a founding owner, Laur Blumberg commented on the approach the VCs took: "It was bittersweet, but we felt burned. We put a lot of sweat equity and energy into the company, but we got severely diluted. The VCs are going to have a good outcome, but they diluted us to death. It was like they wanted to strangle us, but not strangle us to death." Syntonix explored additional sources of funding after the B round of financing. According to Laur: "It's not like we hadn't tried to get other sources of funding over the years. We approached almost everyone we ultimately licensed, particularly Amgen and Serono, but the clinical development wasn't far enough along to gather immediate interest. There were some reservations in the whole industry about the likely success of pulmonary delivery, and this was before Pfizer gave up on Exubera®. Until that issue (pulmonary delivery) was solved, we couldn't get much traction."[3]

Here, a difficult financing environment combined with the need to raise significant capital to get the product on the market (a common requirement of pharmaceutical start-ups) led to large rounds at low valuations, leading to dilution of the founders and significant resentment. There is no secret to avoiding dilution, but the following might help: 1) wait as long as pos-

---

3. Raymond M. Kinnunen, Susan F. Sieloff, and Robert F. Young, "Syntonix Pharmaceuticals," North American Case Research Association, Case NA0034, *Case Research Journal* 28 (3) (2008).

sible to raise dilutive capital by exhausting the nondilutive sources first, but don't wait so long that the company becomes desperate, resulting in a low valuation, 2) raise as much money as you can during the present round since a) the company will probably need it and b) it may help reduce dilution by eliminating a possible down round, and 3) explore other sources of capital that may have different valuation approaches (e.g., venture philanthropy or corporate venture capital).

Conflict of Interest and Conflict of Commitment

Given the number of start-ups that have spun out of universities over the past decades, most universities have come to some understanding of conflicts that arise around a faculty founder and a start-up they found. Many have developed policies, guidelines, and review panels to monitor and manage these conflicts and the policies can vary widely from university to university.

Before we consider these conflicts, it is worth emphasizing the separation between the company and the faculty member and his or her lab. This separation is an important concept as it frames the discussion about conflicts of interest and commitment. Too many times, faculty members cannot conceptually distinguish themselves from the start-up, especially in the early days when they may own all or a significant portion of the company. The start-up is a legal entity whose purpose and function differ from those of the typical academic research lab. It's raison d'être is to bring a product to market in a way that creates value for shareholders. Faculty members and their research create new knowledge and educate students. They focus on discovering knowledge that can have an impact in society, not necessarily via a commercial route.

The extent of the separation between the research enterprise and the corporate enterprise is dictated by 1) the polices and procedures of the university and 2) the nature of the entities' respective activities. Many universities stipulate a complete separation, to the extent that start-ups must use nonuniversity computers and e-mail addresses, and off-campus space for meetings. Others welcome start-up activity on campus but manage it through close review. For example, a lab conducting very applied research (e.g., in sports rehabilitation) might have significant overlap with a company spinning out of that lab (e.g., a company developing a new rehabilitation device). That sort of overlap makes the separation difficult, but it can be achieved with the appropriate oversight and review.

Conflict of interest arises when a faculty member has a financial interest in a company and that financial interest puts the faculty member in a position where he/she can make decisions or provide input as a university employee that will have bearing on that financial interest. The University of North Carolina at Chapel Hill's policy on COI defines it this way:

> Conflict of Interest . . . relates to situations in which financial or other personal considerations, circumstances, or relationships may compromise, may involve the potential for compromising, or may have the appearance of compromising a Covered Individual's objectivity in fulfilling their University duties or responsibilities, including research and teaching activities and administrative duties. The bias that such conflicts may impart can affect many University responsibilities, including decisions about personnel, the purchase of equipment and other supplies, the selection of instructional materials for classroom use, the collection, analysis and interpretation of data, the sharing of research results, the choice of research protocols, the use of statistical methods, and the mentoring and judgment of student work.[4]

Each university has a different wording of its COI policies, but it's important to see the range of conflicts the universities are going to be sensitive to. For example, the policy quoted above states "may compromise, may involve the potential for compromising, or may have the appearance of compromising." The phrase "may have the appearance" indicates that perception is reality in seeing a conflict.

For a faculty founder with equity in a start-up, the following are typical areas where COI is an issue:

CLINICAL TRIALS. If a start-up (or, for that matter, any company where the faculty member is a shareholder) is conducting a clinical trial and the faculty member is involved in it in any way (e.g., in study design, patient recruitment, or data review), a conflict of interest can occur. The faculty member might be in a position to make decisions about a trial that would lead to his or her financial gain (e.g., manipulate data to gain FDA approval). This is one of the most severe COI situations and is treated the most stringently by universities—almost universally, faculty members are prohibited from participating in trials that test products derived from their research.

EDUCATION. In the early stages of the start-up, graduate students and postdocs provide a significant source of both intellectual capital and

---

4. "University of North Carolina at Chapel Hill Policy on Individual Conflicts of Interest and Commitment," p. 2, http://policies.unc.edu/files/2013/04/Individual-COI-Policy.pdf (accessed 15 January 2013).

experimental results related to the start-up's technology. In many cases, what the research students are doing is compatible and aligned with the start-up. A publication in *Science* or *Nature* will provide excellent publicity for the start-up. However, some research needed by a start-up is not publishable, either because it is not research quality (e.g., an optimization or reproduciblity study) or because it is confidential. Faculty members have to ensure their students' academic training is not compromised by the students' conducting experiments that will not further their education.

PURCHASING. Some start-ups provide a service or a product very soon after launch. A COI can arise when a faculty member owns a start-up and he/she decides to purchase the service or product from the start-up.

Most universities will establish department-level COI committees that meet regularly to discuss these issues.

Most COIs are considered personal conflicts, but COIs can also be institutional conflicts. They can occur in cases where "a financial relationship between the university and an external entity compromises the integrity of institutional decision-making."[5] This comes to bear when the university has a financial interest in a start-up, typically as a shareholder as part of a licensing agreement. The university has to ensure that it makes no decisions that could appear to be influenced by its ownership of the start-up and potential financial gain. To this end, some universities have established separate research foundations that handle the IP and equity owned in the start-ups.

Conflict of commitment is harder to define and enforce. It relates to the "distribution of effort between university duties or institutional responsibilities (primary and secondary) and external professional activities,"[6] external activities in our case being working with the start-up. Some universities will stipulate the amount of time faculty can devote to external activities (e.g., a day a week). Others leave it open to the employee's supervisor (chair, dean). Similarly, the use of university equipment facilities and infrastructure for the start-up can pose a conflict. Clearly, a start-up housed in the faculty founder's labs needs close oversight usually through an agreement between the company and the university. However, use of university e-mail, computers, software, and offices for meetings is harder to regulate. Many university

5. "The University of North Carolina at Chapel Hill Policy on Institutional Conflict of Interest," p. 1, http://policy.sites.unc.edu/files/2013/04/Institutional-COI-Policy.pdf (accessed 15 January 2013).

6. "University of North Carolina at Chapel Hill Policy on Individual Conflicts of Interest and Commitment," p. 5.

policies permit occasional use of university property but stipulate that action will be taken in the case of inappropriate use.

The Value of Networking

For many faculty, the world of start-ups is new. Although many resources exist for learning more about a start-up (like this book!), there are important lessons to be learned from those who have gone before. Many universities are developing entrepreneur-in-residence programs to bring experienced entrepreneurs on campus to coach students and faculty through the early stages of the process. Faculty members who have gone through the start-up process are a useful source of information. Most are more than willing to tell you about their experiences. Be forewarned: given the failure rate of start-ups, many of the stories will be negative and discouraging. Don't despair. Focus on the lessons they learned through the process and ask them what they would have done differently.

In addition to the networking on campus, doing so at local and regional events can lead to important relationships and resources. Many areas of the country offer start-up showcases that feature local businesses and attract entrepreneurs and investors. One can also attend local roundtables and panel discussions on topics ranging from start-up funding, to regulatory approval, to accounting.

Many faculty members find it difficult to carve out the time to attend these events, but they also resist attending them because they will be meeting with people they do not normally interact with. Interacting with scientific colleagues at a technical conference is second nature, but working a crowd of business professionals, entrepreneurs, and investors can be intimidating.

Networking can also be done through the Internet. The easiest way to do this is to get an e-mail introduction. For example, if you need an accountant to help set up the books for an SBIR grant and a fellow faculty member has recommended a local accounting firm, have the colleague introduce you to the accountant via an e-mail. The e-mail not only makes the initial contact for you but also greatly increases the likelihood the firm will respond.[7]

---

7. A common courtesy for e-mail introductions is to reply to the person who made the introduction, thanking him for the introduction, telling him that you are moving him to blind carbon copy (BCC) and then introduce yourself to the person you are being introduced to. This eliminates the e-mail traffic of introductory exchanges and the back and forth of trying to find a time to meet.

The University: Friend or Foe?

It is essential that a university start-up work with the university, primarily for licensing the technology but also for engaging in any university-sponsored programs such as grants or incubation space. In these cases, the university can be seen as a friend. Given the complexity of this relationship, however, the university is often also seen as a foe.

People see the university as a foe for a variety of reasons. In some cases, the university is unfriendly to start-ups. This may be for historical reasons, where certain policies have been established and never updated in light of the current state of academic entrepreneurship. There may be legal reasons the university is less supportive of start-ups, such as state laws prohibiting the use of public university facilities for private enterprises. In other cases, the expectations of faculty and entrepreneurs are unreasonable. The faculty has invested so much time and energy into the research that they may not possess the objectivity to understand a university's or a TTO's position. For example, budgetary restraints or cutbacks may severely limit the patent costs a TTO can carry, which translates into a frustrated faculty not having his or her patent filed. In addition, most TTOs operate within the office of the vice chancellor/vice president for research, which manages millions of dollars in research grants and the associated compliance. As such, the TTO may not get the resources it needs to adequately perform its function.

Lessons Learned

In an informal poll, we asked faculty members who have spun companies out of universities to answer the question, If a young faculty member was in your office seeking guidance and counsel about starting a company, what advice would you provide? The following are their (unedited) responses.

Not every good idea should or can be commercialized. Never trust your own judgment; always go to qualified people in the field to critique your idea. I did this with both of my companies (independent of the university), and it was both the reality check and encouragement that gave me the courage to move forward.

Companies should be pulled out of universities, not pushed. If it requires [a] large effort [and a ton of] finances and resources from the university to move a technology into the commercial sector, the technology is of questionable value. The best technologies have investors and partners begging the university to allow them to take [the technology] out, and consequently deal structures can be more amicable.

Know your limitations. Scientist, engineer, and technologist faculty members, with or without MBAs, are rarely the right people to lead the development effort required to fully commercialize a product and certainly not [to lead] the whole company (founder/CEOs should be discouraged—I know from experience). They should acknowledge their strength[s], [i.e.,] the intimate understanding and enthusiasm for the technology and hopefully eloquence and enthusiasm in presenting it (which often leads to CSO position for a while) and step back and let the business folks take care of investors, finance, human resources, business, and product development (scale-up, supply chain, pricing, etc.).

Pick the right partners. Fully vet management teams and investors to ensure that everyone is on the same page and suited for the difficult tasks ahead. Management should have some familiarity with the specific product being developed (e.g., former biotech industry folks for protein development). Investors should bring "smart money," meaning they are familiar with the industry sector you operate in. At some point in the future they will change the direction of the company; it is inevitable, but you, the founder, should feel comfortable with where they are likely to go. In addition, when the going gets rough (and it always does) personalities, goals and objectives have to align, as there will be other challenges that require urgent attention, and sidebar disputes will be a distraction.

There will always be takers if you offer things for free (an almost verbatim quote from one of my friends, an investor in Oriel, Mitch Barron, CEO of Trudell Medical). When you are first approached to work with industry partners or even [when you are] trying to raise capital, there is a tendency to offer to do feasibility studies at your own expense. This tendency should be quashed as soon as possible. If people are interested, they should pay. It doesn't matter how much but the principle is[;] . . . they should part with something as a sign of good faith. Otherwise, you will blow your entire runway pandering to folks who simply don't want to say no but have little intention of working with you. NOTE: Business development folks are not allies in this activity. They like to say they are working with as many people as possible to give the perception of success and, consequently, [they] encourage this sort of activity. In the end this is a dangerous strategy as it can rebound when the "partners" disappear and public perceptions as well as finances rapidly spiral downwards.

I would tell any faculty member considering his or her first entrepreneurial venture three things: First, the benchmarks for success in academics and in the business world are completely different, so be prepared for doing a lot of unsexy work to get your idea developed. Second, you need to develop a broad network within the entrepreneurial community and pay attention to what they are telling you. [Third], don't expect to be the CEO (you don't have the time and probably don't have the skill set), and don't be greedy with equity.

The early decisions, many made for expediency, turn out to matter. Choices you make about HR, IP, licensing, etc., all become big deals later (if your company is lucky enough to have a "later"). Since no one person can really understand all these early decisions, [it] is critical to involve good people in your company from the zygotic stage for help with decision-making. (Corollary: I think personnel is the most important resource of a company. Money cannot overcome a team of losers.)

Half of something is better than all of nothing. Some people spend so much time worrying about equity, dilution, who has how many shares, etc., that the company can get paralyzed and never get anywhere (or perhaps never even get started in the first place). Over and over again, we have had to make deals on how to share future gains, and then just keep on going. . . .

Summary: Scrutinize your decisions, even ones that seem mundane, with help from talented others, but don't be overly contemplative in decision-making, especially about who gets what.

Typical founder shares are common, so, in addition to the subsequent dilution, liquidation preferences put the founders at the end of the list for compensation. Most naive founders, [and I did], certainly, [think] that this applie[s] in the case of bankruptcy, but of course, [it] also applies when a company is sold. Only in the case of an IPO, which is far less likely, [would] all shares have been equal. No one, neither the lawyer, the accountants, [nor], sadly, the university [ever] told us that the most likely outcome is a sale to another entity. The functional result is that the founder's shares are typically worthless unless the company is sold for some astronomical sum. The university should be protective of the scientist founder so that even though the founder shares would dilute with additional investors, the liquidation preference should change to be equivalent to the most recent investors, or to the investment round immediately prior to the most recent.

It is very difficult to find a decent CEO. The university should use [its] experience to vet CEO candidates. Although I am not free to discuss our first CEO, I will say that any conversation I might have would involve the phrase "ten foot pole."

Never say, "I don't care if I make money, I just want people to use my technology." Build start-ups to succeed on the business side.

[A start-up] is a lot of work, and requires a lot of time.

Even after taking courses and attending other seminars and webinars, there's a huge amount about business that we, as scientists, clinicians, or academicians, don't know, and never will. We are not trained to think that way. So you need to get advice about your idea from a lot of qualified experienced people, and build a good network.

Successful businesses require a lot of different skills . . . that means people with different skill sets who work well together. I think many start-up businesses fail because that's a rare combination.

You will encounter unforeseen problems no matter how well you plan. You must be flexible, and persistent.

Sometimes it's the best way to take your idea to the next level. You will gain a new perspective on your idea, which is very worthwhile.

My advice takes the form of this drawing that attempts to convey some separate but related issues.

I am struck that the inventor sees technology as the most important aspect of the company, and that he expects that it be valued as such. However, the easiest way to see the value of technology in and of itself is to look at the UNC express license. The remuneration to the inventor is about 1–2%. This says that 98% of the value is in the "business." However, if the technology fails—of itself, not being able to be productized, etc., then the business topples.

The role of team. It was easiest for me to understand the role of team from an execution standpoint, but I did not foresee its role in communicating the potential of the company. Those outside, such as investors— or partners, do not have time to vet every issue of every company. Their quick way of assessment is through the team. If they know Mary—and she is engaged with the company—then it must be a great opportunity. The building of the company through the progressive accumulation of an ever better team is due to every later member looking at the earlier entrants to gain assurance. This includes especially investors—hence they see team first.

The strategic partner, in our case, a sales/distributor, is driven first by the existence of the market, hence they see this first.

The value of the company—seen from above—includes all of what is seen. This horizontal view builds over time. Note that the technology is not seen—what is important is the IP and the product.

If we could make this drawing 3d—I would have given it a side from which IP is seen first. There is an argument that the IP gives the company its greatest value—at least that is what our IP lawyer tells us!

Business people will tell [you that] your success is mostly related to the business plan. I disagree; success is mostly about the science. Spend most of your time perfecting the science, the rest will follow.

Gather your advice from all of your business experts/consultants/ pitches. . . . Don't discard any advice, [and] don't taken any blindly and definitively, but work with those ideas to move forward. . . . At a minimum have a reply for those criticisms as they will reemerge at a later date. . . .

You're the creator, visionary, and have what THEY NEED. . . . They have the money, which YOU NEED, . . . but don't lose sight of your uniqueness . . . don't minimize your contribution . . . don't be diluted to nothing. . . . It won't be worth it to you in the end. . . .

Patience and optimism . . . got to have it. . . . There are MANY dark days, but they quickly turn bright when someone else "gets it" and wants to share your vision.

Get out of the university . . . to understand your product, customer, and market. A common mistake, and I see it almost 100% of the time, is thinking your invention, discovery, or research is actually a marketable product. Does somebody want it, and if so, why? And if somebody does want it, what will they pay for it? Are there enough customers willing to pay enough for your invention or discovery to build a company or a product line?

The only way to answer these questions is to get out of your lab and office . . . outside of your comfort zone . . . and engage your market, your customers. If you are seriously considering building a company around your invention or research and haven't had critical, serious, and thorough discussions with at least 10–15 real decision makers/customers who have the authority and means to buy your "product," do it today . . . and I mean TODAY. Right now!

It does not matter what you think, what I think, what your friends and colleagues think . . . the market always wins. It will decide the success or failure of your company. So go find out what it has to say!

Find a good corporate manager—you need someone who knows what they are doing to run the business.

Do not let your university lab focus get distracted—your lab is much more likely to be successful 5 years from now than your company.

Find a really good corporate lawyer that can explain things to you.

Keep the VCs out as long as possible.

Bend over backwards to be fair to you lab mates at the university.

Keep separate as much as possible your university work and the business—limit company work on campus as much as possible—if not, there will always be jealousy.

Kiss your free time good-bye. Your department chairman still expects you to teach, bring in NIH funds, and, if you are a clinician, see patients. If you are in the Department of Medicine only 8% of your salary comes from state funds, and some of that time has to be spent teaching, so if you are lucky you have 5% to spend on this. That isn't enough, so something has to give. You can cut into your research time, but then you will lose your grants and eventually salary. In my case I increased my work-week from 67 hours to 80 hours. That has taken a toll. [The] take-home message: No free lunches [and] be prepared to make sacrifices.

The valley of death is very real. It is no joke. Most VCs (I presented to 45 different firms) want to fund a project that is through toxicology studies. That means if you are dealing with a protein drug or any biologic, you have to raise one million [dollars] for GMP [good manufacturing practices] manufacturing and one million for tox before you get VC funds. [And] that doesn't count proof of concept and MOA [mechanism of action] studies, which can easily be another million. Figuring out how to raise the 3 million is not easy. We partnered with a big pharma company, which had major tradeoffs but got us the funds we needed. Angel money is an option, but it comes with a steep price tag.

You are only as good as your idea. You can play politics and if you are a good talker, you can raise some money, and you can get lucky, but in the end you won't make it up to [Phase II] human trials without a very good idea. The best person to bounce your idea off is somebody who has done this before. You can talk to faculty, big pharma experts, VCs, etc., but if they haven't actually started a company from scratch starting with no financial backing, you cannot rely on their judgment. Maybe their ideas will be of some help, but when it comes to filtering those ideas and choosing among options, find a veteran as a mentor and stick with them.

Unless you can raise extraordinary amounts of money, you will need to use a lot of consultants as well as contractors and will [need to] operate in a virtual mode. This requires a skill set that is very different form the skill set that it takes to succeed in academic research, where the brunt of the work is done by postdocs and grad students.

There is very little open-ended creative research in this space. You have your idea, now you have to run with it, like it or not. This is not an academic exercise. It is all about application and performance.

Cheerleading takes on new meaning. Some days you are the only person cheering. You have to be a proactive optimist and a realistic doer at the same time.

Your choice of a CEO is the most important decision that you will make. Get help finding one and try for someone who has done a start-up and understands the bumps in the road. Get someone who is in the top 1% in financial management skills. You will need that expertise.

Little things that appear trivial to a good scientist like formulation are extremely important. Bad advice from a CMC [certified management consultant] cost my company $750,000.

Get the best patent lawyer you can afford. Try to go outside the TTO recommendations. There are a lot better firms out there, and it makes a tremendous difference. If you have to use TTO-recommended firms, pay for an outside opinion yourself. It could save you a lot of money and save your invention.

Don't start a biomedical company for the money. If you want to make a lot of money, there are a lot [of] easier ways to do it.

Business Leaders

The second group of stakeholders are the business leaders, business-oriented people who are either starting the company with the faculty member, joining the faculty-founded start-up, or licensing a technology from the university to start a company with peripheral involvement from the faculty member. These people are bringing their business/commercialization/technology experience to help launch and grow the university start-up. They come from a variety of backgrounds and experiences: they are, among others, serial entrepreneurs, former big company executives wanting to get into the start-up world, and consultants who have enough time and energy to devote to getting a start-up off the ground. Whatever their backgrounds might be, working with a university start-up provides them with unique opportunities and challenges.

Finding Innovations at a University

Most innovations at a university flow through the technology transfer office, since faculty members disclose inventions to the TTO and the TTO patents the invention and then seeks a licensee of the technology.[8] Many TTOs list their technologies on their website for public perusal. The quality and age of the listed assets vary by TTO; they can range from an outdated technology with little interest from a licensee (and only put on the site after extensive marketing) to a recently updated list of assets for license. Some TTOs provide public innovation seminars or showcases where they present cutting-edge research or start-up companies. Finally, a visit with a TTO licensing officer can provide an in-depth review of technologies available for starting a company. Each officer specializes in a certain field or covers certain departments so it is important to meet with the one(s) that cover the scientific area of most interest.

The next stop for a business leader should be a meeting with the faculty member. This is important for several reasons. First, there may be a difference of opinion between the faculty member and the TTO about a technology in terms of commercial potential, enabling features, novelty, utility, or other aspects. These differences arise because the faculty member might be humble in his/her opinion of the technology or he/she might not understand how to assess commercial value. On the other hand, the TTO officer might be marketing the technology hard, and perhaps inflating its value. A visit to the faculty member might also lead to the discovery of other research that is in progress, perhaps related to and strengthening the disclosed technology, or another line of research that might have greater commercial viability. The visit will also provide some insight into how well the lab is funded. The

---

8. The requirement that faculty disclose inventions and discoveries to the university is often part of the university's IP policy. Enforcement of the requirement is often difficult because a) the faculty may not know they have something that needs to be disclosed or b) faculty are not interested in commercialization and prefer to publish all their research results.

number of graduate students, postdocs, technicians it supports, the kind of space it occupies, and the equipment available will all be a good indication of its funding status. Another reason for the visit is to assess faculty members' interest in starting a company. Some are very interested, some are too busy to be interested, and others are just not interested. Finally, a visit will help assess chemistry. Starting a company with another person requires that the parties have an excellent working relationship, where egos need to be put in check and the people involved are aware that they need to work together to achieve a common goal. The question to ask is, Can I spend the next five years working closely with this person?

A business person searching for innovation also needs to consider the extent to which it is being marketed to a large corporation or being considered for a start-up. Many factors are at play here. The innovation might have already been shopped to large companies who have expressed little interest and therefore is being considered for a start-up as the last resort, rightly or wrongly. Or a faculty member may have a strong interest in a start-up and at the same time a large company has expressed an interest. This creates a tension for the TTO who on one hand needs to keep the "customer service" hat on and please the faculty member and on the other hand has responsibility to get a deal done (and a licensing deal to a large company will likely result in a much larger short-term revenue gain compared to a start-up).

Working with the University and Its Intellectual Property

For an entrepreneur considering starting a company around university IP, there are a number of things to keep in mind. First, for a university, publications are the currency for success. They figure into a tenure package, they demonstrate scientific capability and innovative capacity, they provide the proof to funders that their money is being well spent, and they provide the fuel for future grant funding. But this need to publish has to be balanced by the requirement to protect intellectual property (per the Bayh-Dole Act). The university does this by filing patents prior to publication, usually at a very early stage of technology maturation, which starts the patent-exclusivity clock ticking. Second, the preliminary nature of the patent may not cover all embodiments of the invention. (By contrast, a private corporation files the patent application as late as possible to capture as many years of exclusivity as possible, and they include in the application a wealth of examples and broad claims.) The following scenario demonstrates how a university might handle its IP:

1   A faculty member is getting ready to publish her seminal paper on a very exciting area of science.
2   She contacts the TTO to file a patent application around the technology.
3   The TTO rushes to file a provisional patent ahead of the publication deadline.
4   A year later, the TTO wants to file the nonprovisional patent but does not have very much additional data from the faculty member. The patent application is filed nonetheless.
5   Marketing the IP yields little interest from potential licensees.
6   The deadline for the national phase filings approaches, and because of either university policy or lack of interest, only U.S. patent protection is sought.
7   In the meantime, the faculty member has made significant, commercially relevant improvements, wants to file additional IP, and wants to start a company.
8   An entrepreneur comes on board to provide the initial management. In examining the patent portfolio, he discovers that the first filing might be considered prior art for foreign filings of the second filing. The entrepreneur has reservations about starting the company around the university IP.

This scenario illustrates some of the realities of university IP. Universities don't have large patent budgets, so they aren't able to file on all disclosures or are only able to file for limited protection (e.g., United States only). At this early stage and given the limited domain expertise of the TTO, it's hard to pick winners. Finally, the most commercially viable technology may be a second or third iteration but there is no way to predict this.

As noted, the quality of the IP can vary greatly from university to university depending on how early it is filed, how much data is available at filing, and how much the university has to spend on patents. The quality of the IP is also related to the competence of the patent attorney in terms of his/her understanding the subject matter, as well as in identifying potentially interfering patents and constructing the claims appropriately. Some universities have comparatively little to spend on patents, so they might not get the top-shelf attorney or much of that attorney's attention. One way an entrepreneur can make an initial assessment of the IP is to meet with both the TTO officer and the outside counsel to determine what has been done in terms of patentability searches, office actions, and so on. Bringing in independent counsel to review the patent file is worth the investment.

Licensing Technology from the University

The following are aspects of the technology licensing process for a start-up that distinguish it from the licensing process in private industry:

UNDERSTAND THE UNIVERSITY'S MOTIVATIONS. TTOs are trying to balance a number of factors in licensing a technology to a faculty-founded start-up. On one hand, they want to strike a fair deal in the eyes of the faculty member, since, at a certain level, they are there to serve the faculty members. On the other hand, they are trying to extract maximum value from the deal to achieve a good return on the research investment. Pulling TTOs in another direction is the university's mission to commercialize the technology so that cutting-edge products get on the market to solve significant problems. Another layer of complexity is the funding structure of the TTO. If income from licensing covers operational expenses for the TTO, or if the office is cash-strapped, the TTO might be more interested in short-term cash (e.g., up-front payments, reimbursement of patent costs). On the other hand, if licensing income does not impact the office's budget significantly or the office is well funded (e.g., income from a big licensing deal), then the TTO may favor long-term upside over short-term cash (e.g., equity, royalty).

UNDERSTAND THE UNIVERSITY'S PERSPECTIVE. As the founder of a start-up licensing technology from a university, you need to appreciate the TTO's perspective. Most TTOs work is with established companies—that is, companies who have cash, usually pay their bills on time, and employ professional licensing executives. In working with a start-up founder, the TTO might begin with an agreement that is used for most of the university's big-company deals, and thus the terms may be far away from those needed by the start-up. In addition, TTO officers come from many different backgrounds. Some have years of experience in doing deals; others may be novices. Some come from a legal background (e.g., former attorney), whereas others come from a science background (e.g., former postdoc with no industry or start-up experience). The background of an officer will determine not only his/her level of competence but also his/her level of independence. Experienced officers, for example, will have latitude to negotiate, whereas inexperienced ones will likely need to get approval for certain terms, which can delay negotiations. By understanding their background, you can get insight into how they operate and negotiate. In most cases, however, few TTO licensing officers come from a start-up background (e.g., VC experience or worked in start-up), so their perspective of start-ups is limited. Having never experienced difficulties in meeting payroll or having a product failure, they may not understand or have any patience for when payments to the university are delayed or milestones are not met.

UNDERSTAND THE TIMELINE. When Don Rose took his position at the university, after more than a 25 years in private industry, one of the first conversations he had was with a faculty member who was a former pharmaceutical executive. She commented, "Understand the university works at a different pace than industry. It's been here 200 years and it will likely be here another 200 years." With the exception of grant application deadlines, she was right. Time flows at a slower pace than it does in most corporations. For those running a start-up, where time is of the essence, this can be very frustrating. Frustration can be reduced by starting early in negotiations and understanding the process up front in terms of who has to sign off on agreements and how long it can take.

CERTAIN TERMS ARE NONNEGOTIABLE. Since most of the university's research funding comes from the federal government (NIH, NSF), certain terms are not negotiable. For example, the university will almost always reserve its right to use the licensed technology for its research or educational purposes. Although it is rare, the government might have certain rights to the technology or might have control over where the products are manufactured. Furthermore, the university will usually reserve the right to publish in areas related to the IP. The only compromise possible is stipulating that the start-up has the right to preview the publications (e.g., 90 days) prior to publication. This may allow for additional patents to be filed.

CERTAIN TERMS ARE VERY IMPORTANT. Certain licensing terms can make or break a start-up. The first is exclusivity. If exclusivity cannot be obtained in the widest fields possible and broadest geography (worldwide), then seriously consider walking away. Investors rarely invest in start-ups with a nonexclusive license. Sublicensing terms are important for start-ups since the lack of capital and the typical broadness of university IP usually point to partnering down the road. Poor sublicensing terms may preclude partnering. Most faculty continue to do research and make discoveries, so keep in mind that access to future improvements is important but will be difficult to get in the license since universities cannot predict those improvements or their value. One solution is to negotiate an option, or a "first right of refusal," to future improvements. In some cases, a "pipeline agreement" can be put in place that automatically gives the start-up an option, for a limited time, to new discoveries coming out of the lab, whether or not they relate to the original licensed subject matter. License payments are either up-front, milestones, or royalties. For a start-up, back-end loading the payments (i.e., paying more on royalties in exchange for a small [or no] up-front payment) is desirable. Diligence milestones need to be realistic and measurable. TTOs are going to focus on these, especially the early ones, to make sure the start-up is making progress (they don't want a milestone several years away only to find out the company has not made any progress). The university will typically want to retain patent prosecution and prosecution rights.

Working with Faculty

Working with faculty to start a company can be a deeply rewarding experience. They are very smart, experts in their field, and inherently curious. However, what comes with that is limited time and energy as they chase the next grant, serve on a committee, teach students, or seek tenure. And once in a while you will run into the occasional huge ego. It is also important to understand that faculty have been working for years in their ecosystem where the rules of the game and the associated incentives and rewards are different from those in the business world. Peter Schuerman does an excellent job of laying out these differences using Dan Pink's book *Drive: The Surprising Truth about What Motivates Us* as a frame of reference.[9] Schuerman argues that extrinsic incentives like wealth creation are not enough to motivate faculty. Faculty are "knowledge workers" who are motivated by Pink's three intrinsic motivators, in the order of decreasing importance: mastery (recognition from peers), autonomy (research funding), and purpose (legacy). Business people and corporations are motivated by the same motivators but in a different order of priority: purpose (creating value through selling products and services), autonomy (revenue from sales), and mastery (recognition in the market place).

Another difference between faculty and entrepreneurs is their knowledge

---

9. Peter Schuerman, "Aligning Interests between Academia and Commerce," *Negotiate the Future: Realizing the Potential of Technology Transfer* (blog), 17 March 2014, http://negotiatethefuture .com/aligning-interests-between-academia-and-commerce/ (accessed 14 May 2014).

base. Most faculty are a mile deep and an inch wide in their understanding of a subject area. Entrepreneurs, by contrast, are generalists. Many have learned through experience and have gained knowledge in a wide range of areas, from intellectual property, to finance, to product development. The faculty's lack of business understanding combined with different motivations can lead to distrust between the two. Faculty and entrepreneurs often don't value what the other brings to the table. Therefore, entrepreneurs need to build a certain level of trust with faculty as well as educate them about how the business world works.

Finally, because of their different backgrounds, faculty and entrepreneurs often see the world differently. Because they work in a world of data and knowledge, faculty often see a much more black and white world, a landscape built on precision and accuracy. Entrepreneurs, by contrast, work in a world of subtleties and chaos. They are used to a certain level of risk and uncertainty not usually experienced in the academic world. How faculty and entrepreneurs describe the product or technology is illustrative of this difference. The academic will describe the capabilities in terms supported by the data. The entrepreneur may use more glowing terms and perhaps extrapolate the capabilities in an effort to get investors excited.

We note these differences not to denigrate either party but rather to point out that the academic founder and the entrepreneur have *complementary* skills, expertise, and backgrounds. When they have a healthy respect for what each brings to the table and check their egos at the door, a great partnership can be established, leading to a highly successful company.

Lessons Learned

We asked entrepreneurs who have spun companies out of universities to answer the question, "What advice would you give a first-time entrepreneur considering launching a start-up around a university technology?" The following are their (unedited) responses.

The key challenges of migrating technology out of a university from my experience:

(a) Acquire as full an understanding as you can of the existing technology and how it must evolve (all inventions do) to have a chance at creating something of potential commercial value. A crude first estimate of funding to get to this point is necessary ($500,000? $1 million? $5 million?).

(b) Develop a clear vision of real product(s) that can emerge from the technology and that customers will pay for—and why, i.e., a value proposition.

(c) It is vital that good personal relationships are nurtured with the faculty inventors and their staffs, as well as the technology transfer folks. Also seek out one or more senior people in the university administration (with some background in business) who can guide/assist/intervene as necessary in the process of getting a license to the intellectual property (IP) on fair terms. Such a person often becomes an adviser to the company and may sit on the early board of directors.

(d) Identify likely sources of cash sufficient to support the acquisition of the license to the IP and to do the early development work on the "raw" technology. Such sources may take significant time to acquire (e.g., SBIR grants, 9 months). Look for sources that are more immediately available (e.g., the university itself, existing faculty research grants that may be tapped, grants and loans from state organizations, investment from "friends and family," and your personal credit card lines).

(e) Understand your capabilities, willingness, and persistence to slug your way through the above four challenges and beyond. Find and convince people to join your efforts and pay them very little or, better, for free for a while. Hire people only when necessary and do so frugally and smartly, focusing on people who have the right experience and track record to get the specific, near-term tasks done well. Hiring good people takes energy and time; firing your mistakes is quick but demoralizing to all.

---

1. Entrepreneurship is hard. No question. You can't possibly anticipate all that will ultimately go wrong with your venture so you must be tenacious to be in a winning position. Survival skills are essential but in the end a bit of luck must come your way and you must develop the instinct to recognize it when it does.

2. Surround yourself and your company with experts in your space and continue to network with the "top of the heap" throughout your venture's development. These people can be very, very helpful and are perceived to be "value additive" by outsiders, investors in particular.

3. Communicate quarterly formally (more frequently is good too) with your investors. They get anxious when they don't hear anything and are usually very supportive when a company head is available for Q&A.

4. Network with CEOs of competitor companies but resist divulging strategic plans or other confidential information. This type of networking may seem counterintuitive but will benefit you in a number of ways. You will elevate your credibility by the company you keep. You will be closer in the event a conflict arises which needs resolution. You may learn something about your competitor that you otherwise would not have. You may be pulled into meetings (regulatory, reimbursement, scientific) that could benefit your company.

5. VCs are not courageous. VCs are looking for easy, short-term wins. They will waste your time and money when they have no interest at all in an investment in your company. Without being rude or giving the perception of arrogance, be strong in your convictions and do some diligence on any investor who may express interest in your company. It is OK to turn down a request for a meeting if you feel your needs and qualities are not well aligned.

6. Don't burn any bridges with anyone. It is indeed a small world and your reputation is a vital element to your success. Resist the urge to humiliate your opponent(s) and keep it friendly at all times. You will accomplish far more with this attitude as trust will trump an adversarial relationship every time.

7. If you can possibly get through your story without a formal board of directors then by all means do so. Leverage the advice of experienced entrepreneurs along the way but avoid having a formal board. If you must have a formal board be sure to have at least one independent director and preferably more than one, for the investor-directors will have their investment, first and foremost, in their minds when giving direction.

8. "It's not how hard you can hit but how hard you can get hit and then get up and keep going . . . that's how winning is done."—Rocky Balboa

---

I am responding with respect to what is in the best interest of the emerging bio-pharmaceutical founder/entrepreneur himself, assuming his objectives are to:

- Minimize the risk of entrepreneurial failure,
- Minimize the time to a clear success/failure outcome, and
- Maximize the odds of successfully and rapidly translating the university's technology to a point at which the final sponsor (a real pharmaceutical company) will take on the technology.

Drug development is a money-eating beast, and to optimize success a lot of it is needed. Getting to IND, which is not a value generating event, takes $3–5 million; to Phase 1–2 proof of concept, the first real value generating event, another $5–7 million; and to Phase 2 efficacy/safety another $10–15 million. So $20–25 million and 5 years is the absolute minimum required to ensure a positive Phase 2 outcome that has real value to the next owner, assuming the technology cooperates right all along the line.

If the technology provides such a compelling and obvious break-through that a pharmaceutical company is willing to license it directly with only early university POC data and a clear scientific rationale from the PI's lab, prior to it being further developed by a start-up/spin-out, it is in everyone's interest for the university to just do this.

If it requires funding at all, then it requires real venture capital in-vestment. Drug development cannot be funded by SBIR grants, angel funding, etc. alone, beyond very basic/early preclinical proof of concept.

Given this, it is better these days to know up front whether VCs are interested in funding the technology. Venture capital is extremely scarce and becoming more concentrated in Boston and San Francisco. If the VCs who invest in this space are not interested in the technology in concept (even assuming it will work as advertised) at this point, scrap-ing together enough boot-strap funding to somehow get to preclinical POC will not change that. Hope is not a strategy.

If VCs when asked about the technology concept provide "helpful" advice such as 1) go get SBIR grants; 2) go get angel funding; 3) find that pesky lead and come back to me and I'm in; and/or 4) come back when you have phase 1/2 data, they say these things to appear to be helpful and to be nice. VCs don't want to tell entrepreneurs directly that their baby is ugly for many reasons. But in fact telling you to get angel fund-ing is a flashing neon sign that really says they have no interest, because drug development cannot be funded by angels or boot-strap and VCs know it. When/if they are actually interested, they get together behind the scenes and work to put together a syndicate of interested parties and the biggest dog takes the lead, even if it is just initial seed funding to get their foot in the door.

Life science venture capital is incredibly scarce and selective compared to ten years ago. Given this reality, building a multi-year preclinical "spec house" and showing it to potential VCs and/or pharma-ceutical companies after 2–3 years of head-down work based on early funding is now too risky to be considered a sound use of time for an entrepreneur.

So given all of the foregoing, my specific advice is the following:

If you are not already financially independent, do not assume the start-up will succeed—early drug development is *way too risky* to rely on for mortgage payments, college tuition or retirement;

Start with the customers (VCs) and ask them what they are interested in funding—use this guidance to shop for technology at the various universities;

Once you select the technology, make very sure the IP protection is solid and long-dated by talking to the patent attorney hired by the university, as this costs you nothing;

Provide the VCs the *hypothetical* "spec house" to gauge real interest, i.e., be Walt Disney sitting on an orange crate in a California desert describing Disney World, but don't buy the land and break ground until the investors actually sign up;

Move to Boston or San Francisco ASAP, even if the technology is sourced from another state, as that is where the capital is and where the big pharma sponsors are increasingly concentrating their technology in-sourcing energies/people.

STARTING A COMPANY

"Don't fear failure. It's not failure, but aiming low that is the failing. In great attempts it is glorious even to fail."—modified from Bruce Lee quote.

"If you spend too much time thinking about a thing, you'll never get it done. Make at least one definite move daily toward your goal."—Bruce Lee

WORKING WITH UNIVERSITY TTOS

Show respect for TTOs and their mission, because "respect was invented to cover the empty place where love should be"—Leo Tolstoy

Communicate often and in as many ways as possible, because "the single biggest problem in communication is the illusion that it has taken place."—George Bernard Shaw

SUSTAINING A START-UP

"Be positive every day, in every way, to everyone, at least once."—Anil Goyal

"The measure of success of a start-up is the ability to adapt to the changing environment of data, funding, market, people, etc."—modified from Albert Einstein

WORKING WITH FACULTY

"Put your ego in "Self Storage" or make your ego porous. Showing openness, patience, receptivity, solitude is everything."—modified from Rainer Maria Rilke

RAISING MONEY

"Leave no stone (aka VC, Grant, Loan, pharma, biotech) unturned . . . if you have turned it once, turn to it again with new data/eyes and ears."—Anil Goyal

"It's not just the first meeting with an investor, it's what you do in the third and forth try."—modified from James Michener

---

Time after time, I see professors at top universities finding a "solution looking for a problem." This is typically because professors have specialty areas of expertise and "discover" things. It is certainly possible to work with TTO and obtain patents and even spin out a company based on a new discovery, but does the discovery really solve a problem for the customer? Typically, the answer is no.

I can give you only one or two examples of cases where good CEOs have taken the discovery that the start-up company is based on and found problems that could be solved for certain customers and eventually sold the company. This, however, is the exception rather than the rule. I can also give you many examples of professors that have spun out companies with solutions looking for problems and who will never find the CEO that can identify the problem, in part because it is like looking for a needle in a haystack, that is: to find the CEO who can then find the needle in the second, larger haystack for a potential exit.

So, in my view, the key to success is *starting with a BIP* (a big, important problem) not with a solution. An entrepreneur who can find a BIP and validate its importance and then study it will typically innovate, develop, or acquire a solution that is proprietary. Then an initial plan can be put together and a team assembled, a team of good people, to go after a growing market niche for ultimate success.

Eugene Kleiner, founder of the top VC firm Kleiner Perkins Caufield & Byers, was an investor in my first start-up company that I founded in 1986 and that had an IPO in 1995. Eugene was also a great mentor to me in the early years of developing the company. In one of our early meetings, he said to me: "Companies that have a growing market niche, a proprietary position, and good people will win every time." In my view, to develop a company of this type, you must start with a big, important problem that can be solved for the customer or end user . . . not with a solution looking for a problem.

I think a few points to the newbie would be the following:

1) Be honest with yourself about your own strengths and weaknesses, and be sure to have the right team on your side. When you go to raise money, both your science and your team will be scrutinized. Your science may be great, but if you don't have an experienced team, you will have a hard time getting funded. Alternatively, you may get funded, but with the stipulation that a new management team is put in place. Are you ready for this? How would you feel?

2) If you're working with faculty, be realistic about the time that they will be able to provide to the company.

3) Universities work at their own pace and schedule. Your company may be your priority, but they're not the university's first priority! Learn to "go with the flow" as long as it doesn't hinder the progress of the company.

Here is my advice.

1. A company has to sell what the market wants, not what the company can make or do. The first step to any company formation should be market research on the likely customers for the product or service, the unique advantages of your product or service and how it stacks up is a sober assessment against today's and tomorrow's alternatives from other sources. Market research doesn't have to be expensive. It can just consist of a series of interviews among prospective customers, but it has to be well thought out, thorough and honest.

2. Get examples from the marketplace of similar product or service offerings ("comps," or comparables) to base your pricing on. Compare likely costs to the price being achieved and determine whether you can make a profit at your scale of operations. If you think you can charge more than competitors, you need to back up your conviction with customer market research.

3. Make sure the intellectual property (IP) is strongly linked to patent applications with a high likelihood of being approved. If the IP is not patent protected or the claims in the approved patents are not well formulated and enforceable, and if the patent lifetime is not well over 10 years, you will not find people other than "friends and family" that will fund the company. If the IP must be licensed from the university, do that before trying to raise any money. Investors will want to know

the milestone payments and royalty stream the university will get before evaluating your business plan.

4. In license deals, never accept terms for royalties on net sales of the entity that ends up selling the product. Rather, agree on royalties of any revenue your company makes or expressed as a percent of royalties you receive from third parties. The reality is that your product or service may very well end up being sold by another company that you licensed it to. Therefore, you can only promise to pay a portion of what you receive, not a portion of what the third party may receive.

5. These days, company ideas have to be quick to revenue to attract angel or venture capital funding. Depending on a merger/acquisition (M&A) in several years as the sole exit is a long shot. On the other hand, if you can build a story of early revenue generation and cash-flow positivity within at least two years, an M&A becomes more likely and the company becomes more fundable.

6. When looking for investors, do not neglect the credentials of the leadership team. No one will invest in a team that has not demonstrated previous success in business areas similar to what the new company will be pursuing. In fact, many investors look at the strength and plausibility of the leadership team in getting the job done before they look at anything else.

7. Do not assume that the scientific founder will make an acceptable CEO to an investor. It is extremely rare that this works out in practice.

Research faculty are trained as scientists, which means they make decisions based on rational thought and data and they prefer working in a world of black and white. Some aspect of this training and experience are good for working in a start-up (data-driven decisions) but some aren't. Networking, negotiations, fund-raising, and deal-making involve emotions, relationships, ambiguity, aligned incentives and lots of areas of grey. Faculty who can navigate this softer side will be successful.

First of all, ensure you have a good relationship with the technology transfer office. Just like any other negotiation the better you know each other's motivations the more efficient your negotiation will be.

I learned the hard, long way that technology commercialization is tough and it's especially tough with university technologies. In spite of the great potential and promise university intellectual property possesses it tends to be very nascent. Because of this it is best to not use investor's money for proof of concept but seek out gap funding within the university and/or government grants for the earliest funding. Once you have good preliminary data and proof of concept then you're in a better position to seek external funding from investors.

Before fund-raising ensure you know how external investors will make money; remember this is not a research project. And investors don't want bank type returns; they want multiples on their investment. This type of gain only typically occurs when a larger company acquires your technology or you have an IPO (Initial Public Offering). Most university technologies will be acquired by a larger player, so know who your potential acquirers are in advance and how your technology gives them a competitive advantage. Get direct feedback from industry (potential acquirers) at conferences, etc., and ask if they'll be open to talking to investors about the need your technology fills.

A solid business plan is a must, with your financial plan being the most critical. Your financial plan doesn't have to be complicated; a simple spreadsheet with expected revenue and expenses and cash on hand is all you need in the beginning. Be prepared that without fail your revenues will be less and happen slower than expected while your expenses will be more! You cannot run out of cash.

Some closing thoughts:

- Perseverance and optimism are musts for an entrepreneur, however, there is a difference between optimism and denying reality.
- Sometimes doors close for a reason.
- Don't let critics dictate your path.
- Believe the universe is conspiring in your favor.

Office of Technology Transfer (OTT). It may be counterintuitive but OTT offices prefer to work with start-up companies as opposed to large corporations because the license deal includes equity in the start-up. The equity has the potential to provide the university a much bigger return than royalties alone.

The challenge in negotiating a license varies from university to university. Classic license terms that include royalties, sub-license fee and % equity tend to be aggressively University centric. License terms that are not viewed to be fair will make it difficult to raise venture capital in the future. Low royalties are the most critical term since these costs will be assumed by any potential acquirer. Sub-license fee is less important since most company's business strategy does not include sublicense. % ownership tends not to be of concern to future VC investors since this cost is absorbed by the founders. I typically try to negotiate to 2% royalties, 10% sub-license fee and 10% equity. I use a 3rd party legal organization to front the negotiation as the "black hat." I set the desired terms and step in to complete the negotiation when we get close on terms. Such negotiations have taken as long as 8 months and up to $20,000 of legal fees. (I will discuss legal fee strategy below.)

A key goal of OTT is to get the licensee to pay forward-going patent costs, usually 6 to 12 months after execution of agreement. In all cases this provision has been problematic. USA patent costs are minimal, but international costs can run between $30,000 to $60,000 plus yearly maintenance fees. The only funding I have been able to raise for these formation-stage companies has been grants. Such grants cannot be used to pay patent costs except with the grant fee. This fee is usually minimal and has not been sufficient to pay patent costs. In all cases the companies have defaulted on the license agreements and had to renegotiate the license terms from a position of weakness. My recommendation is to delay licensing technology for as long as possible to delay the patent royalty clock. Alternatively, make sure you have identified the funds to pay the patent costs when they come due. Note that this is a complicated situation. The OTT office rarely will file international patents without a licensee. If international IP protection has been relinquished, there is substantial damage to the IP and will make it difficult to attract institutional investors. A comprehensive IP strategy should be established with the launch of the start-up.

Technology. The technology being licensed has been advanced far enough to enable a Ph.D. student to get his/her degree but is rarely market ready. Students will rarely conduct research that does not directly contribute to their degree. For example, a formulation that has a 3-day shelf life is sufficient for a student's research. If the solution turns bad, the student just makes a new batch. In contract, a company requires a shelf life of 6 months or more. In one case it took over 12 months to develop the purification protocols to achieve this shelf life. Three out of four companies failed typically after 1–2 years because of technology fatal flaws. In one case after a year of trying to duplicate the Ph.D. student's results, we concluded the patented technology never worked. It was not that the student falsified data; instead it turned out that the data collected was impacted by the probe used to collect the data. In a second company the technology worked well in lab scale but lost critical performance characteristics when attempts were made to scale it for production. The 3rd company failed because the technology that worked very well in buffer solutions released when exposed to blood an ion poisonous to humans. In all cases very bright Ph.D.-level individuals were surprised by the outcomes.

Founding professors. Professors are extremely bright and creative; however, they tend not to have a lot of business savvy. They are most valuable in solving tough technical hurdles: Preparing SBIR/STTR grant proposals, performing proof of concept studies to support these grant proposals and providing technical credibility in front of potential investors. Research is conducted by Ph.D. candidates and in some cases post-docs. The professors manage the research, but the students have the hands on skills. These students when they graduate are the best candidates for employees. They have the hands-on experience and the desire to advance their research to the market.

Sponsored research. I have never been able to manage sponsored research to success. Funds have been provided to founding professors on multiple [levels] to accomplish specific tasks. These tasks were never achieved. The only success was achieved by locating a company employee in the professor's lab to work side-by-side with the graduate students.

Facility-use agreements. Universities that license technology have a vested interest in the success of the licensee. For that reason they may bend backwards to assist the company. One way they can help is a facility-use agreement. In one case I have been able to locate 5 employees in university facilities and use all equipment and greenhouses for fees far less than that required to set up a stand-alone facility. This arrangement is especially valuable for life science start-ups for which capital equipment cost is difficult to fund.

Legal support. Lawyers are expensive. Seek out legal firms that are willing to defer fees in exchange for equity. I recommend financing of > \$1.5m before such defer fees are paid.

Fund-raising. It is nearly impossible to raise money for a university formation-stage spinout. I have funded these start-ups initially with small state-supported grants and loans. Additional funds have been obtained from SBIR grants from NSF and NIH. Such grants take 6 to 9 months to be awarded and have a probability of success of about 1 in 6. Successful grants require proof of concept data that will need to be provided by the founding professor. Grant applications can be submitted 3–4 times per year. You need to continually submit grants to have a hope of keeping a company funded while you mitigate the risk for equity investors. In one case, a company went into hibernation for 18 months while awaiting a Phase II SBIR award. This was painful because experienced employees were lost when the funding ran out.

Executive salaries. Bottom line: there are no funds to pay executive salaries during the formation stage. Founders or outside executives need to be willing to work for equity.

Anticipate the long-term progression of the company early in the process and ensure that your near-term data objectives support the long-term plan.

When bringing in outside financing, avoid the temptation to go to extraordinary lengths to limit dilution. You must ensure that you are funded past the next value milestone and anticipate things taking longer and costing more than you anticipate. Never put yourself in a position of having to go back to your investors and having to ask for additional financing when you have no leverage.

It is critically important that those with the core scientific knowledge stay close to the company during its early evolution. This extends to grant writing, patent applications, study design, etc.

Raising capital is time intensive. Approach investors strategically, look at your opportunity from their perspective and ask yourself whether it is a fit prior to investing your (or their) time.

University Research Administrators

Much of the book has focused on how university-derived innovations get to the marketplace through the start-up route and the people who make it happen, namely faculty members and business leaders. However, spinning a company out of a university can be greatly enhanced by university policy, procedures, and infrastructure. Walter Valdivia, a fellow in the Brookings Institute's Center for Technology Innovation, makes the case that university start-ups are an important part of the technology transfer function. He argues that most TTOs strive for that blockbuster patent licensed to an established company, generating millions of dollars in licensing revenue. The reality is that few TTOs break even, and the ones that make money are the elite universities receiving royalties on a single product. This revenue reality combined with a need to both diversify risk and respond to increased political pressure for universities to show impact from research dollars (jobs, products, revenue) have resulted in the emergence of what he calls the "nurturing start-ups model" of tech transfer: "This new model of technology transfer involves creating the incentives and organizational capacity within universities to support the entrepreneurial efforts of their faculty. By devoting resources to support campus entrepreneurs, by introducing career incentives, and by partnering with local business incubators and capital investors, universities are creating a nurturing environment for these nascent enterprises."[10]

This new model, as compared to a traditional model of predominantly licensing to established companies, has a number of pros and cons that can positively or negatively affect university finances as well as others' perceptions. Valdivia continues:

> One disadvantage is that nurturing start-ups may consume the resources available to the TTO to find licensors for their high-fee patents. At the same time, high-risk low-fee patents will more easily find a market in the same start-up firms that the university is helping establish. While nurturing start-ups will not displace the standard license-to-highest-bidder model, in an environment of scarce resources the TTO may gradually redirect resources from finding licensors to finding buyers for their start-ups. In addition, while the new model defers income further into the future—because instead of cash fees they will take stock in the new companies (or stock options)—it does not necessarily place a heavier cost-load up front. The costs of nurturing start-ups need not break the bank if small funds can be used to leverage support from local and state businesses and government. The costs for the TTO will not be significant compared to "angel capitalists"—private investors that may include family and friends of the inventors—who bear the brunt of financing initial operations.
>
> Another advantage for the university is that policy makers from their states and from Washington, D.C., will perceive this strategy as an affirmative effort to foster entrepreneurship, to attract high-tech industries to the university's region, and to boost economic growth and job creation. These favorable perceptions stand in stark contrast with the perceived excesses in university licensing—as mentioned above, industry complaining that universities are too aggressive negotiating and other stakeholders denouncing reach-through clauses and other unsavory licensing practices. The strategy of nurturing start-ups poses

10. Walter D. Valdivia, "University Start-Ups: Critical for Improving Technology Transfer," 20 November 2013, p. 2, Brookings Institute of Technology Innovation, http://www.brookings.edu/research/papers/2013/11/university-start-ups-technology-transfer-valdivia (accessed 14 May 2014).

a greater financial risk to the university compared to a more traditional licensing-only business model, but it also lessens the reputational risk associated with commercial activities of the university. At the same time, the university can expect higher returns from its shares and options in a successful start-up and it retains a degree of control over that outcome.[11]

Valdivia points to several important reasons that universities should encourage commercialization through entrepreneurship: 1) to enhance faculty recruitment and retention, 2) to provide a return on the university's investment in the research enterprise, 3) to drive economic development through job creation, and 4) to fulfill the universities mission of having impact in the world. In developing programs to support entrepreneurial commercialization, different stakeholders will emphasize each of these objectives to a different degree. A state legislator might see economic development as most important, while a donor might emphasize university mission, and a vice chancellor for research might see faculty recruitment and retention as paramount. Thus, for universities developing support programs, a complex mix of viewpoints and incentives need to be aligned, which, in some cases, is not always possible.

For a university to support faculty and enhance the launch and growth of university start-ups, it needs to 1) engage faculty members, encouraging them to be part of the start-up process, 2) engage people outside of the university both to assess the technology and to help launch and manage the companies, 3) provide start-up-friendly licenses and access to funding, and 4) provide infrastructure for launching and incubating companies. We'll consider each in turn.

Engaging Faculty Members

Engaging faculty members in the commercialization process can be difficult, as outlined above. They might not understand the process, they might not be motivated to engage in the process, or they might not be rewarded for participating. On the other hand, some faculty members are very motivated and excited to participate, for a wide range of reasons. One can consider four cases in which the level of faculty engagement and the level of commercial potential can determine the trajectory of a start-up. In the first case, if high faculty engagement, which is necessary to drive the early scientific direction

11. Ibid., 14.

for the start-up, is combined with a technology that has high commercial potential, you'll have an ideal start-up. In the second case, a faculty member is highly motivated to start a company but the technology does not have the potential to attract entrepreneurs or funding. This results in difficult conversations between the faculty member and the TTO or entrepreneur, who have to explain why the faculty member's technology is not commercializable. The conversations become even more frustrating for faculty when the technology appears to have significant commercial potential but has not been fully developed and the faculty has limited means for developing the technology (e.g., beyond the scope of academic grants). In the third case, if a less engaged faculty member has a commercially viable technology, external help is often needed to work with the faculty member to identify the best commercial application and get the company started. The faculty member then might play only a secondary role in the company, with the entrepreneur and/or a technologist doing most of the work. In the final case, low engagement and low commercial potential usually don't go anywhere.

Although these four scenarios are oversimplified, they point to ways the university can create movement toward the ideal start-up. First, it can increase faculty engagement through involvement of external people (entrepreneurs, consultants, advisers). Second, it can increase the commercial potential of a technology by finding the best market need for the technology, which does not always involve the demonstrated application, and by providing funding to do the critical proof-of-concept, feasibility, or validation studies that will demonstrate less risk.

Educating Faculty and Students

Faculty and students generally are not well versed in business, particularly in technology commercialization, so education in this area is vital. The key to providing education in this area is to avoid a "one-size-fits-all" approach. Education can occur through a number of different paths:

CLASSES. Entrepreneurship and technology commercialization classes are often taught by the business school or local entrepreneurial organizations. Another source of classes is the National Center for Entrepreneurial Tech Transfer (NCET2). The downside of classes, however, is that many faculty don't have the time to commit to a regular class.

WEBINARS AND WORKSHOPS. A shorter-duration approach is a one- or two-day workshop or "bootcamp," where key topics (IP, fund-raising, management, business models) are covered. For busy faculty, this can be a good alternative to a regular class. For even-more-bite-sized chunks, webinars on specific topics can be offered (e.g., incorporation options, SBIR grants, equity investments, term sheets). Local service providers (e.g., attorneys, accountants) are usually happy to contribute to these webinars. In addition, the live webinar can be recorded for viewing any time at a later date.

BOOKS AND HANDBOOKS. Some faculty like to have a reference they can refer to along the way. A book like this or a short pamphlet or website describing the steps specific to your university can provide good guidance. An example of a "founder's handbook," written by a local attorney and modified for UNC is provided at researchtorevenue.com.

WEBSITES AND DIGITAL NEWSLETTERS. Digital resources such as a website provide easy access to information, especially information that is updated periodically, such as university policies and procedures. A newsletter can also provide the most current information (e.g., grant RFAs [requests for applications], start-up news). The secret to a successful newsletter is providing relevant information to the intended audience. A faculty entrepreneur is going to be more interested in the success of other university start-ups and SBIR opportunities than in biotech IPOs or patent legislation.

Engaging People outside the University

One of the most significant deficits universities have in developing an entrepreneurial ecosystem is relationships with people outside the university, including former executives with significant business experience, entrepreneurs with start-up experience, consultants with specific domain expertise, service providers who work with start-ups (e.g., attorneys, accountants, etc.), and alumni in any of the above categories who want to give back to the university.

There are several reasons for this lack of engagement. First, many of these people don't know the entries into the university, of which there may be few. They might contact the tech transfer office, which may or may not be helpful in getting them engaged with faculty or in contact with a start-up. In addition, they rarely understand university organizational structure and decision-making: For example, they might not know what a provost is or what the associate vice chancellor does, or whether a chancellor or a president is really the equivalent of a CEO. Second, universities have limited the scope of their recruitment to leaders of start-ups; they leave out individuals who can play broader roles as advisers, consultants, and service providers. To this point, it is important for a university to develop ways of engaging a wide range of external people. For example, one can create ways to bring people into the university setting where the risk is low; that is, where the consequences of their actions (poor advice, lack of follow-up, etc.) are negligible. Bringing in someone to advise a student team would be one way to do this. It would also provide the university an opportunity to assess the strengths and weakness of people and the level of engagement they are interested in, thus identifying people who can contribute in a more meaningful way (e.g., as a board member or CEO). The following are some of the ways to engage the community, starting with the lowest-risk option:[12]

SHOWCASES AND FORUMS. These are events designed to attract people who may be interested in university start-ups. For example, a "first look forum" can be organized to present the latest in university technology to a broad audience. These can be presentations of technology to a group of entrepreneurs and consultants who may be interested in a start-up. A useful format involves short presentations followed by one-on-one discussions. Another format would involve presentations about exciting university technologies delivered "TED-style" to a much broader audience where engagement is less important than letting people know about cutting-edge university research and its impact. Another option is a showcase of university start-ups, much like an accelerator "demo-day" or "pitch party." For example, five or six companies could give 10-minute pitches to potential advisers, management, and investors, followed by a networking session for more discussion.[13]

LECTURING, COACHING, MENTORING, AND ADVISING. There are many ways to bring external people into the university to lecture, mentor, or advise. Sponsoring lecture programs or panel discussions is one way. Another option is to host "entrepreneur roundtables" or "lunch-n-learns" where, for example, entrepreneurs can recount their experiences in launching a company or a local attorney can give an overview of the pros and cons of different types of corporate entities.

---

12. Most of these programs, especially the latter three, require a significant network with external people to be successful. That might be difficult with existing TTO personnel and could require hiring in an external person with a significant network (e.g., a former venture capitalist).

13. A word of caution here: Not all faculty members have the gift of brevity or can package their science in such a way that even entrepreneurs without a technical background can understand it. Several rounds of coaching may be necessary to get the presentation to the appropriate level of conciseness and understanding. In some cases, it may make sense for a tech transfer person to make the presentation, focusing more on the features and benefits of the technology than on the technical details.

Coaching and mentoring can take many forms. Some courses (e.g., business school entrepreneurship) have team projects where a seasoned business person can help coach the team. More formal mentoring programs have an "entrepreneur-in-residence" (EIR) who is available to talk to students and faculty about their ideas and start-ups.[14]

In terms of advising, advisory groups for providing feedback on a technology can be organized. In some cases, an "ad-hoc" advisory panel is assembled to hear a faculty member pitch an early-stage technology being considered for commercialization or in the early stages of spinning out. With multiple eyes on these technologies, sound feedback can be provided in terms of competitive approaches, product-development hurdles, industrial partners, and connections to others who may be useful in advising. After the initial meeting, the team could follow up with a session 6–12 months later to provide some momentum and continuity. Ideally, one of the advisers will get interested in the technology to the point where he or she wants to play a more significant role (e.g., CEO, board member, formal business adviser) in spinning out the company. Advisers could also work directly with the tech transfer office. In this case, they could participate in a "patent review committee" composed of several experts with domain expertise in the areas of the filed intellectual property. Committee members could also provide guidance as to the commercial viability of a pending application and help guide the filing process (e.g., in a case where a disease may only be prevalent in certain countries, an adviser with experience in country-specific filings would be helpful).

CONSULTING. All of the activities listed so far have been volunteer activities. These can be a cost-effective way to engage external people, especially since many like learning about cutting-edge technologies or helping their alumni.[15] Another option for engagement is to pay people

14. Entrepreneur-in-residence programs are the rage on many campuses, and they take many forms. Some involve an all-volunteer corps of people who meet with faculty to discuss start-up ideas. Others are paid a small stipend to be on campus to help. Although EIRs can be effective, especially in helping students with their start-up ideas, finding a fit between an EIR and the faculty/technology can be challenging. Many EIRs will have broad industry knowledge, but few have technology-specific expertise (e.g., in commercializing a novel photovoltaic or in the preclinical development of an Alzheimer's drug).

15. The discussion of engagement has been limited to local and regional people, those who can visit campus to attend meetings or meet with faculty. A broader level of engagement can be found with university alumni from across the nation or globe. Technology can bring them to campus in a virtual way to engage in these commercialization discussions. The challenge is finding the people and maintaining the relationships. The university development office is the best place to start.

for services. For example, the university could provide a consulting fee to an external group for a specific task. Our experience is that in some cases, consultants will work for greatly reduced rates for the opportunity to have the university as a client, especially if it might involve future work with the start-up. Consulting groups can provide expertise in areas of regulatory approval, patent landscape, or competitive analysis. A program involving a "deep dive" has been successful on a number of campuses. A local entrepreneur or technologist is given a small grant (approximately $5,000) to take a deep dive into a technology and provide an assessment of its commercial viability. The program can serve two purposes: The university receives an assessment that is likely more complete than one a volunteer would provide, and, perhaps more important, the entrepreneur might be so impressed by the technology that he or she wants to go to the next level of involvement (e.g., incorporate a company or be the CEO).

MANAGEMENT AND FORMAL ADVISERS. From the perspective of someone contemplating a start-up, in many ways, the ultimate goal of these engagement activities is to bring senior management (e.g., president, CEO, CSO) and formal advisers (BOD, SAB) on board. The activities listed above are good tools to identify and build relationships with these people. As mentioned above, it is important to provide a means for "dating" of potential management through a series of informal meetings or more formal advisory engagements (e.g., consulting projects, helping to write the business plan, market research, etc.).

Support Programs for Entrepreneurial Commercialization

The educational and external engagement programs described above will help prepare for the building, launching, and growing of a university start-up. In addition, a number of support mechanisms can be put in place to facilitate the entire process.

Launching the Company

Launching a university start-up has historically been done by the faculty member (with or without a local entrepreneur) working with a local attorney. A C-corporation or an LLC is established with the founders splitting equity. The university might get equity as stipulated in the license agreement but rarely as a founder. Several universities have taken a more proactive approach where they will incorporate the company and serve as board members during the early days of the start-up. For example, the University of Pennsylvania has developed the UPStart program, wherein Penn will incorporate a company around a Penn-owned technology as a Delaware LLC with corporate governance shared by a TTO officer and a faculty founder, both of whom serve on the board of directors.[16] In addition, equity is shared between Penn and the faculty founders. In return for its equity ownership, the university provides support by helping to write SBIR grants, by identifying and hiring management, and by working with corporate partners for sponsored research funding or investing. Although Penn has formed over 100 companies since the program's inception, they are not considered start-up companies in the traditional sense. The companies are started several years before a traditional start-up normally would be formed and are considered university-supported "incubation vehicles," designed to attract management and funding.[17] As such, these companies are dissolved after several years if they fail to attract management or funding.

Incubating the Company

Many university-born start-ups have limited resources to devote to facility rent and laboratory equipment. Some regions have local start-up incubators and accelerators, but few have the lab space and equipment required by technology-based start-ups (e.g., wet-lab benches, sinks and fume hoods, incubators, centrifuges, refrigerators and freezers, or specialty equipment like PCR machines or spectrophotometers). Although a start-up at an early stage may win a Phase I SBIR for several hundred thousand dollars, that amount may not cover all of the equipment needed to complete the studies, and if it is used to buy capital equipment, the more efficient spending for the start-up would be for personnel and supplies for experiments. A number of universities have recognized this need and will allow a start-up to incubate in university-owned space. There are two options for university incubation. With the first option, what we call "ad-hoc incubation," the company resides in the founder's lab, where it has a lab bench and access to equipment in the lab. With the second option, called "dedicated incubation," several start-ups are housed in the same building where they share equipment and common areas. There are advantages and disadvantages to both options:

16. See UPstart's website, http://pci.upenn.edu/upstart/ (accessed 29 January 2014).
17. Michael Poisel, UPStart director, personal communication.

AD-HOC INCUBATION

Advantages | Access to highly specialized equipment
Close proximity to the faculty founder

Disadvantages | Increased risk of conflicts of interest (mingling of graduate research with company research)

Increased risk of intellectual property "leaks," either students to company or company to students

Managing activities is challenging (e.g., enforcing safety procedures across many labs across campus)

Poor external "optics" (an outside observer may perceive significant conflict in having the company in the faculty founder's lab)

DEDICATED INCUBATION

Advantages | Synergies and cross-talk among incubated companies

Easier management and oversight of company activities

Creation of showcase useful for visiting faculty recruits and state legislators

Disadvantages | University commitment to a large space requiring provost or chancellor leadership

The purchase of shared equipment (refrigerators and freezers at minimum)

May require a person in the space to manage the faculties

One of the challenges in obtaining dedicated incubation space is the limited amount of space on campus and the economics of revenue generation. A square foot of lab space used for research (e.g., funded by federal grants) can generate many times the revenue for the university in the form of salary support and overhead compared to a square foot leased by a start-up. However, the short-term economics should only be part of the equation. Other considerations include long-term economics (royalty revenue, jobs generation) as well as the symbolic nature of the incubator demonstrating the university's commitment to entrepreneurship and commercialization.

For either incubation approach, a number of things need to be considered:

OCCUPANCY TERM. One of the advantages of a university incubator is the flexible, and usually short, term of occupancy. Most private commercial spaces require a five-year term, which obligates the start-up to a significant burden, unless the space turns out to be just right in years four and five, which is unlikely (more likely is the start-up either will be stalled or will have outgrown the space by then). An informal survey of university incubators showed that a typical term is two years with a possible one-year extension. The termination term should also be start-up friendly, requiring several months notification prior to termination of the agreement and no further obligation by the start-up to pay rent. The potential area of concern is allowing start-ups to remain in the incubator for years. The objective of most incubation space is to grow companies to the point of graduation to larger space. Some start-ups limp along from SBIR grant to SBIR grant, never having enough traction to leave and the university never setting clear expectations on when it must leave. The issue may be further clouded by university politics; namely, the founding faculty member influencing the decision.

RENT. The rent charge will vary by institution. Some state institutions are required by law to charge the market rate. Others will subsidize the rent to make it affordable to the start-up. The rent charges will also vary by how much space is being rented. A start-up leasing space might rent only a 50-square-foot bench but have access to many times that space in the lab or as part of shared space.

COMPANY SELECTION. In launching an incubator, one must decide the acceptance criteria:

- University-technology-based companies only (excluding faculty with non-IP companies, e.g., service companies, or student start-ups)?
- A license or an option to a license taken by the start-up?
- Funding in hand (VC seed round closed, SBIR grant approved)?
- Appropriate activity (e.g., no radioactive agents)?
- Management on board?

EQUIPMENT. If the space is shared among several start-ups, the most capital-efficient approach is to have equipment available for all companies to use (refrigerator, freezer, centrifuge, pH meter, balance, etc.). In many cases this equipment is donated by a local company or is a hand-me-down from a faculty member upgrading equipment or retiring. The cost of maintaining the equipment should be factored in and could be built into the rent.

USE OF UNIVERSITY SERVICES AND SPONSORED RESEARCH. One of the advantages of a start-up being incubated on campus, in addition to space and interaction with faculty, is the potential access to core facilities. These facilities offer a number of services, from animal studies to DNA sequencing to machining and electronics prototyping. However, many are subsidized by federal grants, so a start-up in private industry would be charged the fully burdened or industrial rate. The rates are usually reasonable for a large corporation but can be a burden for a start-up. Reduced rates for start-ups would help these companies. An interesting approach taken by one university was to provide matching funds for an SBIR grant that could be used as a voucher in any of the university's core facilities.

In addition to university services, start-ups often need to conduct studies in the one of the labs (e.g., the founder's lab). This type of activity constitutes sponsored research, but the typical university overhead charge would consume a significant portion of start-up funding. Some universities waive the overhead on Phase I SBIR grants to enhance success of a Phase II grant.

SERVICES. In addition to space and equipment, the start-up will often need basic services for day-to-day functioning (e.g., waste disposal, parking, computer connectivity) for which the university charges a fee. Other services might include access to coaching and mentoring, accountants and lawyers, or student interns.

SAFETY, LIABILITY, AND INDEMNIFICATION. With an outside entity conducting business on the university campus, there needs to be risk management of activities. The university health and safety unit needs to know the types of activities the start-up is engaged in, and the start-up must abide by the university's health and safety guidelines and regulations. Injuries suffered by company employees on university property should be covered by company liability insurance. In general, the university has to be indemnified in the event of personal injuries suffered by start-up employees or nefarious activities conducted by the start-up.

INTELLECTUAL PROPERTY. Most start-ups incubating on campus are conducting studies to further develop university technologies, so most of the information gleaned from the studies is covered by the patents being licensed by the start-up. However, some companies make discoveries building on the current IP, creating company-generated IP. This IP is usually considered company-owned, but that must be clear in the agreement. The converse may also be true. An interaction between a professor, graduate student, or post doc might lead to a novel discovery, leading to questions of inventorship and ownership.

Start-Up-Friendly Licensing

One of the essential elements of a university start-up is the license agreement between the start-up and the university, which allows the start-up to make, use, and sell products based on the university IP. Until recently, most universities took a one-size-fits-all approach, using a generic license and modifying it for the specific transaction at hand, be it a license to an established company or a start-up. Today, however, many universities have adopted a more start-up-friendly license agreement, some even offering a template or "express" license (see researchtorevenue.com for an example of an express license). These licenses can lower some of the barriers and reduce the time it takes to obtain the license. The following are key aspects of an start-up-friendly license:

NO UP-FRONT FEES. Most start-ups have very little cash, so asking for an up-front fee is a serious constraint, especially when that cash could be used for important early experiments.

PATENT COST PAYBACK SCHEDULE. Given the limited resources of a start-up, spreading the patent costs over a period of time can ease the cash flow for a start-up. A start-up-friendly license could stipulate a modest monthly amount for a period of time (e.g., \$500/month for 6 months), which then ramps up over time.[18]

STANDARD LANGUAGE. Negotiations over the language of the agreement (including indemnification, liability, or termination clauses) are often complicated and protracted—and thus incur significant attorney fees. Every attorney has his/her own way of handling that language, which, at times, is a distinction without a difference. One way to reduce attorney fees is to work with local attorneys and VCs to agree on acceptable standard language for these clauses.

DEALING WITH THE EQUITY ISSUE. The contention lies in how much equity the university will receive as part of the license. The amount of equity is tied to the value of the company, and trying to place a value on a company that has no assets (other than the IP under discussion) and no revenue is difficult. Comparables help but range widely. One solution is

18. One effect of the payback is that it makes the business more real for the founders in that they have to come up with a small amount each month. Founders paying for this out of their pockets is also a good demonstration of their commitment and "skin-in-the-game."

to set one amount of equity, say 5 percent, for all start-ups that is within the range of most university licenses and, given the difficulty in assessing value, have it nonnegotiable. Another solution is to assess a fee at the time of liquidity (acquisition or IPO) that is close to the fully diluted position the university historically has at the time of liquidity (e.g., a fee of 1 percent of the purchase price for an acquisition). This approach takes value out of the equation.

Strategies for Patent Costs

As TTOs take more of a role in promoting start-ups, one of the financial consequences is paying for patent costs where the potential start-up never forms or the start-up has little capital or has trouble raising capital. In these cases, the TTO may have to "invest" in patents that don't provide a short-term payback (unlike an established company that has the ability to pay up-front fees and reimburse patent fees). Of course, one approach is to view the TTO as a customer service organization where patent costs are the cost of meeting the university's mission of service, creating jobs, and faculty recruitment and retention. As such, the university might budget a certain amount of funds for patent costs, expecting little if any return, and in the event of a return, can use the funds in a discretionary way. Of course this approach, if there is no selection criteria in place, can lead to out-of-control patent costs. The following are ways a university can control patent costs:

U.S. PROTECTION ONLY. The university can file the provisional and then at the national phase cover only the cost of U.S. filings. This eliminates the foreign filing fees and places the burden of foreign protection on the start-up. For many technologies, this may be satisfactory in that the United States is a sufficiently large market. However, for some products (e.g., pharmaceuticals), the lack of international protection can severely hamper a start-up's ability to raise money or partner.

PATENT REVIEW PANEL. The university can make an assessment of both the patentability and the commercial potential of the IP early in the patenting process. Traditionally, the assessment has been done by the individual tech transfer officer, perhaps in discussion with the faculty member and the TTO director. A more robust approach involves bringing in outside people who have technical/industrial experience in the area and who have already spun out university technology into a company. This approach not only brings relevant domain expertise to

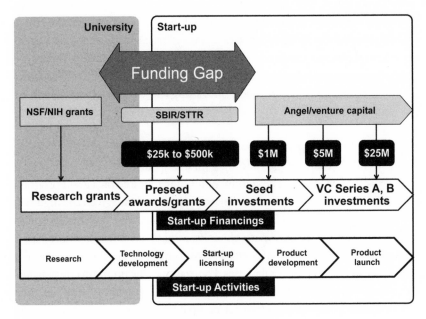

FIGURE 5.1 The funding gap in university start-ups

bear on assessing the technology, but it also takes some of the pressure off the TTO, who can be accused at times of making arbitrary decisions about what to patent and what not to or of yielding to faculty influence. There are pitfalls to this approach, however. First, the external people are usually volunteers and often don't have a strong incentive to understand the technology, so they might not understand a nuance that is critical to its novelty. Second, for many university technologies, the state of development may not be sufficient to make a reasoned commercial assessment, especially if the commercial viability hinges on technical risk (i.e., if this works, it will be a huge commercial success).

Creating an Integrated Funding Program

As shown in figure 5.1, and described in Chapter 2, a significant funding gap exists for launching a university start-up. Federal research dollars are typically limited to research or discovery. Funds to de-risk or demonstrate feasibility or validate the discovery are usually outside the scope of federal funding. Traditional investors (angels or VCs) do not invest this early because of the high risk of failure, plus the amount of funding needed at this stage (preseed) is usually too small. An excellent source of nondilutive capital has been SBIR/ STTR grants, but the acceptance rate is very low, acquiring the funds takes time (usually nine months from submission) and to be successful, some type of preliminary data is important. Obtaining preliminary data does not require much funding ($25,000–50,000), but raising those funds externally can be extremely difficult.

University Grant Program

To help fill this early-stage funding gap, many universities are developing internal grant programs. The amount of funding required for a grant program is relatively small since 1) many of these projects will fail, given the high risk of the technologies, and 2) the infrastructure for doing the studies at this stage is usually at the university, thus the costs of execution are reduced. A grant program should be integrated across the entire funding gap, wherein funds are deployed in several phases. For example, the program could award a large number of small grants to early-stage projects/companies, but then award larger grants to those project/companies who meet milestones in the first phase.[19] The data from these studies usually supports the initial patent filing but can also serve as preliminary data required for an SBIR/STTR grant or even increase the attractiveness of the technology resulting in a license to an established company. As such, these are often called "technology development" or "technology enhancement" grants and are given to the faculty member to conduct studies in his or her lab or in a university "proof-of-concept center" or perhaps to outsource the studies to a local contract lab. An amount of $10,000–50,000 is usually sufficient to complete the study. One approach combines these grants with funds from a patent review panel that identifies and funds the critical experiment ("the killer experiment"), which, if successful, will demonstrate technical and/or commercial feasibility of the technology.[20]

---

19. Note that projects and companies are both considered at this stage of funding, mirroring the region between university and start-up shown in figure 5.1. Funding at this stage should be somewhat flexible in this regard. A project is identifiable IP that has commercial potential but a decision about whether to commercialize it has not been made (e.g., form a start-up company). Likewise, a start-up at this stage may be nothing more than several founders incorporating a company in order to write an SBIR grant.

20. One thought experiment for TTOs is to take half of their current patent budget and disperse it as technology-development grants with the view that some portion of the technologies will fail but the ones that are successful will have a better chance for licensing, thus justifying patent expenditure.

Another need within the funding gap is funding for nontechnical expenses, those associated with company inception (e.g., incorporation, corporate counsel), commercial assessment (e.g., regulatory consultant), or market research. Funding for nontechnical activities can be important, but the question is whether it is essential for getting the start-up to the next step? Is it on the critical path? Funding for patent expenses is a critical need, and SBIR/STTR grants allow a small portion to be used for discretionary purposes, which can be applied to patent expenses. However, using a university-funded grant to pay university-associated patent costs would not make sense since it appears to be a lot of work to recycle money within the university.

A Start-Up Venture Fund

As a university start-up progresses and continues to meet important commercialization milestones, its funding needs become greater. A university grant program may not be able to provide funding at the levels now required by the start-up. As such, many universities are beginning to develop investment or venture funds that will make investments in university start-ups. There are a number of reasons for a university, or a university-affiliated foundation, to create a fund. First, university start-ups may have reduced the risk of investment through university or federal grants, but the opportunity is still too risky for angel or venture capital investors. Thus, a university fund may be the only source of capital available to get them either investor-ready or to the point of generating revenue. Second, most grants, especially SBIR/STTR, limit the use of funds to technical studies, and the aims of the studies must be aligned with those of the granting agency. Some start-ups have significant nontechnical expense such as patent costs, consultants fees, or management salaries, which can't be funded through grants. Funding through a venture fund provides this needed flexibility. University-associated venture funds vary widely, depending on the source of money, the return expectations, the investment strategy and scope, the fund structure, the amount of the investment, and the investment vehicle.

Source of funds and return expectations. The source of funds and the related return expectations are the major determinants of type of fund. A university venture fund could get its funding from four possible sources, listed roughly in order of decreasing return expectations (high to low): 1) investors, perhaps alumni and friends of the university, 2) contributions from the university endowment, 3) donations from friends and alumni, or 4) revenue from the TTO. With individuals making an investment in the fund, the return expectations are generally high. These investors have the opportunity to invest in several funds and are trying to maximize their return. They see the exciting companies coming out of the university as an opportunity to achieve those returns. Likewise, even though the endowment sees the investment as an "alternative investment" asset class, it has a responsibility to seek the highest possible return. Donations from alumni and friends of the university are a philanthropic source of money, so the return expectations, both in terms of amount and timeline, are relatively low. A donor will take the tax deduction and feel good about promoting entrepreneurship on campus. Likewise, a TTO's return expectations are low because its main goals are unlocking innovation, creating jobs, and retaining faculty.

For the first two sources, it is easy to understand the need to generate a return. For the latter sources, the question is, Why show a return; why not just give the money away as grants? There are a couple of reasons to make investments with an eye on a return. First, generating a return ensures a source of capital for future investments. In this case, the return is less than a typical investment but enough to keep the fund "evergreen."[21] Second, donors with a background in business and investment might want to see the money treated like an investment, where the rigors of due diligence are used to make the investment decision.

Investment strategy and scope. It follows that the return expectations will drive the fund's investment strategy: the greater the return expectations, the greater emphasis on the biggest opportunity with the least risk. This translates into making investments in only the start-ups that are the farthest along (i.e., have lower risk). This strategy, however, might preclude investing in much earlier, riskier companies. Thus lower return expectations (e.g., evergreen) can take greater risks. Another aspect of the investment strategy related to risk management is the area of co-investment. Some university funds will co-invest with an outside investor into a company (for some funds, this is a requirement). When a university invests with outside investors, the amount of capital invested increases, and another source of due diligence is available. However, given that the investor is external, it is likely he or she will have high return expectations, again precluding higher-risk investments. In terms of scope, most university funds invest only in the start-ups spinning

21. There is a reasonable argument to be made for simply endowing the fund and using the return on the endowment as the source of investments and/or grants, keeping the principle whole. This approach may be driven by the desire of the donor or the amount of the donation.

out of the parent university, although some invest regionally or among several associated campuses within a university system.

Fund structure. The structure of the fund is determined by the amount of independence the fund intends to have from the university as well as the source of money and return expectations. This degree of independence might be driven by legal or legislative mandates or the fund's desire to create independence in the decision-making process (i.e., to insulate it from university political pressures). At one extreme, the fund might be part of the TTO, in which case it is making investment decisions from within that office, perhaps using an external advisory board for guidance. At the other extreme, the fund might be an LLC, independent of the university with a professional investment manager who is incentivized to achieve certain return goals. In this case, several university officials may sit on the board or the investment committee. In general, the more professionally managed, the greater the return expectations of the fund. The most common structure is for the fund to be set up as an independent entity (like the LLC) with one limited partner, the university, who can be providing the funds from a number of sources (endowment, donations, TTO revenue).

Fund size, investment amount, and vehicle. The size of the fund and the amount of each investment are determined by a number of factors. In general, the fund needs to be large enough to make enough investments so that it has a chance to see a success. Assuming the chances are roughly one in ten to one in twenty of getting a company to a successful point, and that the average investment needed to get it there is on the order of $.5 million–1 million, then a $10 million fund has a good chance of having a few winners. Under this scenario, it could make from 10 to 20 investments, where one or two may be a home-run, thus paying for all the failed companies. A $2 million fund, however, would be challenged to show a return under this scenario.

Annalisa Croce et al. analyzed university-associated venture funds for the period 1973–2010 using data from the Thomson One database (formerly VentureXpert).[22] The dataset consisted of 26 funds (11 in the United States and 15 in the European Union). Table 5.2 shows a number of descriptive statistics drawn from their analysis.

22. Annalisa Croce, Luca Grilli, and Samuele Murtinu, "Venture Capital Enters Academia: An Analysis of University-Managed Funds," *Journal of Technology Transfer*, 20 July 2013, http://link .springer.com/article/10.1007%2Fs10961-013-9317-8#page-1 (accessed 7 April 2015).

TABLE 5.2 Statistics drawn from an analysis of 26 university-associated venture funds, 1973–2010

		U.S.	EU	TOTAL
Number of portfolio companies		258	112	370
Total invested		$424M	$168M	$592M
Number of portfolio companies	mean	23.5	7.5	14.2
	median	7	5	6
Age of fund (yrs.)	mean	17.4	12.4	14.5
	median	9	11	11
Amount invested	mean	$38M	$11M	$23M
	median	$15M	$4.8M	$6.2M
Amount invested per portfolio company	mean	$2.8	$1.3M	$1.9M
	median	$1.6M	$1.0M	$1.4M
Number of managers	mean	4.8	4.9	4.9
	median	3	4	4
Number of co-investors	mean	4.4	4.1	4.3
	median	5	5	5
Number of co-invested investments	mean	22.1	5.8	12.7
	median	7	5	6
Current company status Number of companies (% of total)	Still in portfolio	55 (21)	105 (94)	160 (43)
	Failures	51 (20)	2 (2)	53 (14)
	IPOs	46 (17)	1 (1)	47 (13)
	Acquisitions	106 (41)	4 (4)	110 (30)

Source: Adapted from Croce et al., "Venture Capital Enters Academia."

Concluding Remarks

The importance and acceptance of entrepreneurship has increased dramatically over the past years to the point where starting a company has almost become a mainstream concept. City and regional governments have embraced entrepreneurship as an engine for economic development. Warehouses are being converted into coworking space, incubators, and accelerators. Courses on entrepreneurship are being offered across the educational spectrum, from middle-school to undergraduate classes. The cost of starting a company has never been lower. Low-cost services and advice abound, and the cost of creating prototype products has dropped due to cloud-based services and 3D printing. Several decades ago, a failed company would have been considered an embarrassment. Today, it is considered in some circles a rite of passage, a badge of honor.

This entrepreneurial fervor has begun to seep through the halls of academia. Many universities have embraced entrepreneurship on the educational front, offering courses and curricula for students interested in start-ups. Some complement the classroom with experiential learning for student-led start-ups by offering a wide range of programs on subjects ranging from pitch sessions to business plan competitions, for start-up dorms to mentoring programs and makers spaces. Embracing entrepreneurship as a means for commercializing university innovations has not developed as quickly for a number of reasons. Technology transfer offices, the nexus for university innovation development and deployment, are rarely staffed with people who have experience with start-up companies. Thus, these offices have limited abilities to support university start-ups, much less develop comprehensive programs for the care and feeding of early-stage companies (e.g., incubation space, funding and mentoring programs). Furthermore, many offices are funded to favor the short-term, low-risk revenue generated from licensing deals to established companies over the long-term, higher-risk potential of start-ups.

We believe the tide is changing. Many young faculty expect to be involved in a start-up and expect support in spinning companies out. Older faculty are seeing start-ups as means for applying decades of research to solve important problems. As such, universities are using the entrepreneurial approach for faculty recruitment and retention. Universities would like to see a return on their investment in the research infrastructure, and start-ups offer an alternative to licensing to established companies. State governments, many of whom support research universities, view start-ups as a source of economic development and job growth. All of these emerging factors point to start-ups as playing an effective role in unlocking university innovations. We would argue further that start-ups may be the most effective means for bringing these innovations to market for several reasons. First, most university innovations are immature and need further development. A start-up provides the ideal structure and incentives for raising risk capital to develop technology into viable products. Furthermore, these incentives help to engage and align faculty inventors and entrepreneurs in the process of building a successful business. Second, university innovations tend to be broadly applicable. A start-up company provides the flexibility to pursue multiple commercialization paths. In addition, the start-up can build on the initial innovation to develop improvements and enhancements never conceived by the university or its inventors. Finally, the broader entrepreneurial ecosystem has created fertile ground for university start-ups. The availability of talent, capital, and space in a region helps the spinout process.

The obstacles to launching a successful university start-up are gradually fading. We are moving away from a time where being involved in a start-up was seen as tainting the purity of the academic mission. We are moving toward a day when start-ups are seen, or even expected, as a means for making research "real." This shift has created on opportunity for faculty members to engage in start-up activities and for entrepreneurs to partner with faculty and universities. Our hope is that *Research to Revenue* will be a valuable field guide in unlocking innovation . . . one company at a time.

Index